SUNDAY
MISCELLANY

A selection from 2003 and 2004

SUNDAY
MISCELLANY

A selection from 2003 and 2004

Edited by Marie Heaney

In association with RTÉ

TOWN
HOUSE
DUBLIN

First published in 2004 by

TownHouse, Dublin
THCH Ltd
Trinity House
Charleston Road
Ranelagh
Dublin 6
Ireland
www.townhouse.ie

4 5 6 7 8 9 10

A CIP catalogue record for this book is available from the British Library.

ISBN: 1-86059-230-9

Typeset by Typeform Repro

Printed by Creative Print & Design (Wales) Ltd., Ebbw Vale

CONTENTS

A SENSE OF PLACE

A SENSE OF HUMOUR

A SENSE OF A PRESENCE

A SENSE OF POIGNANCY

A SENSE OF THE PAST

FOREWORD

When I was growing up, Sunday mornings were synonymous with my father turning breakfast into an extended extravagance: the grill working at a ferocious hot red to keep up with our demand for toast while the pan worked away on an equally hot electric ring. It would be filled to the brim, frequently, with the mixed edibles recommended by Theodora Fitzgibbon in one of her recipes from *A Taste of Ireland*. It made Sunday mornings memorably different from weekday mornings, when it was my mother who took charge in the kitchen and got the five of us set up for another day and out to school. This was the 1970s, and the soundtrack to those mornings in our canary-yellow kitchen was Ciarán Mac Mathúna's *Mo Cheol Thú* followed by the signature tune of *Sunday Miscellany* and that week's selection of 'music and musings'. It didn't matter whether we were away on holidays or at home, the sound memories of Sunday mornings remained constant. The inimitable voices of Ronnie Walsh, Anthony Cronin, Benedict Kiely, Hilary Boyle, John Jordan, and Val Mulkerns drew me, and so many others, into their worlds. Just as I remember Paul Durcan's unforgettable delivery of his poem 'That Propeller I Left in Bilbao' (long before I came to know that city), I hope that other voices bringing us new poetry today will equally linger in listeners' minds. Listening to those contributors made me wonder what it would be like, one day, to make such a seemingly easy formula into such popular radio listening in the future.

Years later when I was living in the north of Spain, I accidentally came upon RTÉ Radio 1 on my radio and heard familiar programmes, including *Sunday Miscellany*, making me feel a little nostalgic. But nostalgia alone does not make good radio. The best programmes need to both protect what's good and push out the boundaries to embrace the new. That is what *Sunday Miscellany* aims to do and it is typically what listeners tell us the best material submitted for inclusion on the programme does all the time. Through the magic of radio, we are made to see the familiar, but with an added dash of newness. We are introduced to complete strangers and brand-new experiences in the same way as we are reminded of lives and times we thought we knew and times and people we hope some day we may come to know.

Today, as producer and compiler of *Sunday Miscellany*, it is my privilege to be the first to read the material that comes on air. When I was asked to consider taking over the programme, I spoke with more experienced colleagues about what the assignment might entail. In the same breath as telling me how satisfying and pleasant a programme it was to produce, they warned me of the enormous amount of material that comes in from potential contributors. I had been told that you have to keep very fit and constant to be able to give each contribution due consideration while at the same time making sure to have the week's programme recorded, edited and ready for broadcast for the coming Sunday. Still, I really had no idea about the sheer volume of the submissions until the envelopes, the e-mails and the hand-delivered manuscripts started to arrive.

What has been gratifying is the general desire of contributors to have their material worked on, their delivery directed and their pieces given a fitting place in the programme. I have found myself sifting through contributions in order to find common concerns that draw particular material together and it is one way I have found of selecting and editing pieces for programmes when there is so much material available. This has also helped in the pleasant task of commissioning writing, another feature of the programme, as well as bringing poetry back into *Sunday Miscellany* once more.

Music has always been part of *Sunday Miscellany* and it has played a subtle but vital role in the programme. I must admit it was one area of the programme that gave me concern! I had never before had to select so much music for any radio programme. I knew I wanted music that would complement rather than dominate the spoken contributions. Again, invaluable suggestions and guidance from musically literate colleagues, friends and contributors have guided my choices. I now listen to more music than I have ever done before in my broadcasting career and enjoy it immensely. Hopefully, in the process, I have begun to introduce listeners to some contemporary composers alongside more recognisable musical creators and arrangers. Early in my stint at the helm, it was gratifying when, unprompted, a friend's young child remarked that one of the music choices was 'happy music'. I had, as it happens, agonised over finding something appropriate to follow a humorous spoken piece before I stumbled upon that particular piece of music, which had made me smile too.

I like to think that those tuning in to the radio today recognise *Sunday Miscellany*'s signature tune and know that it signals in a relaxed mood. Nobody has to be anywhere in particular: there's no crèche or school to get to or train to catch, Sunday is starting up. For me, the ritual of hearing another programme and hoping it will translate on the air into memorable radio has come around again. It is my hope for today's listeners and for future generations of listeners that they will hear material that will connect them with new worlds in a new time. An encouraging development in that direction is the number of contributors now involved with the programme who were not even born when I first heard *Sunday Miscellany* back in the 1970s.

Any project, be it a radio programme or the publication of a book, demands co-operation and hard work from a lot of people. Essentially, I would like to thank all those who contribute to and participate in *Sunday Miscellany*. The support and advice from colleagues throughout RTÉ is always appreciated. In particular, I would like to mention Peter O'Connor, Paul Bradley and all the technical staff; Blánaid Bodley and all the radio presentation staff; Jennifer Taaffe and Sandra Byrne, who make sure the public know about the programme; Patricia O'Dwyer, Donal Moriarty, Gabrielle Holohan, Mary Curry and Fionnuala Hayes for keeping administrative work shipshape and everyone in the sound library and archive.

I would like to thank sincerely Adrian Moynes (Managing Director, RTÉ Radio), Eithne Hand (Head of RTÉ Radio 1) and Lorelei Harris (Arts, Features and Drama Editor, RTÉ Radio 1), who have given me the opportunity to work on *Sunday Miscellany*. Their commitment to the programme's progress makes all the difference. I would also like to thank Brian Fay and our daughter Nora for their constant encouragement and support.

Just as I have had the good fortune to inherit one of RTÉ Radio 1's flagship programmes from a long line of inspirational producers, most recently Kevin Hough and Peter Mooney, it is this book's good fortune to have as its editor Marie Heaney, who edited a previous collection of contributions to the programme: *Sunday Miscellany – A Selection from 1995–2000*. I would like to thank all at TownHouse for their commitment to the publication. Treasa Coady, in particular, is to be saluted for her foresight and determination to see the genesis of a bestselling book in the first collection. That collection made material from the programme available once more to those who heard it first on the radio, and introduced it to the many more who had the pleasure of coming across the book. The contents of this latest volume should do the same. It is, after all, what *Sunday Miscellany* takes pleasure in bringing to listeners every Sunday morning on RTÉ Radio 1.

Clíodhna Ní Anluain
Compiler and Producer, Sunday Miscellany
RTÉ Radio 1

INTRODUCTION

Sunday Miscellany: A Selection from 2003 and 2004 is the second selection of pieces from RTÉ Radio 1's celebrated programme. This volume covers a period of broadcasting that is shorter than that of the previous one, *Sunday Miscellany: A Selection from 1995–2000*, but it resembles the earlier volume in its range of topics and in the quality of its writing. I have used the same methods of choosing the material and arranging it as before and you will find in this new book the familiar mix of writing that is the hallmark of *Sunday Miscellany* programmes and anthologies.

The subject matter encompasses a wide range of human experience and moves across the barriers of time and space. To give some cohesion to such a diversity of material I have arranged it thematically into six categories. Each category broadly accommodates the variety and complexity of the pieces within it while still maintaining an element of surprise.

When it came to the difficult task of choosing scripts for inclusion, my criterion was that the piece must work primarily as a piece of writing. There is a difference between what works on air and what works on the page and some contributions that were memorable on radio may not appear in this selection. This is because intonation, delivery and the timbre of the voice – qualities that are so effective on the airwaves – do not translate on to the page.

In *Sunday Miscellany: A Selection from 2003 and 2004* you will find, as I did, anecdotes that will make you smile and others that will bring tears to your eyes. You will be transported to places you have never visited and to times long past. You will get to know people you will never meet, historical figures from the past as well as those who might otherwise be forgotten. Your views will be challenged, perhaps, and your horizons broadened, as mine were when I discovered that significant moments in some of the writers' lives had become significant for me because of the conviction of their writing.

If you are a regular listener to the Sunday morning radio programme, this selection from the last half of 2003 and the first half of 2004 will give you the chance to recover, in a permanent form, stories heard fleetingly and remembered imperfectly. If you are not familiar with the programme, *Sunday Miscellany: A Selection from 2003 and 2004* will introduce you to a world of writers and raconteurs who will share their experiences with you for brief, but memorable, moments.

Marie Heaney

A Sense of
Occasion

BUNGEE BIRTH
Cyril Kelly

Everyone is familiar with the pernicious 'itises' which can afflict a body from time to time: school-itis, Monday-itis, work-itis, the list is endless. The symptoms, disconcertingly enough, have no outward manifestation, so the sufferer can be cruelly labelled as hypochondriac, malingerer and very often a lot worse. But still the shooting pain persists. Most worrying of all, search as you might in sources as traditional as *Pear's Medical Encyclopaedia* or as modern as Ireland's health.com, there is no hope of a diagnosis.

My own peculiar brand of 'itis' happens to be TV-itis. Among my friends and my acquaintances, it is a well-known fact that I cannot sit before a television set for any protracted period of time – like, say, a quarter of an hour. Especially if the television in question happens to be turned on. God forbid that a cross-channel soap or anything with the bray of canned laughter should be transmitted – ten minutes watching such stuff can induce palpitations. One time, three and a half years ago, I stuck with Éamon de Buitléar for twenty-two minutes while he skulked behind a lump of granite on some godforsaken coastline waiting for a hermit crab.

However, I sat in front of a television set for forty minutes the other night and I haven't been the better of it since. It was all my daughter's fault. In common with half the young people of Ireland, she has bunked off on a year's adventure in the Antipodes. I mean, you spend twenty years rearing them and a sizeable percentage of your disposable income trying to educate them and this is what you get.

Just as the tourist in Ireland has to visit certain idyllic sites, the visitor 'down under' has similar innocuous pastimes which are *de rigueur*. For instance, in New Zealand, one must-do is the bungee jump. The daughter's souvenir bungee video arrived the other day, so I was prevailed upon to sit in front of the TV to watch.

I could see it straight away; that peculiar practice of standing upside down, as they do in the southern hemisphere, was not conducive to sanity. While the TV screen was still blank, this soundtrack of relentless jungle rhythms began to hammer on hollow mango trunks. There was the distress call of some bird that, like the dodo, sounded as if the poor creature was on the verge of extinction. And, if I wasn't mistaken, that was my daughter's alarmed laugh in the middle of the cacophony. But then this primitive contrivance appeared on the screen. A scaffolding of bamboo cane, forty metres high, swaying in a forest clearing. In quick succession, Maori men wearing skimpy loincloths and tethered to the top by what looked like a *súgán* began to jump from the platform. Arms crossed at the chest as if they were going to meet their maker, they sailed first up, then out and finally down – sublime parabolas of serenity – until they swung, suspended by the ankles, their skulls within a whisker of the jungle floor.

Finally, in close-up on the screen, that face I hadn't seen for over six months. My daughter was smiling nervously. The camera panned away and I could see that she was standing on Karamu Bridge. This was a box-iron contraption, buttressed by outcrops of volcanic rock 100 metres above Skipper's Canyon.

Clinging all the time to the bars on either side, she slides the toe of one petite runner out to the ledge. When she cranes to view the void below, her pendant, a twenty-first birthday gift from myself, dangles from her neck. The laser of reflected sunlight scorches the trillion butterflies clamouring my ribcage in demented vertigo. I'm the archetypal Kerryman in the joke, watching the video replay, hoping against hope for a better result. I'm screaming silently. Move back! Don't jump! Come home!

Defying death and G-force logic, she leaps. Spread-eagled in the crazy Queenstown air, she's plummeting past the blur of manuka shrubs and rimu trees huddled to the rock face. Till at last, in slow motion, the white umbilical tie line unfurls in her wake; hauls in the headlong plunge; bestows ecstatic liberation. The infant whose birth I witnessed is reborn, supple, swinging – her own unfettered woman.

A SECOND CHANCE

Maureen Mahon

I have recently rediscovered the delights of motherhood. No, it wasn't like the unexpected arrival of the stork with his precious bundle; it was more like an awakening within me which caused me to re-evaluate the mother I had become.

It all started on a cold, wet and dreary November day. It was a typical Monday morning for me, a working mother, indeed for the thousands of women who juggle full-time careers and cope with the responsibility of rearing a family.

My ear was finely tuned to the traffic reports. A wet morning meant heavier traffic, an earlier departure, fighting traffic at the school, driving up the outside lane and trying to cut in to the right lane, frustration building, my mind racing ahead to a busy day, deadlines to meet, my precious lunchtime shrinking before my eyes.

It only takes something as mundane as a missing school tie or mislaid football boots to throw your schedule out. On this particular morning, things were whizzing along nicely. My eldest son had departed for secondary school, taking with him all his teenage hormones. A glance at my watch told me it was time for me to turn my attention to my youngest son…

A small, white face peered at me from beneath 1,001 Dalmatians. All was not well with this little nine-year-old. I felt a sinking sensation in my stomach. Perhaps it wasn't as bad as it seemed. I chatted normally and encouraged him to get up. He'd feel better after a shower and something to eat. I went through the motions. He went through the motions, uncomplaining, quiet and ill.

The breakfast was untouched, the school-bag ready, the lunch packed. I looked at him again. I thought of my hectic work-filled day ahead; I thought of his truly miserable day ahead. I gathered him in my arms, loosened his tie and started to undress him.

I didn't go to work that day, nor the next, nor the next.

I read to him and listened to his stories about school, his teacher, his friends, his world, realisation dawning on me that it was a world of which I knew very little.

I sat up late into the night, my thoughts swirling around in my head. Of course, there were financial considerations, which in turn would lead to a change of lifestyle. But deep down I had already made my decision. I wanted to play a bigger role in my children's lives. In fact, I wanted to be cast in the main part. After all, I was their mother.

One year on, and my only regret is that I didn't do it sooner. I still cringe when I listen to the traffic reports in the mornings, pitying all those unfortunate commuters their weary battle every working day. These days our biggest consideration is whether the weather is fine enough for us to walk to school. I hate to use the car. We have long chats on our walks and, instead of practically pushing my son out of the car in what I now consider to be the old days, we hug at the school gates and I remain until his little head, covered with his red Man U cap, fades from my view. When I collect him in the afternoons, I see his large brown eyes searching me out in the crowd of mothers hovering at the school gate and I'm immediately rewarded by that wonderful loving smile.

Membership of the gym is long gone, yet I have never been so fit. Walking is cheap and an integral part of my day. My bicycle, which had stood dusty and unused in the garage, is now back in action. I love the feel of the wind on my face as I cycle the countryside. I have discovered a passion for cooking, and the kids delight in my culinary efforts.

In truth, I have rediscovered myself.

A ROUTINE OPERATION

Peter Hutchinson

It was to be the usual routine operation. Nothing to it. I go in one day for tests and, all being well, I am operated on the next day. A further two days resting up and then off home with me. As I say, nothing to it. Just a simple operation.

But as the old saying goes, there's no such thing as a *simple* operation. Once they get you on that theatre table, anything can happen and without blame to anyone. In my case the operation went well and soon I was sitting up and smiling. And then something went badly wrong. The 'something' turned out to be a stroke and, for ten days, I slept.

Funny thing is, at times during that long sleep I became aware of what was happening around me. No, I didn't hear my family gathering around my bed, nor did I know about the priest and the last rites. But I *did* faintly hear nurses coming off their tour of duty and, as they passed my bed, bidding me not a cheerful 'So long' but a gentle 'Good luck'.

Another thing, I became blearily conscious that my son was on his knees beside my bed. I half-turned, mumbled something about being tired. He said nothing, just nodded, and I drifted off again. Was he there day and night? He was, after all, my youngest, and his mother, my wife, had died in the recent past.

Not to sound too morbid, but I don't fear death any more if it's going to be like those ten days of sleep. Unlike death, however, and inexplicably, on a morning of sunshine I came back, not knowing what day it was, but conscious that I was tired no longer, only warm and hungry. The surgeon suddenly appeared and congratulated me on my recovery and I didn't realise even then what it was all about.

At a convenient time I was wheeled down to physiotherapy to learn to walk again. Four days fixed that. From a standing position, I could sway and swerve without stumbling. Where did they get that dedicated therapist? And all the time I knew that I was being watched by nurses to make sure, I suppose, that my recovery wasn't a temporary thing.

I began to realise the escape I'd had. And soon everyday things lost their everydayness and became events and people to savour, to delight in, and ordinary life was now an extraordinary experience.

Whatever faculties I possessed were intensified. From my hospital bed I became aware of the enchantment of cloudless nights. Outside my window the grasslands stretched into dark distances until they were edged on the horizon by the city lights, necklaces of jewels sparkling along the perimeter of a wonderful world.

On one such night, on a whim I'm sure, a young nurse who had said her goodbyes on that day long past looked into the ward as she commenced her tour of duty and saw that I was still there and in one piece. What I interpreted as sheer professionalism lit up her face. She stood there, apparently marvelling at the resurrected. I rose from my armchair. With my therapy treatment behind me I raised my arms and commenced a Greek movement that could only be described as stupid. She grinned and came to me, her eyes shining, disbelief still so evident, and we danced in the moonlight.

I never saw her again, but that night I had witnessed what it is to have a job that you love and care about and to have a commitment that gives you joy.

SUMMER STUFF
Chuck Kruger

After breakfast I look west across Cape Clear Island's south harbour, over swaying masts and wheeling gulls, and spot a tractor with a buckrake depositing a haycock beside a stone-bordered foundation. A flock of children playfully trample pikefuls laid flat by three men.

In no time I've joined the summer ritual and I'm trampling away with the kids. Bits of hay, bits of banter, cover us all. The reek rises. Now and then someone checks the stack for straightness.

'That corner's a bit proud,' I hear from the artists below.

Tramp, tramp, tramp. With every step I try to compress the hay without jostling the stack. Back and forth, back and forth. I'm in the rhythm of a beast of burden, trudging round and round a menial yet essential task. The stack grows too high for the safety of all but the oldest boys. The work becomes more serious, especially with a wet, heavy fog rolling in from the Fastnet. Periodically, I place my pike along the edge of the stack, step on it, and a barber below, with a long-toothed rake, combs out loose hair.

As the haystack grows, my trampling slows. Three men pike up to me. I spread and position the hay, as well as pack it. The boys descend. I lay occasional pikefuls across the middle so that the hay interlocks with that from the other side. The fog skins off north, blanketing Roaringwater Bay. Now the reek begins to tower, to jiggle like slow-motion jelly beneath me. And, as if on cue, a parade of women bustle down from the house carrying kettles, jugs, platters. They spread tablecloths on the grass. Thick egg-salad sandwiches ooze between my fingers. Below, the harbour mills with yachts preparing for a nearby race. A farmer curls asleep beside the reek. Another tiptoes over, dumps an armful of hay on his face. Wild shouts, gesticulations, laughter.

Kids scampering about. Recriminations. I hear one of the seventy-year-olds say, 'This is the way it used to be.'

And we're back at work. Tramp. Reposition. Conversation drifts up to me. Push the corner out. Too low to the southeast. Haircut time. Have we enough hay to finish her off? Is that a drop of rain – or a gull? This cock's too much wet in it. Lay it flat, man, not so much at once.

At the top, twelve feet high, I have to reach my pike down and snag efforts from below, pull 'em the rest of the way up. Someone who really knows his stuff joins me. Two on top, two piking, two hauling the cocks from adjacent fields, kids raking the fields to collect the last wisps. A mug of water's pushed up to us on the end of a pike.

Using our pikes like grappling irons, we two on top snare an old fishnet, folded in half, pushed up. Presto, the reek's secure, covered tight with bright orange and blue and black twine. We beat a few more humps out, climb down the rickety ladder, tie stones and heavy pipe along the edges of the net so that winter gales won't blow our creation to the Scilly Isles.

And it's finished, the cattle are guaranteed hay through the winter. We trudge to the house, where yet more food, *uisce beatha* and banter are passed around as we sprawl in the yard.

I return home, take my first late afternoon nap of the year. When I wake, I peer out the bedroom window. And there, across the harbour, she stands, foursquare, straight, golden.

THE PIANO LESSON
Mary O'Donnell

It was the month when everything flowers, when night-time has shrunk to a twilight bank of darkness and the birds start staking out their territory just after 4 a.m. It was the month when I foolishly imagined – as I do most years – that summer is here, that it's time to down tools and relax a little.

But the month of May was also marked out by something else: the approach of the annual piano examination. Once it was me hammering away on those major and minor scales, those arpeggios and contrary motions, occasionally giving the piano base a vital kick of frustration. Just under four decades ago, yes, it was me, panicking at the last minute, feeling my hands collapse from a mixture of under-practice and final, last-minute over-practice, as I tried to play the third, upbeat movement of Mozart's *Sonata in C Major*. The exasperated nun, at her wits' end, was literally crying. She had thrown me out of the room – telling me not to come back until I could play the piece – convinced that I could neither sight-read nor play. But I could, and I did. I got through, was not allowed to give up music and went on to the next grade.

In secondary school, with a different teacher, I was sailing in more temperate waters. Sr Enda, whose room always smelled of lavender water, was calmer than my first teacher. She had time for a bit of a gossip about contemporary matters both before and after each lesson. She was interested in my fair hair but did not approve of the length of my school tunic. She was also good at pushing girls on to achievements they never thought possible. Gradually, music became less of an obstacle course and more of an exploration. I discovered a space in which to manoeuvre myself – a private, uncomplicated and exciting world where I could excel in the same way the Latin aces of our class excelled. But something else too: a private world where the work of

11

repetition led to something beyond the self, and was not useless and redundant. At the end, there were always music pieces learned by heart, but more importantly, *felt* in the heart. Coming up to the music exams, Sr Enda's interest intensified. It was a pushy interest, but one that was inspired by a combined appetite for music *and* results.

The final days before the exam became a kind of quest, a search for the nearest thing to perfection on the keyboard. There were also bonuses that inspired and encouraged: the chance to practise on the school grand piano, which had a strikingly different feel from the ordinary upright one – the ivory keys, subtle and velvety to the touch, and a sound that was mellifluous and complex as it rose into the high space of the school concert hall.

The examiners were usually pleasant, and not the grizzled, dried-up old sticks I automatically expected. The best of them made me want to show off, to perform. If the examiner had a foreign accent, that was a further point of intrigue, making something special of the exam. Europe was coming to Ireland, it seemed. One year we had a Dutch examiner, who observed and listened with just the right degree of attention and non-judgement. Afterwards, he chatted about each piece. It was my first experience of discussing music with someone who asked questions as if speaking to an equal. What such discussion signalled to me was this: that music was important. All that practising was about something very deep and simple in human nature, it was about recapturing the slippery fish of our own souls, and it was all right to undertake such a journey – regardless of the practical, grade-orientated nature of the outcome of the exam. Some of the other exam subjects – like Latin and maths – seemed like crude exercises in mountaineering for the inexperienced. In comparison, music was like skiing on dry, compacted snow, with the wind in my hair and uplifting thoughts in my head.

That's what worked for me. Now it's my daughter's turn. As I write these words, she's downstairs working her way through one of the minor scales. It's the week before the music exam and her teacher has got her to increase the tempo of a piece called 'The Clown'. Suddenly, it has sprung from sedate accuracy to something else, and I can hear this clown and his work in the circus of joy and fun. I don't know yet how she feels about her music. What I do know is that Britney Spears is every bit as important as *The Valkyries* or *Romeo and Juliet*. The Britney video that accompanies her hit 'Everytime' is full of imagery of youthful beauty and premature death. These are worthwhile images that, sometimes, perhaps *only* music can respond to, like a sacred ship throwing a mystical anchor deep into the soul, where it resides with passion and pain and is never forgotten.

VOX HUMANA
Iarla Ó Lionaird

It begins in the mouth, that flat taste, the unleavened, weightless host stuck to the roof long enough for its white moistening odour to make itself known from the inside out; it must be Sunday. I am already sitting up in bed, then my semi-awake body lands heavily on the cold raspberry lino two yards down from my bunk perch, the memory of my father's call to action still pealing in my head. Sunday clothes, bathroom queuing, the staired descent and then shoes – more than most would see other than in a shoe shop. Twelve pairs to be exact – their heels, tongues, toes and eyes still glinting aromatically – a burnished rawhide exhibit, elbow-greased into formation in front of the Rayburn. The fumbled closings and fastenings of best gear, the ensuing special warmth of once-a-week attire, hair-combing, a must in those days, and then bundled hastily into the VW minibus, the only family-owned one in the parish, and off we go. Before long we are heading down the hill of Tóchar on our three-mile south-western odyssey to mass. Tóchar, the road of angry bulls and silent farmers, telegraph lines and shelterless rain, of bursting tar bubbles on sunny days. Tóchar, causeway and winding road, where the sally stakes that fence this grass-centred track took root and blushed into trees again.

Two miles on we take a sharp left at Muirneach Bheag past Ó Riada's house, the tree-slung parch chimes snapshot into mind, their tubular polyphony reverberant as we glide past the lower gate and on to the little chapel of Cúil Aodha, the Sulan River flowing against our flow on the other side. Churches in this part of the world have a double life, life within their walls and yet another hanging around the chapel yard, and, as we arrive, we pass the familiar row of broad-backed farmers holding up the outer wall – their hummed and mumbled discourse, phonic emblems of their trade, horse dealers, politicians and fixers – theirs will be a ceremony mediated by the crackling megaphone clinging nest-like to the porch eaves overlooking the door. I take my place with the youngest in the front, facing the keyboard, and kneel on the carpet-tiled floor. It's almost time. Father O'Connor appears and floats across the altar, his serried fingertips peering out from beneath his vestments. The swell paddles move apart; the pedal bellows fill as ankles coax the harmonium into life. My eyes scan the words 'Mason & Hamlin' emblazoned in gold as with each pull the black-and-red organ stops release otherworldly tongues: 'Diaphason Dolce', the sweet translucent tone; 'Aeolian Harp', each note a pluck of air; 'Seraphone', the song of divine beings; 'Vox Celeste', a heavenly voice; and lastly the tremulant 'Vox Humana', surely *our* God-encrypted cue. I rise to one knee then stand and a stream of voices ensues, a ruddied mix, the weft and warp of an elemental cloth once again made new.

> *Críost liom, Críost romham*
> *Críost im' dhiaidh*
> *Is Críost os mo chionn-sa*
> *Agus Críost fúm.*
> *Críost ina Chónai im'chroí-se.*

> Christ with me, Christ before me
> Christ behind me, Christ above me
> And Christ beneath me.
> Christ living within me.

I hear my child song within a weave of voices folded around me, and in this atemporal space, each strand's particularity maps a compass point perfectly matched to its source; each grained discrepancy marking a shared course, so that even with my eyes momentarily shut I can still see clearly the maker's mark by their sounding. I can sense behind me, to the side and all around me, the peopled components of this circumfluent sensorium of flesh, wood and stone. It is in this place that the song in me took root, sheltered in a grove of sound.

As mass progressed I would repeat a familiar recycled pose, studying between songs the harmonium's butter-and-black keys, then flexing once more to a standing position, each cycle of movements culminating in a gentle lifting of chins and then, all enjoined in song – 'Go mBeannitear Duit a Mhuire', 'Ár nAthair', 'Ag Críost an Síol', 'A Rí an Domhnaigh' and 'Gile mo Chroí' – as those attending moved imperceptibly, inevitably, to the altar steps and then I too would find myself there, where sense and memory condense into one final tasted affirmation of what could not be understood and yet somehow the body had known.

And then, always with that sense of having sung, I walk to the church porch, my father's old penny, its weight grounding me once more as I thumb its bronzed hen feathers all the way to Scannel's sweet shop and home.

A SUMMER SERENADE
Mary Collins Dolan

In the early 1980s, I worked in the Rockefeller Centre's International Building, one of the first of the Art-Deco style skyscrapers to be built in the 1930s by the multi-millionaire John D Rockefeller. It was a glorious early summer's evening, well before New York's heat and humidity had taken hold and, having stayed on in the office a while to finish something, I waited to take the elevator down from the fifty-first floor.

I had recently begun reading *Ancient Evenings*, a somewhat impenetrable book by the American writer Norman Mailer, which I was having difficulty 'getting into' even though archaeology and Egyptology were subjects close to my heart. And so I determinedly buried my head in the book while I waited for the elevator and continued reading as I descended, leaning against the back rail of the cab, its sole occupant.

The elevator stopped after a few seconds and I was vaguely aware of a small group getting in, engaged in conversation, but I continued reading until I recognised a voice. I knew before I looked up who it was, and when I did look up, there he was – Richard Harris. Dressed all in black – black turtleneck shirt, black chino jeans and black cowboy boots – with a shock of yellow-white hair that badly needed cutting, and as thin as a rail. I remember so distinctly what he was wearing because I thought it was incongruous with the weather, and the overall effect was that of a scarecrow!

He had broken off conversation at the same time, noticed my book and asked me how I liked 'Mailer's latest'. I mumbled something about it being very difficult to follow, and he nodded as he said: 'Keep at it – it's worth the read.' Barely pausing to catch his breath, he asked me if he should sing a song and, without waiting for a response, launched into something from *Camelot*. Memory tells me it was 'If Ever I Should Leave You', but I can't be sure because I know Robert Goulet sang that song in the stage version. But it doesn't matter, because Harris sang it with gusto and obvious delight while his companions stood there bemused – partially, I think, because Harris's powerful voice was rebounding within the confines of the elevator, but also no doubt due to my blushing countenance.

The serenade lasted but a minute. We reached the ground floor, the doors opened and Harris's friends stepped out. With a grandiose flourish and bow, he beckoned me to precede him, thanked me for my company, wished me a most pleasant evening and walked off whistling the tune, hands in pockets, to join his friends.

And I, dumbstruck throughout the three-minute encounter, watched him go out into the sunshine and disappear on to Fifth Avenue, swallowed up by the throngs of summer strollers.

Now it should be pointed out that we New Yorkers are well used to bumping into all sorts of characters – good, bad and indifferent – and are generally very blasé about it. But now, twenty years later, living here in County Leitrim, when my daughter and I marvel at Richard Harris's portrayal of Professor Dumbledore in the Harry Potter adventures, I like to think that it was my yellow linen suit and softly upswept auburn hair that moved him to serenade me in an elevator on a pleasant summer's evening in New York.

VERONA, 1990
Áine Mulvey

It was midday in August 1990 and I was seated at the top row of the steps in the Arena di Verona. The sun beat down fiercely on me and 3,000 other singers, arrayed in rows, spread out like an eagle in the Arena. Far, far down below us, the Moscow Philharmonic Orchestra sounded like a distant brass band, and our conductor, the internationally renowned Lorin Maazel, struggled to control an enormous choir that sounded more like a football mob than a group of musicians worthy of his baton.

I was one of 3,000 choristers from around the world who had come to perform Verdi's *Requiem* in Verona's Opera Festival. Pavarotti was billed as soloist and, from my vantage point at the top of the Arena, I watched him arrive for the rehearsal. Old ladies leaned from balconies calling excitedly, 'Luciano!' and he waved back, magnanimous. His arrival inside the Arena disrupted the entire rehearsal for several minutes while the huge amateur choir went wild.

But the logistics of the immense choir and the enormity of the Arena were causing problems. There was a sound delay of several seconds from one side of the choir to the other – the fugue during the 'Libera Me' was disastrous. Unable to hear the orchestra, we must have sounded like some lumbering mammoth, dragging along several seconds after the beat. Lorin Maazel became more and more irritated – I'm sure he must have regretted committing to this ludicrous idea. We were all on holiday, but his professional reputation was on the line.

By the following day, the sound engineers had performed wonders. We could hear the orchestra! The alto line still sounded as if it was coming from the other end of the university, but it was better. I spent the rehearsal amused at the incongruity of the furious 'Dies irae' sung by a choir where the ladies were dressed in bikini tops and shorts and the men had handkerchiefs knotted over their bald spots.

The first of the two *Requiem* concerts was performed against a backdrop of a beautiful Italian evening. As the sun went down, the audience of 25,000 lit candles, and we looked out at a perfect ring of glimmering lights. As the night grew dark, the candles went out slowly, until there was only the darkness of the night, the light of the stars and the mosquitoes that landed on our scores and refused to move before the page turned. It was a magical and funny atmosphere.

We bought the papers the next day and marvelled at the photographs. Someone attempted to translate the Italian review. The gist of it was that the enormous choir was more of a visual spectacle than a musical success, but we could accept this reasonably cheerfully.

After the final concert, a few of us joined dozens of other fans stationed outside Pavarotti's dressing room, hoping for an autograph. He made us wait and most gave up. An hour or so later, there was still no bribing the security guard. So we decided to sing – we were choristers after all! And some moments after our three-part arrangement of 'Danny Boy' had faded out, the message came through: 'Let the singers in.'

We entered his room, momentarily stunned to be in his actual presence. And a vast presence it was too – bigger than he looked on television, dressed in a loud, red and black smoking jacket. Pavarotti was the soul of benevolence, dispensing autographs with wry charm and patiently posing for photos – an occupation that must have been as dull for him as it was riveting for us.

Dizzy with success, we sang our way down the cobbled streets to the piazza where the rest of our contingent had retired for a post-concert glass of wine. Jubilantly we boasted of the photos we had taken and proudly displayed our autographed programmes.

When I look at the photo now, I smile at the girl with the mile-wide grin, arm around Pavarotti's huge shoulder, clearly delighted with herself. Still – it remains a beloved memento of the time when I sang Verdi's *Requiem* with the Moscow Philharmonic on a balmy Italian night lit by stars and candles.

SALOME AT THE OPERA HOUSE, VIENNA
Kevin McDermott

Is it any wonder that Oscar Wilde was drawn to the story of Salome? I see it appealing to his taste for the grotesque, all those lurid ingredients – obsessive desire, eroticism, the fear of the flesh, revenge, a bizarre dénouement. Salome addressing the severed head of John the Baptist, kissing it, caressing it – and the gruesome, murderous ending. Right up Oscar's street, wouldn't you say? Not one for understatement, our beloved Oscar.

And when Richard Strauss used the play as the libretto for his 1905 opera, the effect was explosive – 'blasphemy', 'infamy', 'pornography', the protesters cried.

Richard and Oscar. The odd couple. Both publicly humiliated – Oscar for the 'crime' of homosexuality ('I never saw sad men who looked/With such a wistful eye/Upon that little tent of blue/We prisoners call the sky') and poor Richie, in his eighties, undergoing a process of de-Nazification.

How savagely our civilised world upholds its values; how deeply we fear our artists.

I thought of both Oscar Wilde and Richard Strauss when I sat amid the splendour of the Opera House in Vienna, attending a performance of *Salome*, as a shaft of blue light from the stage fell on the rapt and beautiful face of a woman in the audience upon whom my gaze was trained.

A week before, I had paid €7 to sit in a litter-strewn cinema in Dublin and here I was, having paid €9, sitting in a box in one of the finest opera houses in Europe. €9. A cinema seat in Dublin. A seat in the opera house in Vienna. *Quel dilemme.*

To be honest, I wasn't sure what our €9 had secured for us. So when we handed our tickets to a young hussar, we were delighted when he invited us to ascend the wonderful baroque staircase. To walk there, among the good citizens of Vienna dressed up to the nines in their fur coats and gold jewellery, was worth the admission charge alone. And then, another hussar directed us to our box. We occupied the second row, with a full view of the auditorium and a partial view of the orchestra and stage.

No matter, for when the curtain rose and Strauss's magnificent music filled the auditorium, we were transported. An hour and forty minutes of enchantment. 'Your skin,' Salome tells the prophet, 'is as white as the snow of Judea.'

Afterwards, we followed the fur coats to a coffee house, The Landtmann, where Sigmund Freud was wont to sit of an afternoon, unravelling dreams. We sat opposite a maharajah, whose vermilion silk robes were embroidered with golden thread. It seemed apt, somehow, after the extravagance of *Salome*.

Snatches of conversation drifted our way.

'Had she not married him,' the maharani told her prince, 'she would have ended up a common housewife selling cosmetics in Bombay.'

I'm not sure what makes art great. I'm not sure what makes a great artist. I do know, however, that listening to Richard Strauss's *Salome* in the opera house in Vienna, on a weekend when the marble city was covered in snow, was a glorious reminder of the human capacity to create beauty – a reminder of the power of art to put us in touch with our best selves – and to take us beyond ourselves.

And I salute you and I thank you, Richard, Oscar.

THEATRICAL TOUR
Ann O'Dwyer

In the spring of 1960, Cyril Cusack Productions formed a company of actors to take George Bernard Shaw's play *Arms and the Man* on a tour of a number of international festivals on the Continent. The tour would open in Belfast, then take in Dublin and on to Europe, culminating in the Sarah Bernhardt Theatre at the Paris International Theatre Festival.

I was asked to audition and, after a gruelling session with Cyril Cusack and the director Godfrey Quigley, I was cast as Louka the servant girl, a very good part with some lovely scenes.

The first day of rehearsals arrived, always a very nervous and intimidating affair, but even more so as I was the young, inexperienced player among a group of established actors. Cyril was playing the main character of Bluntschli, and his wife, the lovely and very talented Maureen Cusack, was playing Raina. Shelagh Richards, one of the most beautiful and accomplished actresses I have ever known, was playing Raina's mother, and Paul Farrell was playing her father. Finally, P J Stephens and Seamus Locke came from London to complete the cast.

We were to open at the Empire Theatre in Belfast on a Monday night in June and play for two weeks. Our first shock: the set was only partly built! Our set designer was the brilliant and sadly now deceased Sean Kenny. He had designed a fine but complicated set, very advanced for its time, with a downstairs room, a staircase, a landing and an upstairs bedroom. Scenes were played on all of these areas and so the set needed to be solid. There was no sign of Sean, as on the same night the musical *Oliver* opened in London and Sean's outstanding set was the toast of the town. Our show was unable to open on the Monday, but we finally managed it on the Tuesday – although, as one critic wrote, 'the last hammer blows could be heard behind the curtain just before it rose.' The two-week run in Belfast was a success and the play gelled into a tight production. We moved to the Abbey, in its temporary home in the old Queen's Theatre, for the next two weeks. Still no sign of Sean Kenny – but the set was holding, good reviews were received and there were full houses nightly.

The following week we set off by air for the Amsterdam Festival. The audiences were marvellous, they understood to perfection the comedy and the lovely nuances of the play. Cyril's performance was a real *tour de force*.

We continued on our way – The Hague, Antwerp, Brussels – but slowly and creakingly our set began to disintegrate. Moving and travelling was taking its toll and still there was no sign of Sean Kenny.

Paris grew nearer and, to our delight, we found we had two weeks free before our opening night in the Sarah Bernhardt Theatre. But to our mystification, just before we arrived, Cyril informed us that he would redirect the play and have rehearsals on arrival. Consternation! How could this be? The reviews for the play and all members of the cast had been consistently very good. However, the director/producer is God and so we rehearsed to exhaustion.

One of the best set designers in Paris, M Daidei, was employed to rebuild our set, which he did admirably and, to his credit, Sean Kenny finally turned up and worked very hard under Daidei's direction. Our set was now superb.

Opening night at the Sarah Bernhardt was a glittering affair. But the audience reaction was different: the comedy did not appear to get across, the redirection did not work. The cast was very upset and wondered if it was just a 'first night' experience, but no, the same thing happened the following night. For my part I was devastated. Louka had two wonderful comedy scenes and there was not a laugh to be heard. Within a day or two, the cast got together (except for the Cusacks, of course) and a decision was made to return to our original 'performances', and hang the consequences. That night the reception was ecstatic. We waited for the bombshell from above. Not a word. No notes. We finished the tour on a wonderful high.

On the last night I went to Cyril's dressing room to say goodbye. We talked as he sat at his make-up table and, when I turned to go, he said, 'Well, my dear, you have learned a lot on this tour, I think.' He looked up at me with that wry smile of his through his dressing-room mirror and added, 'I don't think you will forget this experience.' I backed out of his room. How right he was. But I wouldn't have missed it for the world.

An important addendum to the whole tour: Cyril Cusack was of course nominated for his role and won the coveted Actor of the Year award of the 1959–60 International Theatre Festival of Paris.

MY GREAT GRANDFATHER WAS AN ORANGEMAN

Gerald Dawe

My great grandfather was an Orangeman. The story goes that there would have been a banner dedicated to him but his (that is, my) family demurred. I never met William Bailey Chartres. He was of Huguenot stock and married a woman of another refugee stock (she was a Quartz). He fitted into Belfast life as a man of his turn-of-the-last-century times. Growing up in north Belfast in the late 1950s and early 1960s, I was fascinated by this invisible man. His name was still known around and about and that intrigued me: photographs, news cuttings, cartoons, membership cards of this and that; all these mementoes were kept in the house I grew up in. I have, to this day, a cartoon which shows him, a pair of breeches in hand, an old-fashioned, unadorned sash over his shoulder, tearing across cobblestones under the slogan 'Duty Calls!' When I was a kid, I hadn't a clue what that duty meant. It was just as well that William was gone because we would never have seen eye to eye over his patriarchal Unionism.

Throughout the 1950s, I was taken to watch the Twelfth of July parades. We would stand outside the City Hall, our backs up against the ropes, and wait for the carriages to arrive carrying the grandees of the different orders. There would be a kind of embarrassed banter as the preacher – with his doom-laden, black sandwich-board proverb strapped to his chest – would raise his heavy Bible in the air and stamp his foot, calling vengeance or foreboding upon us all. Were we sinners?

Behind, the kiss-me-quick-hat brigade linked arms and danced in their Union Jack shirts and aprons, the marching men in bowler hats waved umbrellas, and the bands streamed by. Wedged between them, serried ranks of men waved, pointing their sons towards mothers, wives, brothers with infants on their shoulders, and the music cascaded down Royal Avenue, veered right and left again, and on down the Dublin Road.

'Kilty' bands, military bands, flute bands, bands from Scotland which were called *hucky-mucky*, men with shining white gloves, sabres, little trays with icons placed on them, banners of marvellous silks with images of queens, kings, stern men, martial figures, historical settings. Sometimes there would be a delay in the procession, a band would stop in front of you and you could watch the bandsmen and their leader walking around. The banners would sway some more and the young boys who held the black or white or orange strings would twirl them in their hands, or the big drummer would have someone hitch up the drum for a brief rest. I've never seen a Lambeg drum since.

We did not go to the Field. Sometimes we'd return after tea to see the men come back through, but by the mid-1960s, that had stopped. Something different was creeping in. Then we stopped going altogether. I don't know why. All I remember is the Eleventh Night and the flames bursting up into the sky in the Brickies behind our home and, in the morning, the drum-roll as a banner was unfurled in the Grandmaster's back garden, which I could see from my back window. Tea was served and then the lodge joined up with its band and they made their way along Jellico Avenue and Alexandra Park on to the Antrim Road towards Clifton Street and the beginning of the Belfast procession. It would take a great film director like Antonioni or Buñuel to capture the unbelievable clash of pomp, propriety, machismo, bigotry and pride that went into those Twelfth celebrations in the 1950s and early 1960s.

Years later, all this ceremony was becoming known worldwide as standing for only one thing, a triumphalist sectarian bazaar. I wrote a sequence of very short poems about growing up in upper north Belfast, called simply *Six Scenes*. This is 'The Banner':

> *The Past Master's*
> *taut face gleams*
> *like the window*

of his makeshift
glasshouse.
The teacup shakes
from stiff gloves
he has on as
the banner unfurls
to a swaying scene
of Slave and Queen.

ZAPRUDER

John O'Donnell

Like many captains of industry, Abraham Zapruder was, in part, made famous by the persistence of his secretary. Zapruder ran a dress-manufacturing business in downtown Dallas, just across from a building called the Texas School Book Depository. He'd planned to go to watch the cavalcade, but believed he'd no chance of actually seeing the President on his visit to Dallas that November morning. But his secretary Lillian Rogers persuaded him to bring his camera, just in case. So he went home to fetch the Bell & Howell 8-mm movie camera. Zapruder had originally bought the camera for making home movies of his grandchildren. Just before lunchtime, however, the little camera would have recorded one of the most significant pieces of live footage of the twentieth century – the assassination of President John F Kennedy.

In a sense, Abraham Zapruder's film is an A to Z of what happened; what the assassination really meant. In colour and (for its time) surprisingly clear, it shows graphically how a dream can turn into a nightmare. We see the gleaming open-top limousine cruising slowly down the street. The tanned young President is smiling and waving to the crowds, his wife pretty in pink beside him. They shimmer in the midday sunshine as they glide towards us. No matter how much we know now, nothing can prepare us for what happens next. The car emerges from behind a road sign and suddenly Kennedy is clutching at his throat. His wife turns to look at him; something is wrong here, something is terribly wrong. But the car keeps going, bringing them nearer and nearer. A second or two later, Kennedy's head 'explodes like a firecracker', as Zapruder himself put it, before our disbelieving eyes.

Some photographers jumped for safety when they heard the shots, others were too shocked to press the shutter. But Zapruder kept filming. Shaken, he returned later to his office, locked the film in a safe and called the police. Word soon got out: there was a film of the Kennedy assassination. The FBI made copies. *LIFE* magazine (described by some as the CNN of its day) quickly concluded a deal for the original, in which Zapruder would receive $150,000 over a period of five years. Zapruder gave the initial payment of $25,000 dollars to the Firemen and Policemen's Benefit Fund, with a recommendation that the money be donated to Mrs Tippit, the widow of the policeman Oswald had shot – shortly after the President's assassination – outside the cinema where he was ultimately arrested. Others were less conscientious. *LIFE* magazine had said they would never sell the broadcasting rights of the film. Inevitably, however, bootleg copies began to appear. Ultimately, the magazine returned the original tape to the Zapruders; the US government then acquired it and finally concluded a multi-million dollar compensation deal with the Zapruder family in 1999. It is now kept in the National Archives, though copies licensed by the Zapruder family are still commercially available.

And Abraham Zapruder? Well, as you might imagine, life for him was never quite the same. He knew, even as Walter Cronkite was reporting gravely that Kennedy was rumoured to have been seriously injured, that the President was dead. 'They killed him, they killed him,' he shouted as the sirens and the engines roared, carrying the fatally wounded forty-six-year-old Boston-Irishman towards Parkland Hospital, away from Dealey Plaza, away from the small green hill and picket fence where Zapruder stood which would afterwards be known as 'the grassy knoll'. When the Warren Commission investigators came to interview him in 1964, he broke down as he tried to recount what he had seen through the viewfinder. He gave the camera to the FBI, and later on to Bell & Howell – it too is now in the Archives. He died in 1970 aged sixty-five. His legacy is a spool of tape that runs, without sound, for less than twenty seconds, a silent witness to a moment in sunny downtown Dallas when the world changed forever.

A CHILD'S WAR

Joan McCabe

Despite the fact that I was only five years old, I did realise that the wail of the siren was not to be ignored. When it sounded over Belfast, the grown-ups had only one thing to say: 'The Gerries are coming!' This was followed by a flurry of activity. Those words struck terror into my heart and a fear that this time they would definitely get me. I wasn't too sure just how this would happen, but my main scenario seemed to picture hundreds of stark black figures slowly dropping from the inky sky, white silk parachutes drifting above them. Their faces would be hidden behind black goggles, unseen and intent on murdering us all in our beds. Hadn't I seen them myself in the newsreels in the Saturday morning show in the Curzon Cinema?

I knew the flat roof over our coal shed would be an ideal landing place for them, since the big house across the entry from us had been taken over by Yanks and the Gerries would be able to fight them from our roof. I could see the Yanks in the yard opposite, peeling their way through big sacks of spuds and vegetables, yet ready for action, should the Germans strike. I could hear them talking and singing in their Roy Rogers voices in the weak May sunshine. Sometimes they drank a dark liquid from funny shaped bottles, which I later learned to be a drink called 'Cola'.

Now and again the Yanks would see me peeking and would wave in a friendly, easy way. I would jump back, mortified at being caught out, but was drawn back again and again to spy on them. Then I began to wonder what would happen if the Gerries found out I was friendly with the Yanks. I decided to keep away from the return room and to mind my own business in future.

The warning siren usually went off at night, and it was the signal for our family to leave warm beds and head fearfully for the space under the stairs. Sometimes called 'The Glory Hole', it was the choice of shelter for most Belfast families during the air raids. It also served as a safe place for the family treasures. During a raid I loved to pass the time inspecting the old musty boxes, with their treasure-trove of china, silver and ornaments, all carefully wrapped in pages from *Ireland's Saturday Night*.

One particular night I was wakened by the dreaded siren blaring loudly. In great fear we all tumbled into our hidey-hole to await the German planes. From the wee door I watched my father preparing to join the men of our street in the nightly watch. I followed his large comforting shadow in the dim candlelight, dreading the moment he would disappear into the unknown, not sure if he would ever come back to us.

At these times my greatest comfort was our large and extremely fat black cat, Felix. During the raids it was the custom to open all windows and doors in the hope of lessening the effect of any blast from a falling bomb. Satisfied that all was in order, my mother would join us at last. Ignoring the distant whine of the enemy planes, we curled up with the *Dandy* and the *Beano*. Felix lay between my knees, purring and dozing. Suddenly he rose and headed for the open door and the freedom of the night. I was too young to understand the workings of the feline mind, or what drove that cat to his nocturnal wanderings. All I felt was terror for his safety, as he sailed nonchalantly into the hell that was Belfast that particular night.

I could hear the Gerry planes droning over the city and I could see the flash of arc lights searching out the enemy. I clapped my hands over my ears as the drone grew louder, and an insane fear for my beloved Felix gripped me. I opened my mouth and screamed. No one could pacify me, I wanted that cat and nothing else would do. Where were the Yanks when you needed them?

Finally my mother gave in and crawled out to a cold and draughty kitchen. Wishing all cats to hell and back, she felt her way into the pitch-black yard, calling softly to the missing Felix. After what seemed an eternity, his black shape danced up the yard wall, down on to the mangle and in through the door.

Purposefully he ran between my legs, tail stiff as a ramrod, and straight into my waiting arms.

Ecstatically I buried my face in his cold musky fur, feeling the damp black weight of him on my lap. He had escaped the Germans and their bombs! A deep resonant purr filtered from his soft body to mine as his claw rhythmically kneaded the arm of my blue woolly jumper. In the soft flicker of the candle I watched his green eyes narrow and close. In the distance I heard the fading drone of the departing German planes. We would live to fight another day!

THREE CHEERS FOR DEMOCRACY
Norman Freeman

Whenever I hear someone say that they're not going to vote, or they give out about the flaws in our democratic system, I'm reminded of a voyage I made many years ago. I was the radio officer on a ship which went to South America to load beef for the British market.

Our first loading port was Buenos Aires, capital of Argentina. On our arrival, the shipping agent came on board. Like many Argentinians, he was a man of Italian background. He had an important warning to impart to us all.

'We gotta the military rule here in Argentina. In a bar or some kind of dive, don't get into a fight, OK? Otherwise police come, everybody gets arrested. Who knows what happens!' He shrugged his shoulders to indicate menace.

With these warnings in our ears we strolled about the streets of this great city, a vibrant place full of life and energy, resounding with the rhythm of the tango. But we were careful. We saw the bullet marks on the front of the Casa Rosada, the presidential palace that had been stormed by the army in its successful coup.

We then set off for Brazil, passing almost within sight of Uruguay, which was also under military rule at that time. We arrived at Pôrto Alegre, in the southern part of Brazil. We had hardly tied up alongside when a blond man, representing the agents, came on board. Like many in that part of Brazil, he was German. Almost the very first words he uttered were a warning.

'We now have in control the colonels. A *putsch*, you understand. The President is ousted. Military rule. Better for nobody to get into trouble in bars and... other places.'

So here we were, going about with some caution in one of the largest and most populous countries in the world, a country of endless diversity, of great wealth and poverty, of colour, of the smell of coffee and exotic tobacco, of the sound of the samba and Brazilian-accented Portuguese.

We eventually set sail for Europe. Brazil is so vast that it took us five days to clear the coast of this country where the military ruled. After another five days we were abreast of Africa. In the radio room I began hearing signals of the marine radio stations in the Canary Islands. They and the Spanish mainland were then under the repressive dictatorship of General Franco. At much the same time, the stations in Madeira and in Lisbon could be heard. At that time Portugal had been under the dictatorship of one Dr Salazar for decades. The jails of the Iberian Peninsula were full of political detainees.

At long last, after three weeks sailing in the shadow of military rulers and dictators of one kind or another, our ship reached the Bay of Biscay. That evening I switched the main transmission aerial into the receiver. With earphones on head, I managed to tune in and amplify the sound of Radio Éireann on the medium wave.

There was a report of that day's proceedings in Dáil Éireann. Some deputies complained that they could not get in or out of the Dáil without running the gauntlet of groups and individuals, some with placards, protesting about a variety of matters. One TD, whose name I cannot recall, was reported as saying: 'I can't go outside the Dáil without some fellow giving me dog's abuse about the price of a pint.'

Now, while I could never condone our elected representatives being subjected to 'dog's abuse', at the same time I found myself saying, 'Three cheers for democracy.'

JOURNEY TO AFRICA
Jane Wright

My parents were married in Skibbereen in 1938 and, shortly afterwards, my father departed alone to take up a medical post in East Africa. My mother planned to follow him as soon as she could, but all her early attempts failed. War then broke out, and it was not until 1940 that she found a Danish ship, *The America,* sailing from Newport in south Wales, which could take her to Kenya. Quite a few other passengers embarked with her, many of them Irish, and they had all been assured they were travelling on a bona fide passenger ship. Any vessel carrying arms would be considered a legitimate target by the Germans, so it was with some trepidation that they stood on deck the night before sailing and saw the munitions being loaded under the cover of darkness. The passengers were, in fact, being used as a front and the danger they were in became even clearer to them when they were told they must always sleep in their day clothes in case of submarine attack.

The voyage began with a detour designed to throw the U-boats off the scent: they went up the Irish Sea and out into the North Atlantic almost as far as Iceland. There they encountered a terrible storm. My mother was the only passenger who was not seasick and, when she went down to the dining saloon as usual for her meal, she found only a single steward on duty. As she sat at her table the ship suddenly began a great sideways roll: the sea rose right up over the porthole glass and she innocently asked the attendant if this was normal. He replied by mutely flapping a terrified hand at her and spread-eagling himself against a great clock that was chained to the wall. The chain broke, as did the one holding her chair, and they were both thrown across the room. When the ship eventually righted itself the steward told her that he had been sure his last hour had come.

Afterwards, the passengers learned that a submarine had indeed been tracking them but had luckily lost them in the storm. Their journey continued, down the Atlantic, along the west coast of Africa, round the Cape of Good Hope and into Durban Harbour. On leaving Durban, however, the main engines failed and they had to return to port using an auxiliary one. It was then found that two of the engine-room crew were Nazi sympathisers and they were arrested for sabotage.

Over a year later, my parents were staying in a hotel in Mombasa when they heard about a ship being repaired in the Mombasa docks that had suffered from unusual engine trouble. It sounded very familiar and my mother told the authorities of what had happened to *The America*. Further investigation revealed that one of the two men jailed in Durban had somehow become a crew member on this second ship and he was arrested once again.

The culprit was a Hungarian and my mother always suspected that he might have been blackmailed into becoming involved. Shortly before the war was over, to her great and lifelong discomfort, she came face to face with him when he was dying in the Nairobi military hospital. He looked at her and realisation dawned.

'Oh,' he said. 'Of course! It was *you*! I could never understand how they found out.'

DESERT BARBECUE
Arthur Reynolds

I had gone to Tory to record a method of herring-netting from open boats which was rapidly dying out elsewhere. While virtually all herrings caught around Ireland are taken by trawlers using bottom or floating trawls, the Torymen set a buoyed net in a circle around shoals often located by birds diving. This was because the fishermen were compelled to use boats that could be hauled out of the water by tractor when bad weather threatened. That's what I had gone to record, but the story I brought back from that rain-drenched County Donegal island proved to be much more interesting.

There were no other visitors there at the time, so the resident priest was keen to invite me into his home on a few evenings to talk about almost everything under the sun. As it turned out, the story he told me certainly had to do with very hot sun – never experienced near Ireland.

He said that before he came back to his native Donegal he had been a chaplain with the Royal Air Force stationed in the Gulf of Aqaba. With not much to do, he had learnt Arabic well enough to speak with the many nomadic desert Arabs who came to the base with their camels from time to time.

So, when the RAF needed to extend its premises, it was decided to ask the Arabs if they would bring along their camels in six weeks' time to help unload a ship, which would carry the building materials. A few days before the vessel came, the nomads arrived with many camels and set up camp at the base. Forming a continuous train, they used the haughty beasts to carry the bags of cement and blocks to the site. They certainly did not need to bring in sand, for there was scarcely anything else there.

When the task was finished some days later, the base commander arranged a night-time barbecue, with lambs roasting on spits over big fires, and the priest was given the task of making a speech to thank the nomads for their willing help.

Then came a surprise.

One old man with a face wizened from the harsh desert winds, who owned the most camels and the biggest tents, stood up and replied in English, saying that they were glad to help the airmen, as the base had always been helpful to the desert wanderers, particularly with mechanical repairs and medical attention. He had taken on the job of organising the operation.

And when he sat down, the priest went up and embraced him saying that he was sure from his accent that the man had learnt his English from a Donegal man.

'Indeed I did,' he replied. 'I'm from Stranorlar. I came out here with Lawrence of Arabia in 1924.'

LIMERICK TWINNING

Mae Leonard

The coach stops outside a large school and the courier consults his clipboard. He calls out, 'Ze band,' then he pauses, frowns, looks at his list again and adds, 'and, a Madame Lay-on-ard.' I look at him open-mouthed. There must be some mistake. I am supposed to stay with a French family – I have a bottle of Irish whiskey and a box of Irish chocolates for them.

'No, no, Madame,' the man assures me with a typical French shrug. 'Zer is no mistake – you are with ze band.'

So what can I do but collect my belongings and step down onto the pavement, closely followed by twenty men in skirts – well, kilts – the Curraghgower Pipe Band to be precise. We are part of the Limerick contingent visiting Quimper, Brittany, for the twinning ceremony of our two ancient cities.

I'm escorted to my room on the third floor and left to my own devices. I close the door and get this awful lonesome feeling. I am trying to decide whether to open the whiskey or the chocolates to console myself when there's a violent knocking on the door and a shout: 'Ten minutes for the parade.' Parade? What parade? Apparently we are to march to the opening ceremony of the twinning. The alternative is to remain in my solitary room. So the twenty men in skirts – I mean kilts – march into town with Madame Lay-on-ard, one wife and one girlfriend trotting behind them.

There are others from Limerick here but they have all been housed with local families or are staying in hotels. There's a school of Irish dancers, a harpist, an author, a lecturer in all things Celtic, corporation officials and several supporters to swell the ranks of the Limerick representation.

We parade through the thronged streets of Quimper, the oldest city in Brittany. We cross over flat bridges bedecked with geraniums, sniffing the scent of coffee wafting from pavement cafés along the cobbled streets of the medieval quarter with its precarious black-beamed houses, until we finally halt in front of the huge Gothic cathedral of St Corentin.

The Mayor of Limerick – in red robes and gold chain of office – and his councillors (all red-robed too) are seated on the platform, with their less flamboyant dark-blue-robed French counterparts, where the official documents are signed and exchanged. Breton dancers with amazingly tall lace headgear gather with the Irish dancers and the musicians strike up a reel. Celtic embroidered costumes flash and swirl before us. Then what happens? There's a clap of thunder, a stunning fork of lightning, and it rains. A summer shower. But what a shower. It's a deluge.

The dancers scurry for shelter as colours begin to run and lace head-dresses droop. The councillors are ushered back to their hotel as rain runs down the platform like a waterfall. The band members cover precious instruments and we rush back to the school in rain so heavy that it's difficult to even breathe without getting a mouthful of water. I go back to my solitary schoolroom and console myself with a couple of chocolates and a gulp of whiskey and so to sleep.

Next morning the sun rises to the high-pitched screeching of a Breton bombardier band in the courtyard below. My guys in kilts soon join in with squealing pipes and thunderous drums.

This cacophony is my alarm clock for the rest of the week. There's no time to be lonesome. I scurry to the peaceful downtown early every morning to seek out breakfast and enjoy the speciality of Quimper pancakes – crêpes – with a vast selection of fillings, anything from chocolate to fish. And every evening there is a parade with the band.

Driving to Limerick, the sign reminds me: 'Welcome to Limerick City – Twinned with Quimper, Brittany'. It seems like only yesterday I witnessed that twinning. Could it really have been twenty-one years ago?

ALL SOULS' DAY

Frances Donoghue

Hallowe'en is no big deal as a festival in France. Yes, there are witches' hats and broomsticks in the novelty shops, but no barm bracks with rings, or trick or treat. It doesn't really show up in the cultural folklore of the country.

But two days later, on 2 November, there's a ritual which carries far more weight with the French – the rush of family feeling that goes with the celebration of Toussaints, the feast of All Souls. This is the occasion when every son and daughter within reach of the family burial place will pay their respects to the loved ones gone ahead of them. Not just if they happen to live in the same town, but even if a journey by bus, train or car is involved. Flower shops have a boom period. For several days before 2 November, their windows explode in pots and wreaths of chrysanthemums, gladioli, cyclamen – formal flowers in autumnal colours – with striking silk ribbons trailing from them. They are destined for the family tomb or grave, and designed to show how much Maman or Grandpère is missed, no matter how many years have elapsed since the funeral took place. Indeed, the family contributes far more to the occasion than merely buying the flowers, expensive as they will be on this particular day, when the florists handle so much business that they set up temporary stands at the gates of the cemeteries.

The grave is tidied, spruced up and generally spring-cleaned by the hands of these same relatives. This is not a service which is ever sublet to a workman. There's quite a lot to do. Tombs are very common in France and a tomb is in effect a small house. It may be freshly whitened and will certainly have its ornamental metalwork – like grilles or crosses – cleaned and polished. I watched the procedure in my local cemetery with admiration. The relatives arrive in formal church-going clothes but also carrying rubber gloves and detergent and maybe a little pail, as well as their flowers. A man and his wife – he in collar and tie, she in high heels and a hat – had brought a bottle of cleaning fluid and were doing a serious job on the marble tombstone of La Famille Bonnet. It positively gleamed. He sluiced off the stone with fresh water and she polished it with a soft cloth. They added their huge pot of bronze chrysanthemums and restored the little plaques with their tender messages. When the couple had gone, I came closer to read them: 'To our cherished parents… forever regretted by…' and then there was a long line of sons, daughters, in-laws and grandchildren.

People pattered round like busy spring-cleaners and offered advice and commendation to each other. Here and there the tomb doors stood wide open, as if inviting guests in to appreciate the artistic display of fresh flowers, as more cousins and in-laws arrived. Not all the mourners were the bourgeoisie. A young woman with jagged hair and Doc Martin boots, child in hand, came with a single rose in its plastic tube. She placed it carefully on a narrow grave bearing no tombstone at all, just a rudimentary wooden cross with a single name. The child added a little crudely drawn picture of a boat and bent to plant a careful kiss on the wooden cross. Then she took her mother's hand and they left, her twisting backwards for a last approving glimpse of the rose and the picture. Till next year Grandmère.

MRS GORE-HICKMAN
Jamie O'Neill

Our next-door neighbour, when I was growing up, was a widowed lady by the name of Mrs Gore-Hickman. Her house, though ostensibly the same as ours, was an island of Protestant grace in our teeming housing estate. Whenever my father approached her – which he did at every conceivable turn – his accent would rise a tone or two in affectation.

'Oh, Mrs Gore-Hickman! How are you, Mrs Gore-Hickman? Not at all, Mrs Gore-Hickman, sure I was mowing my own lawn. I was wondering, Mrs Gore-Hickman, would you like your gates closed for you?'

Mrs Gore-Hickman gave bridge parties. At that age I had no clear idea what a bridge party involved, save that, seemingly, it required a bountiful supply of sweets. For her house was a treasure-trove of sweets. She had them in open bowls on every table, chocolates and truffles and queer continental confections, whose very wrappers hinted at rare and unimagined tastes. When she holidayed, which she did seasonally, in Wicklow and Sligo, my mother would water her houseplants for her. I would accompany my mother through the rooms, marvelling at this open display, the sheer luxuriance of it – sweets at every turn – and my mother's eagle-eye defying my thieving hands.

One Christmas Eve, my father called me to go visit Mrs Gore-Hickman. 'Who knows,' he hinted, 'she might have a present for you.' So I knocked at her door. 'Sweets' was my first and final thought. It had to be sweets. What else had the woman to give? A box of sweets, an entire box of those incomparable sweets, and all to myself. I could hardly contain my excitement.

Mrs Gore-Hickman asked about my schooling and told me I was growing into a fine young man. Beyond the sweets, I had no feelings one way or the other for the woman. Save, tolerantly, I was willing to forgive her double-barrelled surname – the consequence, so my sister told me, of a shotgun wedding.

She handed me my present. And I knew immediately it was not sweets. It was not sweets nor the smell of sweets, not even biscuits. The hard edge and flat extent told the present was a book. The so-called present. A lousy useless book.

Our home had no books. Shelves we had, great wide sweeps of shelves, with Capo di Monte roses, holiday china, those wooden elephants whose trunks must face the door.

'Why do they have to face the door?'

'It's to keep the tigers away,' my father would explain.

'But there aren't any tigers in Ireland.'

'See?' says my father, 'It works.'

And the only reading was the local evening newspaper, read out loud at the tea-table, religiously, column after column of the classified ads. Even at school I never read – or at least I never finished – the books on the syllabus. I sat exams without reading them. I don't know, but schoolbooks then seemed to be specifically chosen to dampen young spirits. It wasn't that life was too interesting. Life was already dull enough without the further drudgery of book-reading.

So that present was relegated to the high shelf in my room; and there it lay, unopened, unthought-of, gathering dust for the next two or three years. It came to my Intermediate exams and, the way schoolboys do, I thought to cram ten years of idled study into the last two weeks of term.

I cleared all distractions from my room – music, games, everything. The last item on my shelf was that crusty old book. *Ivanhoe*, read the cover, by Sir Walter Scott. There's no point throwing that out, I thought – I'm never going to be distracted by that. Well, of course, that's all I did those two weeks; I read

Ivanhoe. I read it two, three, four times. And I remember the pages turning, thoughtless of turning them, entirely captivated by a story. And the later joy of skipping pages, and the further wonder of delay, of earning an exciting passage, knowing it was on its way. It was a revelation to me. Books can be fun, they can be entertaining, you can learn things out of books. A book can take you out of yourself, take you to places you never imagined. They're interesting things, books.

It was the start of something big in my life, though I could not tell then how big. Whoever would have thought? A scorned present from a kind old lady. *Ivanhoe* by Sir Walter Scott.

CHRISTMAS ISLAND

Pat Boran

It's Christmas morning. You're probably lying there in bed, your head a little heavy from the night before, feeling the pitch and roll of the world, awaiting some kind of signal to get up and get going. In fact, were it not for a voice on the radio, you might well be Captain Cook himself, resting on his bunk, deep in his ship, and hearing close by not the laughter of children, but the voices of sailors and, beyond them, the screeching of gulls.

And where there are gulls, there is land. You can imagine him now, that intrepid explorer, enthusiastic as any child at Christmas, leaping to his feet and rushing out to discover what the day might have in store.

Two years ago our Christmas present to ourselves was a house. Our first house. After months of studying property supplements, the way Cook might have pored over navigational charts, at last my wife and I were standing before the object of our desires: before the door of a thirty-year-old house we tried to believe was now ours.

Unlike us, Cook hadn't set out to discover the sight that greeted him from the deck that Christmas morning in 1777. Having first glimpsed it with great excitement the day before, a second look now took, as it were, the winds from his sails.

'Upon a nearer approach', he confided to his log book, the desolate landmass before him was merely 'one of those low islands so common in this sea'. And yet, despite his disappointment, he decided to explore.

For us, too, that new world seemed alien and foreign – someone else's dim, grey hallway; the jaundiced yellow walls of a kitchen – but a fresh lick of paint would soon make it ours and dispel any lingering doubts.

Cook's third voyage to the Pacific had been, by far, his most challenging, and his manner of dealing with difficulties was often less than fair. On an earlier landing, one of the natives, astonished by the vision of the horses, cows and sheep that accompanied the expedition, had climbed on board to acquire some little keepsake for himself, some little pre-Christmas present. Cook's response was, to say the least, bizarre. He had the left side of the man's head shaved, and then his left eyebrow, before flogging him and dumping him back on shore. For a similar transgression, another unfortunate native lost both his ears.

And yet, even Cook had a reasonable side. Remembering how festive celebrations at sea could leave his people 'none of the soberest', he decided to observe, in the words of one contemporary, 'the old laudable custom of keeping Christmas' and began to examine the ship's provisions with an eye to a suitable meal.

As it happened, for once, luck was with him. That afternoon the shore party 'met with some turtles on the beach' and seized their opportunity.

And so the Christmas menu was set: and a world away from the beef and pudding of his Yorkshire childhood, the Captain with his crew sat down to a dinner of South Sea turtles, some twenty in number, and generous helpings of sauerkraut in brine, the Captain's ingenious solution for keeping scurvy at bay.

Turtles being in short supply, even now in cosmopolitan Dublin, and sauerkraut being something of an acquired taste, in our new house two years back we settled for a cold mince pie and sugarless tea, but we were every bit as certain as Captain Cook himself that we'd arrived at our own near-mythical Christmas Island.

A BETTER LIGHT

Mick Doyle

Some time back, my partner and I were watching television – lights on in various rooms around the house, the radio we hadn't switched off playing to nobody in the kitchen – when we heard a quiet crack and we were suddenly sitting in darkness. The television screen shrank to a dot before hissing out into nothing. It was as if we'd fallen into the pocket of some giant. We sat there, silent, stunned. Then we began to get annoyed that the power cut had robbed us of whatever it was we were gaping at at the time.

Minutes later, I'm fumbling around the kitchen for forgotten candles, irritated by the words of that adage that came to me now: 'It's better to light a candle than to curse the darkness.' I found a candle. A chipped rose candle about six inches long that we'd lit at least once before. Then, a faded box of matches. I made my way back to the sitting-room, fingertips spidering along the hallway wall.

I struck a match and held it to the wick until the flame took. A wavering tongue leaped out of the dark, puck-puck-puckering.

Yellow-tipped, blue at its base, its aura grew brighter and bigger every second. All the familiar things in the room showed themselves again. Only now in a glow. My shadow was an ogre that bent its head and shoulders on the ceiling.

Technique returned quickly. I held the candle horizontally and it bled plump drops, dark as claret, into the cup of a candelabra that stood in a web of dust on the mantelpiece. I planted the candle in the cooling wax, half-turning it a couple of times until it bedded. The flame yellowed the brass on the mantel clock. Like buttercups' yellow, soft skin. Its shadow shivered over photographs and prints.

Outside, all was quiet. It was as if the power cut had instantly restored our suburb to its rural past, transported that planet of housing estates to the still, pitch-black countryside that was its recent history. The silence evoked inky space, the end of all things. It was as if the world had stopped. Then a car snored by on the road, giving us hope.

'The power'll be back soon,' I said to reassure my partner. And myself.

We started talking, a little self-consciously at first, but there's something about a naked flame that draws human beings close. Urges speak from a deeper part of us. Topics seem more meaningful. Even the words we choose, more deliberate. It wouldn't be an exaggeration to say we rediscover ourselves, make some sense of our place in the universe, through the thoughts, the meditative conversation, that fire gives rise to.

We were together, mind-in-mind in this rhapsodic maze, when the power came back on. The spotlights in the ceiling dwarfed the candle's slim flame. Dismissing it. We pulled away from each other, startled, embarrassed almost, at how close we had become. An instant later, the TV unleashed out of nothing some garrulous ad and the radio in the kitchen resumed its self-involved chatter. Lights blazed from half the rooms in the house again.

I got up and blew the candle out. Smoke coiled off the wick to hang just beneath the ceiling. It no sooner faded than the smell of wax filled the room. I sat down again and my partner and I stared at the television.

ICE CREAM IN THE SNOW
Maureen Charlton

My mother had a strong aversion to the twentieth century. What she might have made of this one only heaven can tell! An exile in the present, she imperiously disdained all the gadgets and labour-saving devices which a Dublin suburban semi had to offer when we were transplanted there from the country. She brought with her all the customs and ways of times past, familiar from her rural upbringing.

The move to Dublin had come about when my father had taken up a post as principal of a Dublin southside national school and our new home offered all the important inventions of modern times. Candles after all had long been obsolete!

Lights switched on and off, a three-ring electric cooker stood gleaming and pristine in the kitchen and yet – winter and summer, in heatwave or cold snap – a fire blazed in the dining room with an ungainly kettle bubbling on the hob. Potatoes were baked there in their jackets and often an Irish stew in an ancient black pot. Nor were pop-up toasters needed when you could skewer a piece of bread and in a flash have a most delectable slice of toast.

Electric blankets and the humble rubber hot-water bottle were unheard of luxuries. For, to keep chilly little toes warm and snug on winter nights, a brick reposed in the glowing embers as exercises were got through around the dining-room table. When bedtime came the brick was wrapped in an old piece of blanket and accompanied us to our chilly bedrooms.

Our iron was, of course, made of iron and heated on that ever-gleaming dining-room fire. But children are natural conformists and, when I went to the homes of my pals, I used to watch with a mixture of wonder and envy as kettles were plugged in and miraculously boiled.

But the thing I most envied in those kitchens of yesteryear was that gleaming white cupboard humming away happily to itself in winter and summer – the fridge. How lucky those kids were! I ruefully thought that they could have ice cream whenever the fancy took them, when we would have to cadge the money and scamper off to the local shop for a twopenny or fourpenny wafer.

But my mother even triumphed over this contraption. Only once in my memory, it must be said, and yet, what a delightful memory, viewed however mistily along the corridor of time.

A cold spell set in after one Christmas and that first night we could hear the snow falling faintly and faintly falling, as Joyce so memorably puts it. And next morning – a miracle. A gleaming, wonderful, white world. A soft, fluffy, white fitted-carpet which nature's workmen had obligingly installed over our back garden.

There was no time to be lost. My mother set to. Eggs and cream were whisked. The remaining drops of the Christmas sherry were added and the mixture was placed in a bowl and buried in the snow. And in a few hours it had turned into delicious ice cream.

The Italians are credited with the invention of this scrumptious dessert, as they are with so many other wonderful things – aqueducts and aeroplanes, Olivettis and Vespas. Manly creations. But I bet it was some Italian mama, deep in the heart of the Dolomites, who first thought of ice cream in the snow.

A Sense of Place

BORN-AGAIN COLOURS
Bernard Loughlin

Where do the colours go when they are not here? Do they drain off the Pyrenees in the streams that are quickened and swollen by the autumn rains, to wash into bigger rivers and then away into the sea? Is there a delta of colours that builds up every year in the Mediterranean, where all our rivers end? Do they swirl there, bright and acrid like spillings from dyers' vats, waiting to wash back up the mountains again when the weather warms?

In deep winter, there are mostly only whites, blacks, browns and duns: all the other colours are leached and eroded away.

In spring, the first flowers to appear are the violets, growing in the shelter of trees, along hedgerows or at the edges of copses. Their soldier-boy blue is brave and declamatory, as if they are saying, 'Look, we're back and there are thousands more coming after us.' Next, yellow coltsfoot, flower heads hammered flat and ragged, creep out from under stones and mud along streams and in marshy places, to be followed by the parasols of leaves that were folded down and packed away last year like garden furniture. Wild daffodils waggle tentative fingers of green in the meadows, as if testing the temperature, and are often deceived, their white frills of petals frittered by late frosts. And then, as the trickles of returning colour become a flood, there will be saffron crocuses, azure irises, scarlet pheasant's-eye, mauve geraniums, royal-blue gentians, the yellow and red turbans of lilies – all the colours under the sun, as if they and the sun had never been away.

All-knowing and all-seeing as we humans now are, gazing back at ourselves and our lovelorn planet from all the eyes we have put in space, we understand how the earth tilts and the colours of the seasons run from pole to pole in tides, but up close, down here, where we live, it remains a glorious mystery annually renewed. As it has been for as long as life has existed on the earth, right back to our most primal ancestors, the blue-green algae that were the beginning of the chlorophyll factory that colours our planet, without which it would be as monochrome as the moon.

Even in the primeval sludge, blue algae must have fancied green algae and got together to produce brown algae, which would eventually evolve into brown birds – LBJs as birdwatchers call them, little brown jobs – the warblers that return from migration to add the colours of their songs to the spring effusions.

And all the other, more showy creatures. The face-blushes of goldfinches. The boastful red throats of bullfinches. Butterflies swaggering and staggering about the air, drunk with popinjay pride in their gorgeous apparels. The cicadas that flash do-not-touch-me blues and reds as they bound away. Plasticine-green gecko lizards.

All summer long the colours will be beaten down and neutralised by the fierce heat of the sun, until, by late autumn, the landscape will be dry and brown again, torpid and exhausted from the orgy of pigmentation, whose juices will run off into the streams, thence to the river, and then to the Mediterranean, to fuse there into one vast deep legendary blue, from which, next year, all the colours will be born again.

HARRY MAKES ME SMILE

Barbara McKeon

Whenever I chance upon Harry I smile. Just seeing him sets me up for the day. Usually I encounter him early in the morning by the river and there he is, with his grey head set into his hunched shoulders, contemplating the day ahead. Later on, Harry is off doing whatever herons do, presumably fishing. Harry is a capital angler.

I like to wake early. I open the curtains, make a cup of tea and go back to bed and read a while. But my eye is always drawn to the expanse of sky beyond the window. Occasionally I see Harry fly overhead. I call him Harry because the name seems to suit. I cannot name all the birds I encounter because there are too many of them, whereas there is only one Harry.

I open the window and listen to birds trilling and chirruping. I leave out food and they reward me with their songs. There's the robin whose warbling is so pleasant to human ears but so threatening to other birds; and an adorable little wren whose voice is incredibly vociferous for so tiny a bird. Then there are the chattering starlings, tenacious blackbirds, skittery pied and grey wagtails, and of course the finches – chaffinch, greenfinch, goldfinch, bullfinch – displaying their virtuoso performances and distracting me as I sit writing at my desk by the window.

And in summer who could not be mesmerised by the aerobatic cavorting of swifts and swallows in pursuit of airborne insects? Once I saw a streak of gold skimming over the canal water and into the dense foliage growing along the banks and realised it was a kingfisher.

At the end of my garden, where the river runs by, swans, cormorants, and mallards gather to preen themselves and dry their wings in the sun. There is a colony of about 200 swans farther along the river and the sight of swans flying by always makes me drop whatever I am doing to gaze in awe at the magnificent sight, enthralled by the fearsome sound of their wings beating a steady throb, as if the effort to keep themselves in the air is almost too much.

One time a swan accidentally landed on my rain-drenched patio and couldn't fly off. I had to alert the swan rescue people, who captured the stricken bird in a clean plastic coal sack and released her in the colony that lives by the Claddagh.

On another occasion I saw a seal swim by the end of my garden.

'Look, look, a seal!' I shouted to a passer-by crossing the bridge. Then others passing by stopped, amazed at the sight of a seal so close to the city centre. For this wildlife haven I live amidst is not in the heart of the countryside but in Galway city. My ground-floor apartment has a patio overlooking the Eglinton Canal and the Corrib River.

The English poet William Cowper wrote: 'God made the country and man made the town.' And every time I see Harry the heron, I smile and think, thank God for the waterways of Ireland that bring a little of the countryside into the towns.

HIGH RISE

Gavin Corbett

We were settled on the plain around the papal cross eating crisps and drinking fizzy orange. Earlier my father had pointed out to us, with an exiled northsider's pride, all the main features of the park. Now we were just lazing. It was summer. It was one of those days of letting yourself grow limp in the heat, of feeling the itch of fresh-cut grass, of watching ladybirds idle on the back of your hand. My attention drifted and lolled and drifted until it rested on the huge metallic cross above us. I remember being mesmerised by the reflection of the sun on it. I watched the burning white light consume the outline of the cross and felt it warm and water my eyes; I watched it until the sun had disappeared behind a cloud and I was left with a slowly fading, purple smear. When the smear had faded completely, I saw something amazing. I pulled at my father's sleeve.

'See up there,' I said.

My father's gaze followed the line of my pointing finger.

'My God,' he said.

'Wow,' I said.

There appeared to be two men 'inside' the cross. We gathered up our stuff and walked closer to it to get a better look. The cross had a kind of groove running its whole length. Inside the groove, between the two girders that formed its edges, were, not two men, but two boys, not that much older than I was, whooshing themselves skywards with a sort of peristaltic squirm. Already it seemed they were a mile in the air.

'They'll slip and die,' I said.

'They will if they're not careful,' said my father. 'Messers. The view from up there though. It must be incredible.'

I looked around me. It was true what my father said, I thought. The view must have been amazing from up there. It wasn't too far in front of me that things became vague, in waves that seemed to rise from the ground. It would be clearer up in the air, I thought.

From that time, I became fascinated with the idea of high vantage points in the city. For years I had thought there must have been some very high place in Dublin from which I could look out over the whole of the city. By my early teens I had discovered that the City Fathers had an aversion to high-rise buildings, and that there weren't any such places in Dublin. There was Nelson's Pillar once, of course; but that was gone. There was Liberty Hall too, but that was closed off to the public.

Then at last, in 2000, the viewing capsule at the top of the Smithfield Chimney was opened. I was an early and eager visitor. One of the first places I looked for when I was up there was the cross in the park. And there it was to the west, a forlorn stick in a desert of space. I walked around the capsule in an anticlockwise movement, my hands behind my back, goose-stepping like a dictator. The rooftops of the city to south and east were far below. Out on the docklands, a new quarter was taking shape. The buildings there seemed truncated and ordered, like blocks of wax and Styrofoam laid out and then planed down to uniform size. Gaps in the streetscape revealed flashes of those disgusting, squat, modern apartment blocks along the river, between Heuston Station and the Four Courts. On the horizon, the condemned Ballymun flats stood out like the remnants of a city wall. I wondered would anyone miss them for that civic function: the way they delimit the northern expanse of the capital. I know I will miss them for their height. There is something undoubtedly awe-inspiring about the scale of the Ballymun towers. I think they are among the most beautiful buildings in Dublin.

Now we have a new, tall structure in the city, the Spire. I'm really proud of it. It has one unforgivable fault, namely that you can see the seams where its sections are welded together. But like the cross in the Phoenix Park, it can do funny and wonderful things with the light. And at least it makes you crank back your neck; it sets a new high air-mark for Dublin, so to speak. What I like most about it is that it isn't even a high vantage point. It has no function; it's just there for its own sake. There's no lift to a viewing deck or revolving café. Not that that will necessarily stop me: some day I'll get a pair of goalkeeping gloves and some knee-pads, and I'll shimmy my way to the top.

DONEGAL'S GLASS MOUNTAIN
Bill McStay

R ising abruptly from the surrounding lowlands to a height of over 2,000 feet, the great bulk of Sliabh Muckish dominates the landscape near Creeslough in north Donegal. Up until fifty years ago, the mountain's rich deposits of silica sand were a prized ingredient in the making of high-quality glass. Composed of friable, quartzite rock, the silica sand beds are found in layers, from one to several yards thick some 200 feet below the summit.

There was some small-scale quarrying of the sand beds in 1837, and later in 1901, but it was not until 1918 that an expert analysis of the sand deposits revealed that the silica content was virtually 100 per cent. In 1939, Irish Minerals Ltd secured a commercial mining licence. September of that year was an eventful month, marking the outbreak of World War II. One result of the speedy German conquest of the Low Countries was that the high-grade and easily mined silica sand of Belgium was no longer available.

Denied access to continental sources, the world-famous glass producers Pilkingtons of St Helen's in Lancashire looked westward. The sea journey from the Mersey to Sheephaven Bay was relatively short and, more importantly, small cargo vessels plying between the two places would not have to run the gauntlet of attack by German U-boats. The bay was dredged to provide sufficient draught for 600-ton sand carriers, and a pier was built at Ards on its western shore, some seven miles from the Muckish quarries.

Given the difficulties of quarrying operations at 600 yards above sea level, extracting Muckish's silver sand was never an easy matter, though pneumatic drills, mechanical jack hammers and dynamite had replaced the old manual pick-and-shovel system. Specially reinforced wooden chutes conveyed the sand to the mountain's base. At ground level it was crushed, screened and dried before transport to Ards Pier, where it was loaded on to the docked boats by shovel and wheelbarrow. Labourers engaged in this work were expected to provide their own wheelbarrows and, in the early days of mining, earned one shilling daily.

Hugh McElhinney from Dunfanaghy, now seventy-four years old, can clearly recall his days at the quarry in the early 1950s. Upon arrival at the mountain, it took almost half an hour to climb to the work site. Hail, rain or shine you stayed there all day, with only a small shed to protect you from the elements as you took your frugal midday meal. You were paid £3 for the week. On the days when a boat was in for loading, all hands were mustered to load the cargo. It seemed to take ages, Hugh muses wryly, before you would hear the clump of the sand hitting the bottom of the hold.

Towards the mid 1950s, the whole Muckish operation was becoming uneconomical. Fog, frequent rain, piercing winds and snow in winter slowed production and made for hazardous working conditions. The location itself was difficult to access because of its isolation, and Sheephaven Bay was too shallow to permit navigation by bigger boats. Any further quarrying was going to require deeper and deeper inroads into the mountain. Most significant of all, with the ending of the war, cheaper Belgian sand was once more available. The writing was on the wall.

In July 1954, the whole project was wound up. Today, grassed-over scars in the mountainside and a few rusting pieces of equipment are the only reminders of a unique attempt to wrest the mountain's silver treasure. And Muckish itself, in all its shifting moods, stands ancient and unconquerable, as it has from the dawn of creation.

A PILGRIM'S TALE
Frances Plunkett-Russell

B usáras is a hive of movement and sound. The ticket-seller, a tanned, cherub-faced Dubliner, smiles and says, 'You can't have a return. You have to stay.' I eye him with menace as he passes out the ticket and quips, 'Well! Have a great weekend.'

I take a front seat on the bus and spread myself to deter anyone from joining me. Opposite, straddling three seats, a man in a dirty red anorak sleeps and I envy his ease. Still the sun is shining as I descend the Hill of Howth, scattering the early morning mist. As I pass St Fintan's graveyard I think of my parents and brother who lie there. I have just left the house that my father built, where I was born and grew up and where I now live with my own family.

I am going to Lough Derg in Donegal, a place of pilgrimage since the fifth century. There, feet are left unshod, food is a once-daily ration of black tea, cardboard biscuits or dry toast, and sleep is not allowed. Lough Derg also boasts a micro-climate of near-permanent winter but offers tantalising glimpses of clear blue sky, over the hills in the distance, just to remind you of what you are missing.

The bus hums and rocks through the swoosh of traffic, past roadside verges bleeding violent red poppies and fields of silky grass, populated here and there with contented creamy-coloured cows, sitting and chewing. I fall asleep.

At Ballyshannon, dark, woolly clouds press against the roof. The lakes and rivers are peopled with hillocky islands, sedate and pretty. Fallow fields of yellow weeds and lush green overhangs bring us closer to the lough.

'This is it! The last-chance saloon.' The driver calls to us, indicating a pub called Potter's Bar in Belleek. Nobody laughs and someone mutters, 'We shouldn't even be in Belleek.'

I feel a finger of rain as we take the short boat ride across the lake and a sudden melancholy closes around me. Still there is a something here for me. I always find it. This pilgrim place lays me bare. In my cubicle I keep my shoes on until the last moment. I make my bed for Sunday night and look at it longingly. Outside is grey, cool, threatening rain.

Three stations completed now. A station is undertaken over rough stones, often slithery with mud, walking and kneeling while following a prayerful repetitive format. My knees are sore, my jeans are wet.

Lough Derg is a place of silence for me, and also where I find stillness, reverence, my connection to my God strengthened. We pilgrims recognise each other in our bearing over the rough stones, in our hunger, weariness and lack of bodily warmth. Stripped to the basics, my thoughts are of victims of war, famine, displacement.

The Taizé chants bring tears to my eyes. I love their haunting melodies. I remember my parents and brother in the darkening graveyard and my husband and children back home, missing all of them in different ways.

Last Sunday, my front door was open and a woman knocked and asked if we still did 'teas'.

'We used to come out here, you see,' she said. 'My husband and myself, before we were married.' Her eyes filled. 'We would have a walk and come in here for tea and scones.' The tearooms dominated my summers as a child. I hated the invasion of tourists into my home and the busy preoccupation of my mother. I preferred the insularity of winter. But I know that my late mother would have been glad that her little tearoom was remembered so fondly.

Now I am wearing underwear, two T-shirts, an Aran sweater, leggings, jeans, a rain-jacket, no shoes. I have a T-shirt and thick tights with the feet sliced off for the deep night when the cold will creep up my calves from icy feet.

Night prayer. Benediction. The Vigil Homily. The Rosary. Four more stations. A cool wind is blowing about and the flagstones are colder to the touch. The night is black and heavy and the lough waters look like ink. I hear the bell ring. The night yawns and I look into the cavernous darkness and begin to pray.

A NEW LIFE

Peter Sirr

When the time came to leave and to find another city to live in, I went to the hiring fair, held every year in a hotel in the grounds of Heathrow Airport. Here, clutching the CVs that held the promise of a new life, supplicant teachers queued in front of desks at which the principals of desirable schools sat like tribunes or provincial satraps, bored with their duties.

I glanced across at Vienna, Berlin and Rome, with their long lines, and headed for Bogotá, where I succeeded in getting an interview. I managed the same at Istanbul and Tokyo. Interviews were conducted in the hotel bedrooms. Bogotá was a British school which went in for uniforms and imperial grandeur, paid meagrely and liked its sport. Tokyo was a Catholic girls' school run by nuns. Istanbul was a genial conversation about the difficulties of the Turkish language after it became evident that there was, in fact, no job on offer. The following day brought Kenya, with a fruit plantation, a houseboy and the requirement that, on arrival, I would purchase a jeep from the school to the amount of a year's salary. 'Fine,' I said. 'That sounds great.' I must learn to drive, I told myself as I left the bedroom.

The final interview was with the principal of an American school in Milan, a huge, shaggy man with an unsmiling face who seemed to be going through the motions of interviewing me in case, at some distant point in the future, all of his staff having been consumed by a plague, he might reach a sufficient pitch of desperation to want to hire me.

'Tell me,' he said to me as he contemplated the floor, 'your five worst qualities.'

I groped around to encapsulate my failures as a human being, the ones I could reveal to him that would show me in a good light. I work too hard. I give too much of myself in the service of others.

I don't remember what I did say but whatever it was hadn't seemed to make much of an impression, for it took my interrogator a long time to retrieve his gaze from the carpet and force himself to utter the next question on his list.

It was with some surprise, therefore, some months later, that I picked up the phone and heard his voice offering me a job at his school. His first choice had let him down and his second choice had contracted a rare illness. I wasn't too concerned about the details as I stepped off the plane into the August glare of Linate Airport. I was glad to be somewhere else, looking at new faces, listening to a new language. Something inside me was soaring, was home.

The school was an island of Americanness and, although most of the pupils were the children of the affluent Milanese, the atmosphere, the system and the ethos were firmly American. There was a peculiar doubleness to each day as I moved from one unfamiliar culture to another, tending, unfairly, to regard one as the necessary tax on the enjoyment of the other.

Every morning, wanting to get at least an hour of Italy into my system before the bell rang, I would clamber down the stairs of my fourth floor walk-up, bolt into a bar for a shot of coffee, jump on a tram crowded with Italians on their way to work and run for the bus to the suburb where the school was housed, enjoying the clamour of the Italian kids on the way to their school a few doors down on the via Carlo Marx (an address which did not appear on the school's letterhead). Then I would walk, trot or run from the bus-stop until, finally, I slipped past the team of *carabinieri* on permanent guard outside the gates and into the world – vaguely familiar from high school movies – of home rooms, hall passes, spot quizzes, advanced placement, eleventh and twelfth graders, the high-school principal waiting for me in the hall, shifting in annoyance inside his white suit. The students called him *Il gelataio*, the ice-cream man. *Benvenuto*, I would tell myself every morning. Welcome to the new life.

FROM CORSICA TO PASSAGE EAST

Catherine Foley

Our house in Waterford was called 'Corsica'. When we were toddlers, we loved to try out the three-syllable word, reading the cast-iron letters on our gate. Cor-Sick-Ca. We knew it was where our great-grandfather, Joe Martell, had come from.

He had run away to sea when he was sixteen. That was back in 1873. He didn't want to stay at home. He escaped because he wanted a life at sea. In time he met William Ryan, a Passage East man who was a sea captain. They became great friends and, when both men were in their twenties, Ryan brought Martell home with him to County Waterford. That's where he met William's sister, Mary Ryan. They fell in love and got married in Crooke Church in Woodstown in September 1883. They had four daughters: Rose Ann, Maggie, Angela and Mary Ellen, who was the youngest and my grandmother.

My mother remembers Joe Martell, even though she was only a little girl when he died. He wore a moustache and a soft cloth cap. He had black hair, dark brown eyes and sallow skin. When he got older, he used to make model ships moored against detailed piers, all set against a painted background of the Waterford estuary, with Ballyhack, Arthurstown, Duncannon and Cheekpoint all easy to pick out. He also used to get some of Mary Ryan's grey hair for the wisps of smoke coming out of the funnels of the ships! These elaborate seascapes were housed in great display cases made of glass.

'You'll be beautiful like your aunt Madeline when you grow up,' Joe Martell used to tell my mother when she was small. 'You'll be a lady and ride a horse,' he'd say, as the two of them chatted away to each other. Her brother, John, remembers that he was the first to bring a gramophone home to Passage East from one of his voyages.

It was many years later before we decided to travel back to Corsica. My sister and I were emotional the day the Marseilles ferry sailed into the port of Ajaccio. Day was just breaking but, in no time, as the ship glided in, the sun was beating down on the wide expanse of bay and the white cliffs. The distant hills were a lilac colour, the sea was blue and the houses and hotels of the little town were yellow. Rose Ann and I both had lumps in our throats as the boat got closer to the dock.

Joe Martell never returned home to Corsica, but we were determined to find some links with his past. Maybe we could find some key to his early life and to his family. We had travelled to Corsica to see if we could dig up any trace of him, to see if there was any record of his life.

Our search began as soon as we had docked and checked in to our hotel. Without wasting any time, we headed out towards La Chapelle du Grec and the local cemetery beyond. The place was deathly quiet when we got there in the bright mid-morning; no one was about. We began looking for a Martell plot, wandering through lanes between the large tombs and lavish burial chambers.

We peered at the family names and the sad, framed photographs of the deceased. We squeezed through half-open gates into the forgotten, overgrown parts. In the silent, white sunshine, with the cicadas clacking away in the heat, it was an eerie place. But La Cimetière de Sept Familles yielded no clues and so we walked back towards the centre of Ajaccio.

Over the coming days we went through the census records at the national archives. We also visited the Maritime Museum, where one man shrugged his shoulders, lifted his eyebrows and said with a Gallic flourish, 'Il est difficile à trouver, comme une aiguille dans une meule de foin.'

'Oui,' we said, nodding our heads in weariness. 'C'est vrai.'

And yet, although we didn't find any records of the Martell

family, we did leave feeling as if we had found something. Early on in our search, we had both realised that there was something odd about the old part of the town. It struck us both very forcibly that there was something familiar about Le Vieux Port d'Ajaccio. The narrow streets, the smells, the light and the darknesses, the coolness of the shade, even the faces of the people, seemed to remind us of something we knew. We weren't a minute putting our fingers on it.

Le Vieux Port d'Ajaccio was just like Passage East. The same sea-going vibe, the same breezy aspect, the same narrow, curved streets with their pockets of coolness and warmth. The yellow stones appeared white in the sunshine, reminiscent of the whitewashed houses in Passage East. Even some of the faces of the people we passed looked familiar.

As we left, we were determined we would return some day, and it made us smile to think that our great-grandfather, the sea-going captain who had run away to sea, had not really avoided his fate. He had merely fulfilled his childhood dream of going to sea and, rather than escaping, he had just found a home away from home in Passage East.

PEGGY'S HOUSE
Siobhán Mannion

There's something about spending time in somebody else's house. And when that person just happens to be a member of a notorious dynasty and can count a handful of high-profile artists among her lovers, you're going to be curious.

Wandering through Peggy Guggenheim's home in Venice offers a tantalising glimpse of another era. Peggy herself, an American heiress who had busied herself traipsing leisurely across Europe, bought the Palazzo Venier dei Leoni in 1949. Having opened galleries in London and New York, this residence on the Grand Canal was to house her impressive collection of modern art. Today, the unfinished palace is a bright, modern oasis in the midst of a crumbling, if ever-charming, city.

With its cool, tiled floors and whitewashed walls, this is the perfect setting for works by Picasso, Miró and Dali, to name but a few. In contrast to the abundance of Renaissance treasures in dimly lit churches, Peggy's house is very much a twentieth-century Venetian delight. And alongside the art, photographs of the lady herself are discreetly placed. Standing before such images, in the very spaces where they were taken, is akin to looking at a work by Vermeer. But instead of finding a painting within the painting, the past becomes visible in the present. With a little imagination, one conjures up the impossibly fabulous parties of those long-gone days. Did Anaïs Nin and James Joyce rub shoulders and discuss their latest scribblings? Were Gore Vidal and Jean Cocteau animated dinner guests? Was Peggy herself regarded as an enchanting hostess, important art patron or flighty fool?

One of the pleasures for a visitor to Miss Guggenheim's house is an imaginary entrée into high society. Seeing where somebody lives is a fascinating piece of the jigsaw. But this is no cosy abode. Despite being unexpectedly candid about some areas of her life, Peggy did have her private side. It is difficult to equate the woman whose autobiography is, in part, breezy kiss-and-tell, with the gallery owner who hid away when her home was open to the public. Sexually liberated to a degree well ahead of her time, Jackson Pollock and Samuel Beckett are among those named. The details add to the legend…

And so you can see her sunbathing on her rooftop, sporting her trademark sunglasses. And there she is laughing about the Marini sculpture prominently displayed on her canal deck. This bronze, exceptionally explicit in nature, prompted Peggy to request a detachable phallus. Unscrewed occasionally to preserve the composure of the more sensitive guest, a rumour spread across Venice that she had commissioned the item in a selection of sizes.

Any life boiled down to its highlights evokes energy and excitement – read any obituary. Was Peggy's existence really a wonderful whirlwind or did boredom creep in? Is there more to this saga of pleasure and privilege? A moment of horror registers on each visitor's face as they happen upon a headstone in the garden. How could so many of Peggy's children have died in infancy? There is a second before the realisation that her beloved dogs, and not her offspring, are buried where the visitor stands. Which is not to imply that Peggy escaped tragedy in her life. The early death of one of her children, not to mention the loss of her father on the *Titanic*, punctured her world. Being inside her artist daughter Pegeen's room is eerie, in spite of its stick figures painted in vivid colour.

Decades after her own death, Peggy Guggenheim's spirit lives on, in her palazzo at least. Perhaps this is what gives the house its charm. To be truly taken by it, you have to populate the place with its ghosts, be intrigued by how the artworks came into her hands. Tales of sex and wealth. Today, Venice in the spring. Sharp sunlight on the canal. Every turn in a myriad of walkways tripping over the possibility of the perfect photograph. The city is at its most appealing before the tourist season really kicks in. Take the time to wander a few streets north of the Academia Bridge to be seduced by Peggy's house.

THE HOUSE THAT EILEEN BUILT
Patricia O'Reilly

It's a warm summer's day in 1926. The woman drives her MG roadster into the train station at Roquebrune, parks, and reaches into the back for her rolled-up towel. Anticipating the pleasure of a swim, she crosses the low stone wall and walks along the narrow pathway, looking for a way down the cliff to the beach. After a few minutes, the path fizzles out.

Intrigued by the isolation of the area, she clambers over crumbling walls, through the scattered Levant pines and brushes of wild rosemary and euphorbia, before arriving at a small natural terrace cut into the honey-coloured limestone rocks.

The woman is Eileen Gray, born in Wexford in 1878 to an Anglo-Irish family whose ancestry dated back to the fifteenth-century English peer, Lord Gray. For a decade she has been the toast of Paris for her lacquer work, furniture and interior design.

She is in the south of France looking for a suitable site to build a summer getaway for herself and her current lover, Romanian architect Jean Badovici. For the past three weeks she has been searching up and down the Côte d'Azure. Without success.

Today – and when she wasn't even looking – she has stumbled across the perfect site on which to build her perfect house. She calls it the E.1027. E for Eileen. 10 for Jean. 2 for Badovici. 7 For Gray. And she gifts it to him.

The house was tiered and, carved from rock face, it embraced the natural contours and used light and wind to best advantage. With walls of glass, it looked out towards the ever-changing turquoise of the Mediterranean.

During the three years of construction, Eileen remained on or near the site. Dressed in a trouser suit, silk shirt and a jaunty bow tie, she buzzed up and down the treacherous mountain roads checking on details, ensuring every aspect of her design was adhered to, refusing to compromise.

Seen from the sea, the finished villa, complete with masts, looked like a ship at anchor. Sailcloth membranes protected the terrace from the sun; life preservers hung from the balcony deck and reclining chairs suggested a cruise. On land the design was equally impressive. By using the same wooden floors, plain white walls, shutters and lights, the exterior terrace seamlessly converted to a secluded living room. The furniture was chrome, leather, wood, glass and cork.

Into this house she poured her very soul and she and Badovici spent many summers there, frequently with house guests. One was modernistic architect Le Corbusier who painted – without permission, Eileen maintained – eight sexual murals which she called 'an act of vandalism'.

After the break-up of her relationship with Badovici, she left E.1027, never to return. She was amused to learn, however, that the German soldiers who occupied the place during World War II used the murals for target practice.

Seventy-eight years later, on an equally warm summer's day, I walk in the footsteps of Eileen Gray. I've come by train from Nice. Crossing the tracks, I climb over the same stone wall and wander the quarter mile or so along the now-asphalted pathway. It's dirty and dusty. Littered with wrappers, beer and coke cans, cigarette butts and dog faeces.

A vandalised telephone box and padlocked gates mark the entrance to E.1027. The smell of urine predominates. Yet the Mediterranean, barely visible through the tangled overgrowth and chicken-wire fencing, is still turquoise and still dashing against the honey-coloured limestone rocks.

The E.1027 has become a shipwreck of a house. Crumbling concrete. Staircase off-kilter. Smashed windows.

Recently it has been designated by the French government as a historical monument. Ironically, it owes its salvation to the murals. Without them, rumour has it, it would have been left to rot.

EDGAR ALLAN POE'S HOUSE IN THE BRONX

Mary Russell

Edgar Allan Poe used to live in a small rural village called Fordham not far from New York. Nowadays, to get to the house, you take the D train across the Harlem River to the Bronx and walk across a couple of busy streets till you reach a leafy urban park, and there is the house: a small clapboard dwelling with a veranda and wooden steps leading to the front door. It is a peaceful place, surrounded by sweet-smelling honeysuckle and jasmine.

Poe led a troubled life and the move to the little village of Fordham was intended to bring some tranquillity to his own life and to improve the health of his young wife who was suffering from TB.

Poe was born in Boston, in 1809, to a couple of fit-up actors, but his father soon abandoned the family – in a sulk over a bad review – and his mother died when he was only three. Poe's paternal great-grandfather was from Northern Ireland, but, when he was orphaned, he was fostered by John Allan – a relative on his mother's side – which is why he became known as Edgar Allan Poe.

His relationship with his foster father never ran smoothly. The teenage Poe led an aimless life, drinking and gambling, and he was forever asking his foster father for money. Then he did an about-turn: he joined the army and applied to go to West Point. John Allan was pleased and put up some money for this stage of Poe's career but, six years later, the errant writer was thrown out for bad conduct. Poe was twenty-seven by then and for the last ten years had been writing stories and poems. He was influenced by Byron, and his Gothic tales are full of oil paintings that come to life, creaking doors, spooky mansions, premature burial, death and decay.

His income from writing was sporadic and uncertain, but things looked up when he started to edit a literary magazine. He was living in Baltimore at this point – the city in which his Irish great-grandfather had settled. Poe, in fact, was the fourth generation to live there and he had many relatives. One of them, his aunt Maria Clemm, had a daughter Virginia and, though she was only thirteen and he was twenty-seven, Poe and she set up house together – with Mrs Clemm moving in as well. The threesome moved back to New York and it was when Virginia was diagnosed with TB that they made the move to the little cottage in Fordham.

In theory, it was a sensible move: the air was fresh, they had a view of the ocean and the sound of church bells and seagulls as background music. Nearby was St John's College – now Fordham University – where Poe was able to make a few friends among the teaching staff. Even better was the fact that the rent was $100 dollars per year, just within his budget.

It's a pleasing cottage with timbered floors, old fireplaces, pale blue and cream walls and low ceilings. But this is now and, in 1846, it was far from comfortable, especially since that year brought one of the worst winters for some time. The cottage was damp and chilly since there was never enough firewood to keep the fires going and poor Virginia, coughing up blood, was kept warm with extra coats on the bed and her husband's faithful cat, who used to lie on her bed and keep her feet warm.

Neither was good enough, however, and in January 1847, she died. Two years later, after another bout of heavy drinking, triggered this time by melancholic despair, Poe also died: he was only forty years of age.

If the phrase had been invented then, you could say that a lot of the time Edgar Allan Poe was in denial about Virginia's poor health, and this comes out in one of his stories in which an artist continues to paint a portrait of his ailing wife, blind to the fact that she is, in fact, dying. In another more sinister story – written before Virginia died – the main character tries to kill a cat which has been tormenting him, but, failing to do so, he takes the axe to his wife and kills her instead.

When I visited the little house in the Bronx, it was on a warm, spring day, but on a dark winter's night, with rain lashing the roof and the leafless trees bent before a cold wind blowing in from the sea, it would be easy to imagine the seeds for many a ghost story being sown in the heart of this melancholic writer.

HAMLET'S CASTLE
Greg Collins

The twenty-eight-mile journey from Copenhagen to Elsinore, along the blue waters of the Øresund, with its ships and sails, and the coast of Sweden on the other side, is magical. At the other end, built on a peninsula, is a Renaissance palace with soaring green roofs, dreaming spires and high, pink-brick ramparts. This is Kronborg. Hamlet's castle.

The real Hamlet never saw Elsinore. His true name was Amleth, the only son of a tribal chieftain who had been murdered by his brother for both his power and his wife. The young prince realised he was in danger and would be the next to die, so he pretended madness. One evening he got the bodyguards drunk and, while they slept, entered his uncle's chamber and killed him. Then he appeared before the people and told them of his ruse to avenge his father's murder. In typical folk tradition they jubilantly hailed him as their new chieftain.

The story was first written in a history of Denmark by Saxo Grammaticus. A book on the subject by Christian Pederson appeared in 1514. The publication spread the story beyond Denmark and the English playwright, Thomas Kyd, transformed it into a drama of revenge. Probably inspired by this, Shakespeare wrote *The Tragicall Historie of Hamlet, Prince of Denmark and the Castle of Elsinore*. He was the first to associate the legend with Elsinore.

A Danish festival devoted entirely to productions of *Hamlet* is held annually in the courtyard of the castle. It was inaugurated in 1937 with the London Old Vic Company under the direction of Tyrone Guthrie and a cast led by Laurence Olivier. Dublin's Gate Theatre was invited in 1952, when the fifty-one-year-old Mícheál MacLiammóir played the young prince, with the late Eithne Dunne and Denis Brennan as Ophelia and Horatio. I was fortunate to be there in 1988 when Derek Jacobi directed Kenneth Branagh's *Hamlet*.

Like all such festivals, it has not been without its moment of crisis. On the inaugural night, the Old Vic was presenting the play before a cluster of crowned heads from all over Scandinavia. A special train was to convey the royal party and the diplomatic corps from Copenhagen. The performance was for 8 p.m. At 7.30 p.m., the rain was torrential. Conditions were so appalling that messages were sent to the royal parties cancelling the show. Unfortunately, they were making their scheduled ways to Elsinore. Guthrie decided that a performance in the open air was out of the question. The situation had all the ingredients of a thriller. The half-hour deadline. The decision-making crisis. The royal train steaming relentlessly to Elsinore. But the show, as they say, must go on.

They would perform in the ballroom of the local hotel. There was no stage. They played in the middle of the hall with the audience seated around. Like the circus. 'Theatre-in-the-round', it would later be called. This impromptu performance convinced Guthrie that for Shakespeare the proscenium arch was unsatisfactory. This conviction was to influence the design of many modern theatres. The Guthrie Theatre in Minneapolis is a testament to his vision.

As Elsinore is the setting for *Hamlet*, I have often wondered if Shakespeare visited Denmark. There is no direct evidence that he ever left England. However, a troop of actors from the Globe played there in the 1590s at the coronation of Christian IV. Christian, a wit, linguist and architect, loved music and the theatre. During the summer, actors and musicians from all over Europe were invited to perform in the castle courtyard, which could seat 3,000 people. I asked the castle guide if he thought Shakespeare played there. He had no doubt. The dramatist, he said, could never have described the castle so perfectly had he not come to Elsinore.

When I crossed the moat, and stood in the inner castle with its sea-facing battlements, the enigmatic young prince seemed to haunt the place. My tour of the castle and its endless rooms reinforced this feeling. Entering the turret room under the lighthouse, with its wide view over the Sound, you fancy you're in the 'Queen's Closet'. You look around for the 'arras' from behind which Polonius spied on Hamlet. From here I looked down on the wide lawn that was the 'platform' where Hamlet spoke to his father's ghost one midnight. Two armed sentries patrol there day and night, reminding one of Bernardo and Marcellus. In the great Knights' Hall, with its exquisite tapestries and illuminated by hundreds of candles in gold chandeliers, I imagined Hamlet directing the 'players' to perform the play that would 'catch the conscience of the King'.

As Shakespeare was actor-director and a leading shareholder in the Globe Company, it is feasible that he travelled and played with his fellow actors at Kronborg. About one thing there is no dispute: his creative genius turned a hero-legend into a mirror of mankind and the most profound drama ever written.

The rest is silence.

MY LIFE AS A BED

Elaine Sisson

Tracey Emin must be the most famous loser of the Turner Prize, the British award for contemporary art. Her entry, called *My Bed,* generated so much interest, antagonism and bewilderment that you could be forgiven for thinking she had actually won that year. In fact that honour went to an artist called Steve McQueen, who has had the double injustice of being eclipsed by Emin's notoriety as well as having a more famous namesake.

My Bed is an installation of an actual bed: a base supporting a mattress on top of which are rumpled sheets and pillowcases. Cluttered alongside it is an assortment of items, such as slippers, fluffy toys and contraceptives. The piece caused outrage, described – not only the tabloid newspapers – as a squalid installation of stained sheets, underwear, cigarette butts, empty vodka bottles and other unmentionable items. Underlying the indignation was anger at what contemporary art is supposed to be.

The popular suspicion is that what currently passes for 'art' is a very elaborate confidence trick. However, it was not so much what the piece meant in artistic terms but what it was worth that generated the most debate. The tabloids worked themselves into a hysterical frenzy at the fact that Charles Saatchi, the eminent art collector, had paid over £100,000 for Emin's work. Apart from the exasperation of the 'I could do that' brigade, there was also an uncertainty about what an artwork offers if it cannot be hung on a wall or appreciated for its refinement of line, composition, colour or beauty. People felt cheated that a bed – 'How could you hang that over your fireplace?' – could be the subject of art.

But to focus on the value, the meaning or the commercial worth of contemporary art, or even on Emin's own notoriety is, I think, to miss the point about *My Bed*. Like it or not, buy into it or not, to me, Emin's bed is a meditation on living. The very chaotic nature of it – the messy clothes, the traces of absent bodies – is completely at odds with those pastoral, ordered, tranquil living spaces displayed around us in advertising: the ideal homes, the show houses, the matching bed linen.

Flicking through interior-design magazines or lifestyle programmes on the television suggests that the bedroom and the bed represent contemplative, restful spaces – calm, white, serene, spare, feng shui – but set against the disorder of real life and the messiness of living they appear to be unreal, anaesthetised, vacant spaces. I'm not just thinking about the untidiness of an unmade bed, but that your bed is probably the most turbulent square in your entire home. Bed is where everything happens. We dream, fight, love, squabble, eat, recover, read, give birth, sleep and die in bed. We experience not solely the bed of rest, peace and sleep, but the bed of anxiety, languor, indolence, pleasure, abandonment, and distress. The bed – your bed, my bed – contains our abbreviated lives. And this is why I like Emin's piece so much. Not her bed specifically, not the collection of objects she has chosen to represent her own life, but all beds, every bed on which, in which, you have worried about the day to come or fretted over the day past.

I read somewhere once that we spend one third of our lives in bed asleep. But how much time do we spend in bed awake? That concentrated square arena is witness to every calamity, every pleasure, every grievance, every desire. It is our refuge from the day and yet it is also a place of no escape. When the day dies away we are left captive in our beds, thinking, planning, weighing things over, addressing, redressing, undressing things done and undone.

The poet John Donne, who wrote about the intimacy of the bedchamber better than anybody, says in 'The Good Morrow' that 'love... makes one little room an everywhere'. Thanks to Tracey Emin, I now think of my bed as an everywhere.

Sometimes, late at night, woken by the sound of rain drumming the roof, I imagine my bed as a ship. And for a moment I breathe deep, all that is precious in my life is distilled into this small square parcel. The captain snores faintly beside me and, with the hot fierce bodies of my sleeping children tightly lashed to mine, I see us cast anchor and set sail together, in our bed, for stormy adventurous seas.

THE DISNEY EXPERIENCE
Vona Groarke

It was a bribe: if they would come to America for six months with us, we'd take them to Disneyworld. I'm sure we thought they'd let us off the hook, that if we took them to, say, a Disney movie, that would do fine. As if.

They start us on the easy stuff – Magic Kingdom, with its picture-book carousel; the Peter Pan ride that took us in little carriages over a simulated London night-sky; the raft-ride out to Tom Sawyer's island with its fictional landscape made clamberingly real. 'Oh this is fine,' we think, 'very pleasant, very clean.' So clean, in fact, that we see cast members polish bins. The kids wait until we have our lunch down to reveal the meaning of the knowing looks, the solicitous asking after the state of our feet and feelings; they have the real deal up their sleeves. Imagine two poets, brushing up against middle-age, whose idea of a helluva night out is a new Polish movie, set in a mortuary or prison or, ideally, both. Now put them in the Tower of Terror, falling twenty-five storeys in as many seconds. Or up the front of Splash Mountain, heading south. We should be as disarrayed as the canto of Ezra Pound, as green as early Yeats, as breathless as Ginsberg's 'Howl', but actually, it's fun.

I too have read my Umberto Eco. My intellect responds to his theory of the passivity of the Disney experience. He's right – visitors are corralled and marshalled, their responses pre-programmed and their desires both simulated and exploited with breathtaking (and economically fortuitous) zeal. But I suspect Eco didn't go on any *real* rides: no one who stumbles off those roller-coasters or lunging freefalls could ever focus on their own passivity – they're much too busy pacifying their guts and rearranging their facial features to eliminate the fear of imminent death.

Day two is for Epcot and the embodiment of the American literalism, the World Showcase. When Marshall McLuhan coined the term 'the global village', I think he had in mind an imaginary or intellectual entity. Disneyworld cannot sell imaginary entities, so it has made a real global village consisting of pint-sized versions of foreign countries: the perfect solution for a country where some estimate that the number of Americans with passports is less than 5 per cent. No need to travel away from home – just head south to Florida, the world will come to you.

Not quite the whole world – mostly, in fact, strategic allies of the United States. And then France. Bizarrely, there's also America. The Liberty Café sells chicken wings and hot dogs. The American Adventure is an empty, outdoor amphitheatre, where Arlo Guthrie will sing American songs next week.

All Epcot cast members are authentically derived: English people work in England (although we meet the odd Scot); in France the French speak real French. But in America, the young man selling Old Glories is from Puerto Rico, and the lady in the Revolutionary war costume started off life in Mexico, but has been here eighteen years.

Each of the countries is crammed with visitors of the appropriate nationality – French people buying *pain-au-chocolat* in a village *pâtisserie*; Italians queuing for pizza at the Café Alfredo; Chinese people with baskets full of paper fans and jasmine tea.

In England, we walk through an Elizabethan maze, then down Tudor Lane, over which 'Greensleeves' ripples like Wimbledon applause. In the gift shop, you can buy Union Jack table mats. The Rose and Crown sells pints of bitter for $7.25. And Alice in Wonderland – who looks like a youthful Princess Diana, blond, wistful and pert – is having a tea party to which our children are invited.

They want to collect souvenirs of all the countries they visit. In France they are colouring mini Eiffel Towers when a conversation strikes up between two fathers at the art station. I listen in. They are African-American: one is in the army, the other is a reservist. Both, it turns out, are shipping to a very real Iraq within two weeks. This is a special holiday, five kids between them, none older than our Eve, who is eight. They discuss their units, how long they've been in service, where they've trained, when they're due to depart. After that, there's a thin silence. They don't want their chat to go ahead of them to a country so foreign it doesn't even feature in this Disneyworld. The father closest to me gathers up his sons. They don't want to go.

'You can finish it later,' he tells them. 'There'll be lots of time for that.'

ALL QUIET ALONG THE POTOMAC

Ted Goodman

Visiting Arlington National Cemetery, in Washington DC, a few years ago, I was following the path of many another Irish pilgrim to the graves of John F Kennedy and his brother, Robert. I also wanted to see what I knew to be America's greatest shrine to the dead of all its wars, where they lie at peace by the banks of the mighty Potomac.

It all began with Mrs Lee's rose garden, in the grounds of a rambling old house called Arlington, set in 200 acres just two miles from the centre of Washington DC. How her little garden became the centre of one of the most memorable sites for any visitor to the American capital is a story replete with many of the elements of Victorian melodrama – hatred, vindictiveness and a dispute about property which was to last for more than twenty years.

When the American Civil War broke out in 1861, Mrs Lee's husband, Colonel Robert E Lee, resigned his commission in the United States army to follow the cause of the south and his beloved state of Virginia. But many of his southern colleagues in the United States army chose to stay with the north, among these being one General Meigs, Quarter-Master General of the army. Meigs was to be the villain of the story, a southerner now consumed by a burning hatred for everything connected with the rebel south. The war at first went badly for the north and the great numbers of dead soldiers swamped the existing burial grounds around Washington. By a ruse, the government confiscated the house and grounds at Arlington and Meigs promptly decided to use the land as a military cemetery. He took particular pleasure in converting Mrs Lee's rose garden into the Tomb of the Unknown, a huge stone vault to hold the remains of over 2,000 unidentified northern soldiers.

After the war, the Lees returned briefly to Arlington but never lived there permanently again. Their eldest son brought a case on the confiscation to the Supreme Court and, in 1882, it ruled that the seizure had been illegal and awarded damages of $150,000 to the family. The Lees then assigned the property to the government.

Between 1861 and 1865, some 620,000 men from north and south died in the Civil War, but it was not until 1900 that it was possible to have a section of Arlington dedicated to the dead of the south. It took a further fourteen years to get agreement to the erection of a memorial to them. It bears the apt quotation from Isaiah:

'They shall beat their swords into ploughshares and their spears into reaping-hooks.'

Today, Arlington's 1,100 acres holds the graves of some quarter of a million Americans, almost all former members of her armed forces. Even now about eighteen funerals take place every day and the notes of a bugle sounding 'The Last Post' fall constantly on the ear.

The cemetery has strict controls as to who may be buried there – broadly speaking, any American serviceman/woman who dies on active duty, or who had to retire through disability, or who has been a holder of any of their country's highest military decorations. The deceased spouse or minor child of any of these may also be buried there.

Of course many distinguished civilians also lie in Arlington, among them presidents Taft and Kennedy, the boxer Joe Louis and the crew of the *Challenger* space shuttle.

That Arlington is regarded as a sacred place is reflected in the rules for visitors – no recreational activities are permitted in the grounds. Food and drink may not be consumed, even chewing gum is not allowed. Litter is totally forbidden.

The hushed dignity and reverence accorded to the fallen is caught well in the poignant words of the Civil War song:

> *'All quiet along the Potomac tonight, no sound*
> *save the rush of the river*
> *While soft falls the dew on the face of the dead,*
> *the picket's off-duty forever.'*

THE PHILLY CURSE
Conor O'Callaghan

Last month, Philadelphia's latest sporting hero, Smarty Jones, was poised to become the first horse in twenty-six years to win racing's treble. He had streaked home at Kentucky and Preakness. He was 5-1 on at Belmont. Smarty-mania had arrived. There was going to be a ticker-tape parade down Broad Street. Mounted police were going to be reintroduced for that one afternoon. Then Smarty's legs hit quicksand down the final furlong and a 33-1 no-hoper cruised by with half a length to spare at the post.

We sat in silence in our living room. Our kids' lips wobbled and I stepped out on to the decking to spit silent mournful expletives. Even the lady who owned the winning horse wept at the press conference. She wanted Smarty Jones to win. Myself and my wife went out for a cocktail that night.

'What about Smarty Jones?' I said gloomily to our barman.

'What about him?'

'He LOST!'

'Sure he lost,' the barman said bitterly. 'He's from Philadelphia.'

They call it the 'Philly Curse'. Although the phrase refers only to sports, after six months we have learned that it represents the city's place within the American imagination. She is the dowdy older sister, still on the shelf long after her younger, prettier, luckier siblings have broken countless hearts. According to the old joke, the residents of these streets are too tacky to live in Boston, too scared to live in New York and too poor to live in Washington.

What amazes us is how happy locals are to repeat that joke, to the detriment of their home town. What amazes us even more is

93

their initial surprise, and then gratitude, when we tell them how much we love the place and how handsome we find it. Coming on a year's lark from what my wife terms 'a butt-end provincial town' in Ireland, the City of Brotherly Love strikes us as the heights of glamour.

This year, centre city's Fourth of July shindig is called 'Welcome America', lest you forget that it all began here. It was here that Dutch ships drifting inland, in the same year as the Flight of the Earls, spotted wigwams in clusters on the banks of the Delaware. It was here that such founding fathers as Benjamin Franklin and Thomas Paine lived, that Congress first convened, that the Declaration of Independence was read aloud to passers-by, that the Liberty Bell sounded and the Constitution was written. Indeed, for a whole year and a bit, this was the capital of the Union. It was from here that the first transcontinental train track ran all the way to San Francisco, laid largely by Irish hands. You could be forgiven for believing that all American passages – east to west, upstream and inland – begin here, and all rivers gather back into this one source: Philadelphia.

Whenever family visit, we take them on walking tours and watch their eyes widen at the skyscrapers and street after tree-lined street of sunlit brownstones. We bring them down the Avenue of the Arts to read the roll-call of musicians on the sidewalk: John Coltrane, Dizzy Gillespie, Stan Getz, Chubby Checker, Mario Lanza, Frankie Avalon… We take turns to stand on the steps of the art museum and shout 'Rocky!' at the skyline. We remind them that Eddie Murphy 'traded places' with Dan Ackroyd on these streets and Tom Hanks died of Aids here. We make sure that the way home includes a spell of gridlock on Kelly Drive, if only to permit us to imagine how Princess Grace must have looked as a neighbourhood teenager during the last war.

When we ourselves leave, what images will we pack? The old-timers in Villanova University who still remember Ronnie Delaney training for Melbourne; the toll-free numbers of *American Idol* favourites fluttering under a fridge magnet; the wide-eyed, thick-ankled Amish girls behind market stalls, the braids of their hair tied up into pretzels; the ads for Viagra and the like, sandwiched between kids' cartoons, advising us to call our doctors if arousal lasts longer than four hours; the native American place names: Wissahickon, Conshohocken, and Lanape Avenue, named after the tribe those Dutch adventurers slaughtered.

'This was never my town,' Louis MacNeice once wrote of Dublin, 'but yet she holds my mind with her seedy elegance.' In six months we'll be out of here for good. We may never return. But we know already that we'll remember this with all the aching fondness that you remember an old flame. We'll experience a silent flutter whenever we hear the name, and secretly check out the Phillies' woes in the lower reaches of the Irish sport pages. We will always feel protective of the place, and anyone we cross with a bad word to say about it can expect a curse on their house from us.

A PASSAGE THROUGH THE PANAMA CANAL

Séamus Ó Lógáin

In 1963 I was radio officer on the *City of Brisbane* bound from New York to Auckland, New Zealand. Before starting on the journey across the Pacific, we had to transit the Panama Canal. Just a nine-hour journey of fifty-one miles which, before the canal was built, would have taken us several weeks to travel the 18,000 miles round South America. This transit journey through Panama provided an ever-changing view of the emerald rain forest, where I caught sight of the occasional tropical bird flitting through the trees or the even more rare glimpse of a monkey. Not at all resembling the tropical forest where 30,000 workers had died – most of them due to mosquito bites – during the monumental effort required to construct the canal.

For me the most interesting thing about the Panama Canal was the series of three massive double-locks. I went out on the wing of the bridge to watch the activity when we reached the first and largest of these, the Gatun locks and dam. The canal pilot who had come on board guided us into the lock and the ship was raised 26 metres as the lock filled with water. By use of hand signals and shouted instructions, he stayed in touch with the driver of the locomotive which hauled our ship to the other side of the lock. There she was released into an artificial lake and we continued our journey across the continent.

A demanding task completed, the frown of concentration left the pilot's face and I felt free to ask him about the clockwork precision of the lock operation. Pleased at my interest, he told me that no force is required to adjust the water level between the locks except gravity. As the lock operates, the water simply flows into the locks from the lakes or flows out to the sea-level channels. The dam at Gatun generates enough electricity to run all the motors which operate the canal, including the locomotives towing the ships. I asked him when the story of the canal began and he beamed with pride.

The first plan for a Panama Canal was drawn up in 1534 at the behest of Charles V of Spain. The motivation for the canal at that time was to shorten the time it took to get the plundered booty of Peru and Ecuador safely to Spain. The plan did not go ahead. In 1881 the Frenchman de Lesseps, who had been responsible for the construction of the Suez Canal, began work on the Panama Canal. Seven years later, the French company ran out of money because of the delays caused by disease-carrying mosquitoes and the inadequacy of their machinery. The American government bought them out for $40m. The United States and the new state of Panama signed the Hay-Bunau-Varilla Treaty, by which the United States guaranteed the independence of Panama and secured a perpetual lease on a ten-mile strip called the Canal Zone. Panama was to be compensated by an initial payment of $10m and an annuity of $250,000, beginning in 1913. The construction of the canal was recommenced in 1904 and completed in 1914.

At the Pacific end of the canal, our ship was brought down to sea level by the Pedro Miguel and the Miraflores locks. His job done, the pilot shook hands with the captain, turned to me and, with a broad smile, summed up the story of the canal in one sentence:

'The Spaniards had the vision to think of it, the French the confidence to begin it, the Americans the cash to finish it and, in 1999, we Panamanians will own it.'

HOMECOMING

Helen Fallon

I was pleased when Anthony, one of my students, invited me to spend a weekend with his family in his home village. This was his first trip home in four years. Transport was costly and unreliable. Distances that seemed short back in Ireland took on a new significance in Sierra Leone.

A few weeks prior to our visit, Anthony sent a letter, announcing our impending arrival, with someone who was travelling to the village. One of her neighbours read the letter to his mother. Returning home a university student to a community where most people could not read or write, and bringing with him his lecturer – a white woman from far away – was news indeed.

We set out in the early morning in a ramshackle van called a Poda Poda. It rumbled its way along the pot-holed road, finally disgorging us and some other cramped passengers at a cross-roads about ten miles from Anthony's village. We waited patiently, buying peeled oranges from the many children who congregated around newly arrived travellers. After a few hours, a creaking old taxi with a canary-yellow number plate appeared on the horizon and brought us – dusty, hungry and tired – the final miles along a ribbon of dusty pink road to Anthony's home.

There, his family had assembled to greet us. His father had died some years ago. In keeping with the tradition of his ethnic group, his uncle is now the head of the household. Anthony introduces me to his birth mother and also to his elder sister, whom he also calls mother. A lot of time is spent exchanging greetings and enquiring about my family. A bowl of groundnut stew – a stew made from peanuts, chilli peppers and fish – is passed my way. I eat from the big spoon that accompanies it and then pass the bowl to Anthony's uncle – the one he calls father.

My bedroom has a tiny window with a wooden frame. In place

of glass, a piece of grey mosquito gauze keeps out all the creatures of the night. I fall asleep to the chirping of the many insects that inhabit the choking mass of vegetation surrounding the house.

In the morning I awake to the sound of laughter. Light struggles through the tiny window, illuminating the faces of children pressed against the mosquito gauze. Most of them have never seen a white person before and giggle in wonderment. Breakfast – a cup of coffee and an egg – takes some time. The water is boiled on an open fire set between three large stones. This is a really common way of cooking here and, not surprisingly, it is called a three-stone fire.

Before the sun gets too high in the sky, we walk a few miles to a nearby gold mine, where whole families spend long days knee-deep in water, panning for gold. It's not as exciting as it sounds. If they find anything, it goes to the Lebanese controllers of the mines. The local people might get a tiny bonus in their meagre wages.

In the evening the villagers gather outside. A child is sent to a nearby village to get a small container of palm wine. Like milk in appearance, it has a sharp tangy taste. I sit sipping it, watching stars spread thick across the sky, while crickets, frogs and other night creatures provide a gentle, backing orchestra. The villagers talk quietly in a local language I do not understand.

Our departure is given as much ceremony as our arrival. Eventually a Poda Poda creaks into view. After haggling for a few moments with the driver we agree a price and the long journey back to the city, and my other life at the university, begins.

PORT ST JOHNS

Nieve Viedge

One of my favourite places to visit in the 1980s was Port St Johns, a small town on the east coast of South Africa. This is where the Umzimvubu River flows into the sea. Before doing so, it flows long and lazily along the side of the town, where it widens before reaching the sea.

At that time, we would cross the river by pont, a flat raft-like ferry that one of the local Xhosa or Pondo tribe pushed with a pole across the big river. A long wooden ramp was put down and we would drive on to the pont. For me, this was the most exciting part of the holiday.

My mother-in-law had a lovely house across the river at a place called Ferrypoint Farm. To get to town from her house meant either taking the pont across the river or driving along the side of the mountain for thirty or forty minutes until we reached a small bridge near the town.

Port St Johns was made up of a few hundred people, mostly blacks. There were a few white people who still lived there in large houses that were no longer looking so well kept – remnants of better days.

Port St Johns was part of an area called the Transkei, one of the homeland areas set up by the then nationalist government to give blacks their own areas, but these areas did not have much in the way of natural resources and the blacks had to travel long distances to work in the mines near Johannesburg.

When we would arrive at my mother-in-law's house after the twelve-hour drive, usually at dusk, we could smell the wood fire being prepared as we got out of the car. We had to go through the kitchen to enter the house. There, the two maids would greet us as they prepared supper. They were forever laughing and smiling. My mother-in-law introduced us – they couldn't understand us and we couldn't understand them. Our langauge was smiling and gesturing.

The house was split-level with a lovely veranda facing outwards towards the big river. Looking north, you could see the river flowing into the sea and across the river you could see Port St Johns. At night, you could sit on the veranda and see the lights of the town flickering in the distance. It was magic.

Behind the house, the side of the mountain rose up sharply above us, giving us cooling shadows from the day's heat. Nearby were two lovely beaches. We often got up at 6 a.m. and went swimming. The water was already warm at that time.

Sometimes we drove to Port St Johns to do our shopping. To do this we would drive along the dirt road with the river on our left and the sheer mountain on our right. The shopping was a lengthy, leisurely experience. My mother-in-law spoke fluent Xhosa and laughed and chatted with the locals. The townspeople formed queues in the few shops available. Time seemed to stand still. There was no rush.

The main street of the town was lined with tall avocado trees heavy with fruit which hung at the top like dark green bulbs. There was lush tropical vegetation everywhere. After the shopping, we would go to the Cape Hermes Hotel and have tea. There, we sat outside and looked at the Indian Ocean.

Soon it was time to leave. We would get up very early in the morning so that we could get home before dark. We would say our goodbyes to my mother-in-law and drive down the steep incline from the house to the dirt road. The river would accompany us again until we reached the town. There, we would bid the town and the river farewell and head inland towards home.

HELL'S GATE REVISITED
Madeleine Going

I went back to Hell's Gate last month, after an interval of about twenty years, wondering what changes I'd see. Hell's Gate is the name given to an ancient, long dried-up river bed in Kenya's Rift Valley – well named, I thought, for its desolation, its greyness and its almost lunar landscape. I remembered oppressive heat, clinging red dust, cliffs dwarfing all life in the gorge, cliffs so high and bare that they threw back echoes that got fainter and fainter as they travelled down the valley. But these bare cliffs were home to a couple of pairs of the very rare lammergeyer – that huge, hardly ever to be found, bearded vulture that could carry off a baby lamb in its beak. And that was what we had come hoping to see.

We turned off the road, all those years ago, and drove the Land Rover, bouncing along a track, leaving clouds of dust in our wake. Ancient tree-roots acted as natural sleeping policemen, monkeys and baboons leapt across our path ahead of us and large flying insects crashed against the windscreen. As soon as the cliffs loomed into view, we abandoned the car and walked the length of the valley, binoculars scanning the bare rock-faces for a glimpse of the elusive bird. No luck. We shouted at the barren cliffs, hoping that the echo, ringing up and down the valley, would startle one of the birds and make it fly from its perch. No luck. Disappointed, but not too dismayed, we decided to pitch the emergency tent we'd brought and stay the night – hoping to see the bird at first light.

And what a night. Fearing that the floor of the gorge might harbour a lion or leopard, we clambered up to the most accessible part of the cliffs. Three times we scrambled up with sleeping bags, water, food, etc. Darkness was falling fast, along with the temperature – and our hopes. Was any bird worth this? I thought, trying to warm my feet in my sleeping bag, after a supper of tepid baked beans and lukewarm tea. At first light, again we scoured the cliffs. Again – no luck. So, three more journeys to bring down all our paraphernalia, and back to Nairobi.

Tired, dirty and very disappointed, we got into the car. This had been our last chance. We were leaving Kenya for good the following Friday.

'We tried,' I said to my husband, doing my best to cheer him up. 'Good excuse to come back for a holiday,' I went on, as he didn't seem cheered.

'Suppose so,' he said, turning the car to join the road that would take us back up and out of the Rift Valley to Nairobi.

The sun was rising and the day was warming up. I rolled down the window to let in a rush of air, heavily scented with acacia. 'Stop the car,' I said. 'Quick. The binocs.'

We fell out of the car and stood, binoculars trained on a dot in a sky of the palest blue tinged with sunrise. The spot gradually grew bigger.

'Yes. It must be. Look at the triangular wing tips.'

It was. The bird seemed to be making for the car and, when it was almost overhead, it veered slowly to the west, giving us a stunning view of the pale breast plumage, the curious black feathers around the beak that put the 'bearded' into its name, and flew towards Hell's Gate with the sun on its widespread wings. It seemed to be apologising for the trouble it had caused us. We were dazzled, speechless, triumphant. All the miseries of the previous night were forgotten.

That was then. Last month we revisited Hell's Gate. There were rangers and a public toilet at the smart main gate, and a shop where you could buy curios and Coca-Cola. We ate our picnic off a nice wooden table in a little sunny glade. I had been prepared to be saddened, but somehow the ancient place still worked its magic. The barren cliffs still threw echoes down the gorge. The park was alive with every sort of game and we had the incredible luck of seeing a leopard tracking a baby zebra – a sight I had never seen in all the years I had lived in the country – until it was disturbed by our Land Rover.

The roads were as dreadful as ever, only now we were warned about them, and, for its final act, Hell's Gate put on a magnificent storm for us. From our vantage point, we had a panoramic view of almost the whole of the reserve and, behind it, Lake Navaisha. Huge storm clouds which were clustered over the lake were pushed across the sky by a strong wind. Reaching us, they emptied their contents in sheets over our heads and the reverberation of the thunder put the echoing cliffs to shame. I was delighted. Nobody could tame Hell's Gate, no matter what they did. I had one regret though. All the lammergeyers had gone.

THE GARDEN EAST OF EDEN
Max McGowan

It rolled lazily on the warm waters of the Indian Ocean until it was washed ashore on a beach in India. It looked like a large double coconut and they called it the coco-de-mer (*Lodoicea maldivica*) and so it has been called ever since. In fact, it is no relation of the coconut. It is the largest seed in the vegetable kingdom, weighing up to 40 lbs and, to quote a contemporary guide book:

> '... when husked the nut bears an uncanny resemblance to a naked female pelvis including the most graphic details...'

As I scribble this, there is one on the desk in front of me which I was lucky enough to get when I visited the Seychelles in the early 1970s. It has everything, including 'pubic hair', and from either front or rear it is provocatively curvaceous.

It is considered to be highly aphrodisiac and perhaps it was this quality that inspired General Gordon (of Khartoum fame), who was in India when it floated ashore, to follow the trail of the coco-de-mer across the Indian Ocean to the island of Praslin, twenty-three miles east of Mahe and the second largest island in the Seychelles archipelago.

There is a mystical place there called the 'Vallée de Mai' where the huge fronded 'trees' of the coco-de-mer grow – the only place in the whole world where they can be found. I visited this strange place, where never a breeze blows yet the massive fronds are always 'shivering'. It is always dark there and the ambience is eerie and primeval. Very rare birds, such as the Black Parrots, flit silently amid the foliage. There are no snakes or mosquitoes and other troublesome tropical insects are almost non-existent.

The male catkins are like the phalli of Irish donkeys (when in the mood... the donkeys, I mean) and they point across the narrow woodland paths directly at the huge seeds. The Seychellois do not believe that the seeds are pollinated and impregnated in the usual way but that the trees uproot themselves, after dark, go down to the beach and copulate in the warm waters. No local will visit the valley after the tropical night comes dropping fast.

After his visit, General Gordon concluded that the site of the original Garden of Eden was the Vallée de Mai and that the coco-de-mer was the original forbidden fruit. Its gelatinous flesh is highly regarded and one seventeenth-century king is reputed to have had an offer of 4,000 gold florins turned down for one.

I was taken to a slope in the centre of the valley and shown a small apple tree guarded by a wire cage. Apples do not grow in such climates, four degrees north of the equator, and indeed there was nary an apple on the tree when I saw it. But the impish, Seychellois lady guide told me that the tree does produce *one* apple each year. The implication is that this is the descendant of the famous apple, the bearer of the fruit of Good and Evil, which discombobulated our young lives in the catechism class, *fadó, fadó*. You can make of it what you will.

She also told me that the name of the head gardener in the Vallée de Mai was Adam and that his father before him was called Adam and so on, as far as could be traced in these 'islands of love' where there were no written records until recently.

I was lucky enough to stay in the intriguing Seychelles before the tourist boom started. You could buy coco-de-mer, unhusked of course, from stalls in the streets, as well as hearts of palm to make 'millionaires' salad'. Each 'heart' meant the death of a royal palm. I believe you cannot buy them any more and that is a good thing to hear in this era of nature's destruction.

A Sense of Humour

RESCUE

Helen Skrine

L ong ago, in the age of chivalry, the troubadours of France and the Don Quixotes of Spain regarded it as their vocation and privilege to rescue damsels in distress. Virtue was its own reward. I felt something of the same satisfaction when I received into my household twelve displaced ladies. Actually, I'm wrong – there were thirteen, a baker's dozen. Somebody had added the thirteenth for luck, I suppose, and good riddance. She was very lame and bumped along rhythmically like a bicycle with a flat tyre. They were all extremely quiet and timid, being unused to a country place where there was only the sound of the rooks in the trees.

Where they had come from there had been constant noise like a permanent scream and now the quietness was, yes, *frightening*. They huddled together for reassurance and spoke little amongst themselves. The sunlight, too, seemed to make them cringe, but on entering the house they seemed reassured and more relaxed, though still too intimidated to chatter even quietly in their own language. Also, it was warmer inside, for the clothes they had arrived in displayed enough bare skin to qualify them as models for the Paris Fashion Week. It would take time to tog them out in country clothes.

As always happens, a leader soon appeared amongst them and it was she who blazed a trail into the great outside world, while the others followed with tentative steps. Having so little in common with ordinary folk, they embarked with great anxiety on what we would call a steep learning curve. The first shock was to sample the non-prison food and the second was to make acquaintance with green grass. They examined it with astonishment. But the most agreeable sensation by far was, I think, that released at last from their solitary confinement in very small cells, they could now 'swing a cat', or whatever the equivalent is in their own terms.

After a week of the getting-to-know-you phase, the sun came out one day in its full mid-summer glory and, after breakfast, out they went to enjoy it. And I came upon them, all thirteen of them, lying stretched out on the grass, sunbathing, with their eyes shut, oblivious to everything but the happy conviction that they had arrived in paradise.

After three months they were looking smart in their beautiful new fine feathers and at last I was rewarded by finding an egg for my breakfast. Soon there were enough for an omelette. To celebrate, I introduced a fine cock with handsome green tail-feathers, a shiny orange scarf and a tall red comb on his head. I must admit he received the frostiest of welcomes, and his strutting and crowing were a bit subdued.

But now we're all friends and my reward is a *daily* reward. Their love for me is probably all of the cupboard variety, but mine for them is of a higher order. Or is it? If there's no egg for my breakfast I do feel a bit hard done by. 'I must have eggs,' I shout at them, 'or else – back to the battery!' But it's an idle threat and they know it, as they sing a reply and pluck at my shoelaces.

CLOSE ENCOUNTERS WITH HEDGEHOGS
Trudy Lomax

Many years ago, a friend gave me a lift home to Sligo from Dublin on a winter's evening. At about ten o'clock we were just coming into Carrick-on-Shannon when he jammed on the brakes, leaped out of the car, scooped something up from the middle of the road, climbed back in the car and, dropping a round ball of prickles into my lap, drove on, saying, 'We couldn't leave it in the road, the poor little fellow would be squashed flat!'

'What about fleas?' I squeaked, feebly.

'No problem at all,' I was assured. 'Hedgehog fleas are only interested in hedgehogs.'

So Humphrey, as the hedgehog was christened, travelled quite happily, as far as one could tell, to just north of Sligo town, where he was released in Classiebawn woods. I have wondered ever since whether he, or indeed she (sexing hedgehogs is tricky, for obvious reasons), was torn from the bosom of a loving family and might have preferred to remain in County Leitrim.

Some years later, my husband set off down the pier at Mullaghmore Harbour to go out fishing. Twenty minutes later, he was back with a very disgruntled hedgehog in his lunch bag! The pier always has lobster pots stacked against the wall, often with remains of salt fish, used to bait them, still inside. This particular specimen of the genus *Erinaceus europaeus*, attracted by the smell of fish, must have found his way in through the pipe where the lobsters go in and, like the lobsters, had been unable to find his way out again – at least I have never heard of fishermen baiting their pots with hedgehogs! Anyway, the lobster-pot hedgehog was also released in Classiebawn woods, where perhaps he met up with the exiled Humphrey.

Our daughter Sacha encountered the next hedgehog, which she found on the road with badly injured hind legs. We took him to the vet, steeling ourselves for a verdict of 'just have to put the poor little fellow out of his misery', but we underestimated our vet! Uncurling the little creature, not without difficulty, from my daughter's wrist and examining him gently. 'You'd be amazed how tough these little fellows are,' he said. 'We'll just give him an antibiotic and make sure the legs are clean. Keep him confined somewhere safe for a few weeks and there's a very good chance he'll be fine. Whatever you do, don't give him milk! Contrary to popular belief, it's very bad for hedgehogs, they can't digest it. Give him tinned dog food and bring him back to me if you're worried.'

Thinking back to the previous hedgehog, a lobster pot seemed a handy way to provide an intensive care unit for Hodge, as he was christened, so he was duly installed in a luxury lobster pot on the back porch, where he quickly adapted to his circumstances and developed a passion for Pedigree Chum dog food, which he ate with such gusto that he could be heard all over the house. While he tolerated the rest of the family, Hodge had a definite preference for Sacha and never curled into a ball when she picked him up to check his legs. Both legs healed well, though one was badly mangled and he didn't have full use of it. However, by the time he was able to have exercise runs in the garden, he was able to produce a good turn of speed and, when finally released – hopefully to meet up with the other two or their descendants – we felt he had a good chance of survival.

On a recent trip to Belleek in County Fermanagh, I was intrigued to see a notice in a shop window advertising a bring-and-buy sale in aid of the Hedgehog Helpline. This turned out to be in support of a campaign to relocate hedgehogs from the outer Hebrides, where their numbers have grown to so many that they are thought to be a danger to the native wading birds. Adopt a hedgehog, anyone?

IN PRAISE OF THE GOLDFISH

Anthony Glavin

There is a lot to be said for goldfish as childhood pets – especially when the care and feeding of a pet reverts to parents, as often happens. Compared to a dog, which needs walking, or a cat, which looks to be let out, and in, and out again, a goldfish is very much a low-maintenance affair.

I know of what I speak, as our goldfish, Guinny – short for Guinevere – has been in my charge for several years now. To be fair, the daughters looked after Guinny and her consort Lancelot when the couple first came to us, inherited from a younger cousin who had lost all interest in them at home, only to ask eagerly, 'Can I feed the fish?' every time she visits us now. And it was our elder daughter who renamed them Guinevere and Lancelot, inspired by the Arthurian legends she was reading that summer.

Lancelot passed away a year after he came to us, but Guinny's still going strong, somewhere into her fifth year, we reckon. Though whether it's actually *her* and not *his* fifth year isn't absolutely clear, as Guinevere and Lancelot were so-christened according to size, with the latter, Lancelot, being the larger. Apparently it is easiest to determine a goldfish's sex at spawning time, when the male develops a row of white pimples along his pectoral fins – a feature that, let's be honest, sounds like it might in fact discourage sex. Another way to determine gender is to introduce a known female into a tank of indeterminate goldfish, whereupon any males will immediately 'check out' the new talent, while her sisters pay her little heed. A response pattern, it must be said, that raises the question of how far guys have really evolved from goldfish.

For their part, goldfish have definitely evolved a long way from the freshwater carp first domesticated by the Chinese over a thousand years ago. Generally brown or olive-coloured, freshwater carp can grow to sixteen inches in length, which was nearly the size of the grand-daddy carp I caught and released years ago in a Wisconsin lake, thinking I'd snagged an old automobile tyre as I reeled it in – all weight and no fight whatsoever. As for its diminutive cousin, breeders have over the centuries developed countless varieties of goldfish, ones with bulging eyes, double or triple fins, strange tails and vivid colours, though in fact most so-called goldfish are actually orange.

It is said the goldfish has a memory span of three seconds only, though I sometimes wonder how scientists – in this case ichthyologists – measure for memory. Or for IQ either, given that goldfish are also said to be highly intelligent, able to recognise who in a household it is that feeds them and greeting them upon sight by swimming briskly about the bowl. Certainly that's true for our Guinny, who lashes about whenever she sees me pass by. What's more, we have developed a neat routine in which she (or is it he?) rises to the top of the bowl to accept a massive pellet of fish food I've rolled between my fingers, far handier than feeding her piecemeal.

It seems goldfish can live up to fifteen years – although a neighbour recently told me of the morning his pair expired and swam off into that great fishbowl in the sky. And how his wife immediately sent him into town for an identical pair before their son awoke, only for the four-year-old to meet his father coming in the gate, a plastic water-filled bag in hand. 'What are you doing with the fish, Dad?' the little lad shouted, all amazed.

'Oh, just taking them for a walk, son,' my neighbour *calmly* replied.

AN ENCOUNTER WITH A WILD TOMCAT
Peter McNally

Our small town house in Skerries at one time had a passable-sized back yard. However, over the years, bits and pieces of extensions were built until, in the end, all that was left of the yard was a square the size of a small bedroom surrounded by four high walls. One evening, at the age of about twelve, I was reading in the living-room when my mind was distracted by an odd clinking sound from outside. Curious to find out what it was, I pressed my nose up against the glass. What I saw out there at once appalled and enthralled me. A mangy off-white tomcat was running in crazy circles around the yard with his head jammed in a Bachelor's bean can.

A glance at the rubbish bin told me what had happened. The plastic bin lid lay on the ground along with other detritus scattered by the hungry tom. Somehow, while supposedly licking the bottom of the bean can, my scruffy visitor had managed to get his head firmly jammed inside it.

As I watched, the by now frantic tom ran headlong against one wall then changed direction, plummeting headlong into the opposite wall. Of course, each time he whacked his head into a wall he forced the bean can down even tighter on his head. The penny finally dropped with me that the poor thing was suffocating and I had better do something for him quickly if the bottom of a soggy bean can was not to be his last view of this planet.

I opened the back door gingerly; stepping out into the yard was like stepping out into the middle lane of the Indianapolis, with the deranged tom careering frantically around it. Here was a ball of rotating mangy fur, out of which protruded razor-sharp claws that flailed around like the blades of a food blender – and every bit as dangerous. Catching this whirlwind with bare hands would be impossible.

I vaguely remembered from first-aid class that the brain can last only three minutes without oxygen, even when you are not cracking your head off a stone wall. I had to do something mighty quickly.

I cartwheeled up the stairs and whipped a sheet off the nearest bed. All the way there and back to the yard I could hear the continued clanking of bean can on stone. Emerging tentatively into the yard, I took up position and cast the sheet at the demented cat. I might as well have been trying to trap a withered oak leaf in a hurricane. After missing several times, however, the cat finally tripped head-over-heels over the can and rolled *himself* up in the sheet.

At that point he went perfectly still, so much so that I thought he must surely be dead. I knelt down, put my knee on his limp body, grabbed the can and wrenched it off his head. The explosion which followed would have put the Los Alamos experiment to shame. With a mighty sneeze, the liberated tom sprang up off the ground, flailing his claws in all directions. He took two or three mighty bounds and leapt six feet into the air and straight over the wall, with shards of the white sheet trailing behind him.

I have seen neither tom nor sheet since… and forty years later, I still bend the mouth of every bean can flat, *before* it goes in the bin.

A WEASEL'S TAIL

Brendan Jennings

The little animal stared straight at me with the meanest pair of eyes you ever saw. It was long and lean, about the size of a small cat, its fur brownish-red with white under-parts. it had a whippy tail, a pointed head and a sneering sort of mouth. And those mean, glittering eyes.

We were in the middle of our picnic lunch at Portnakillew, a secluded cove on the north Antrim coast. It was a magical place of woods and rocks, inviting pebble pools and shallow bays. The sea sparkled and the misty blue hills and islands of Scotland shimmered in the distance.

'Look,' I said to my aunt who was sitting beside me.

Aunt Lizzie's eyes opened wide in alarm. 'It's a weasel!' she squealed. 'We'll be eaten alive!'

My mother tried to keep everyone calm but the children were crying, their voices echoing off the high basalt cliffs, and Aunt Lizzie was almost hysterical with terror. I remembered how the weasel had looked at me with its mean, glittering, bloodthirsty eyes and I shivered with cold, even though the day was warm. I knew the weasel could spring on me in a second and sink its fangs into my throat and suck the blood from me, because that's what weasels did.

Aunt Lizzie wanted to abandon everything and flee but, even though my mother was almost in tears, ashen-faced and trembling with fear, she refused to leave the crockery behind.

'Those are the only cups I have in the world.'

By this time, the weasel had disappeared but our terror had not; if anything it had grown and multiplied until it filled our minds, and our only thoughts were of escape.

We scurried fearfully up the cliff path, the same path down which we had hurried with such happy anticipation. Our day of joy had become a day of unspeakable menace. The track levelled out and we entered a great dark wood with gigantic trees that blotted out the sky. The path was hemmed in by weeds and bushes, full of sinister places where a million weasels could have hidden.

We thought we were safe when we met two fishermen going down to their boat in a nearby cove, but our nightmare was only just beginning. When Aunt Lizzie breathlessly told them about the weasel, they frowned and shook their heads sadly. Johnnie McKenna asked if it had put its tail in its mouth.

'It's a well-known fact,' Johnnie told us grimly, 'that when one o' them wee devils is attacked it can put its tail in its mouth and whistle and other weasels will come to its aid. There could be dozens of them waiting for you at the top of the path.'

Away the two men went and, just before they were swallowed up by the dark wood, Johnnie called over his shoulder, 'You'd better pray they don't do the dance o' death.'

And what was the dance o' death? The very words filled us with dread. And could dozens of weasels really be waiting for us?

Weasels were renowned for their evil ways but now we knew they were monsters and brutes of the foulest sort, who would murder us all without pity. We had no choice but to keep climbing the path, terrified beyond words with every step that took us closer to our doom. My mother herded us up that gloomy track, frightened children wailing, Aunt Lizzie slipping and sliding in the dirt, stumbling over tree roots, sobbing and blubbering, praying to the saints and the Blessed Virgin to intercede for us.

At the top of the cliff there was only sunshine, blue skies and safety. Certainly no weasels, for there are no weasels in Ireland – what we had seen was a stoat. There were no hordes of little monsters of any description waiting for us. Such things happened only in the minds of children and hysterical aunts. Weasels putting their tails in their mouths and whistling for help, and the dance o' death, are just tall stories, but I'll never forget that day at Portnakillew when I looked into the mean, glittering, bloodthirsty, murderous eyes of a notorious killer.

SAIGON, SAIGON
Marjorie Wallace

In 1973, the Golf Club de Saigon was a charming French colonial building with a deep, cool, semi-circular veranda, in the middle of the US military base at Tan Son Nhut. My husband Thi, a Vietnamese engineer, was secretary of the club and we spent most Sundays on the course. Golfing diplomats posted to Saigon were usually anxious for speedy membership and Thi was happy to oblige. He even managed to rustle up clubs, bags, shoes and the like for new members whose heavy baggage had not yet arrived. As a result, we were often included in the guest list for Embassy or Consulate functions at the Thai, Philippine, Japanese, Taiwanese, American or British compounds. For a war-torn country, my life in Saigon was a busy, sociable whirl, right up to six weeks before autumn.

My father had been a keen golfer, with a goodly collection of monthly medals to his credit, although he was always disappointed that his handicap was higher than he would have liked. As a child in Scotland, I would join him in the garden and we would practise chipping the ball into a jam jar. On our annual trip to the seaside, the putting green beside the promenade was my favourite spot, and I fancied myself as a bit of a dead-eye Dick. I foolishly thought that, with practice, there was no reason why I couldn't become a reasonable golfer. Sadly, thirty years on, I have to accept that it never happened. Much too erratic and inconsistent. But I do have one claim to golfing fame and it happened in Saigon.

One Sunday, Thi and I were playing with the British Consul General and his wife. At one point, a public road ran through the course, with high perimeter fences on both sides and a sentry post to be passed before the next hole. The sentry's wife had set up a stall selling deliciously cool coconuts, much appreciated in a place where temperatures rarely dropped below thirty degrees.

With a deft slash of the cleaver, the top was removed and a straw inserted. The enterprising lady was also raising a few turkeys that ranged free around the sentry post.

Gratefully revived, golfers now had to walk back, away from the next green. The men had to retreat seventy yards but the ladies' tee was only about thirty yards from the sentry post. We stood out of the way with our caddies while the men drove off. Then the Consul's wife sent one long and straight down the fairway. Desperate not to let the side down, I gave an almighty swipe at the ball, which skewed-off low and to the left... and smack into the head of a turkey. With a gurgled gobble, it toppled and fell, killed instantly.

Out rushed the sentry's wife, making a beeline for Thi. In a high-pitched torrent of Vietnamese she screamed at him that I had killed her turkey, I was a rich American and I'd have to pay for it. Calmly, Thi informed her that I was not American, I was not rich, I was his wife and he was the secretary of the club. Could she please tell him who had given her permission to raise turkeys in the middle of the golf course? Somewhat subdued, the discussion continued. A price was agreed and it was arranged that, when we had finished the round, the club manager would be dispatched to pay her and collect the bird.

At the end of the round, we retired to the clubhouse for a beer. To my surprise, the Consul General had an uncharacteristic, stern expression on his face. Loudly he called for the club manager and demanded the complaints book. In the book he wrote: 'I have played golf all round the world. I am aware of the fact that it is possible to get a birdie, an eagle or an albatross. Only in Saigon is it possible to get a turkey.'

Some time later, we had a turkey dinner for the Consul, the president of the club and their wives. Despite every attention to detail, and Thi was a great cook, the bird was as tough as old boot-leather.

THE DAY I RAN THE HALF MARATHON
Henry Austin

Having a flutter on the horses can be a very enjoyable pastime, when taken in moderation. So can having a drink. But when you combine the two it can be an expensive pastime. When money becomes scarce, one has to go, or maybe even both. But with a certain amount of enterprise, and even with a lack of finance, they can go hand in hand.

Take my own situation for example. I did not know very much about horses, although I was well versed in drinking. My best pal, an individual known as the Vulture – so-called because of his willingness to eat or drink anything he could get his hands on, especially if it was free – was a student of form. One day in summers past, with both of us yearning for a drink to quench our thirst, the Vulture got a tip for a horse. Neither one of us had a brass farthing to our name, but I was wearing a nice suit of clothes my mother had bought me for my brother's wedding several weeks earlier.

The horse was at very short odds of about 6-4 but, as far as the Vulture was concerned, it was a racing certainty. Against my better judgement, I entered the gents' toilet on Marine Road in Dún Laoghaire and I removed my suit. I then handed it over the cubicle door to the Vulture, who immediately headed for the pawn office on the main street.

Because the suit was relatively new, he was able to borrow £2 on it, which he duly put on the nose of the horse in the 2.30 p.m. race at the Curragh. Standing in the cubicle in my underwear, I felt there was a great irony about the whole situation, considering the name of the horse was Shiny Bottom.

Approximately one hour later, the Vulture returned. But his deadpan face caused my jaw to drop and, besides, he wasn't carrying anything, which further compounded my fears. But being the joker that he was, his face soon broke into a smile and he produced a parcel with my suit in it. He got several more tips and, with one exception, they all won.

But the winning distances were getting shorter each time and, in fact, our last winner had prevailed by a short head. I had been getting more nervous with each race and, as a consequence, I decided to take a precaution, in the event of a tragedy occurring – I began to wear football knicks under my suit.

On the last day of our brief sojourn into the sport of kings, neither one of us had a penny to spend, which meant I had to use the free cubicle. It was designed in such a way as to discourage anyone from staying too long. In fact, it was just a hole in the floor and, if you were unlucky enough to slip, you were likely to be drowned.

After following the usual procedure, I waited anxiously for the Vulture to return. Standing beside the black hole of Calcutta was like a month of Sundays. When he finally showed up, his deadpan face was for real. His selection, Speedy Gonzales, finished so slow that it finished last. Although my suit was safe and secure in the pawn office until I could get the money to redeem it, I never did.

But there was one thing about the Vulture that I particularly admired; he was loyal to the bitter end. As I tentatively made my way on to Marine Road, dressed in just my shirt and football knicks, the Vulture borrowed a bicycle, for which he was later to receive a month in Mountjoy Prison. He then cycled beside me all the way home, as I ran the half marathon.

THE AGE OF REASON
Mary Halpin

In the winter of 1959 I was seven and had reached the Age of Reason. This meant I knew right from wrong, truth from untruth. I could work things out in my head and give explanations for my answers. I could shine what my Nana called the 'pure light of reason' on a problem and discover its solution. I had reached this happy state the previous May when I'd made my Communion and it had come not a moment too soon. As December approached, a nagging question had entered my mind which only reason could solve.

Whispers had begun circulating in class, rumours were rife in the playground. One of the big girls had declared that there was no Santa. Only little children believed in him and she certainly didn't. Eventually, the rumour reached me and I was devastated. Surely, this had to be wrong? I tried to put it from my mind but doubts kept flooding in. My anxiety was fuelled by the belief, instilled in me by my sister, that if you didn't believe in Santa, then he wouldn't visit you and you'd waken on Christmas morning with a horrid empty space at the end of your bed where the presents were meant to be.

My sister was six years my senior and an expert on everything. It was she who had told me that, at the end of the world – an event that would happen when all the candles in all the churches finally flickered out – God would initiate a kind of lottery. It wouldn't matter how good or bad you had been, you could go up to heaven or down to hell entirely at His whim. This didn't seem very reasonable to me, but for many months afterwards, whenever I was in church, I would nag my parents with requests for small change to light as many candles as I could fit on the stand below the statue of St Anthony. Eventually, my mother tired of searching for pennies in her purse and questioned my sudden devotion to the saint. Her tongue clicked in exasperation when I explained. 'Don't mind that sister of yours,' she told me. 'I'll have something to say to her later!'

None the less it was to my sister I now turned. She dismissed the rumours out of hand. 'Of course there's a Santa,' she assured me. 'Sure doesn't he bring me presents too?'

But still I worried. For one thing, there was stark disparity in the presents we received. Whereas my bed was piled with toys, dolls and books, and the stocking on the bedpost swelled with fruit and Dinky cars, she only got one or two things. This year she was hoping for an Alice band and Cliff Richard's single 'Livin' Doll'. Did she get less because she believed less? That didn't make sense because I was the one with the doubts. It was all very confusing. 'Maybe Santa likes you more,' she told me when I asked. Though the answer was flattering, I wasn't convinced. She'd been wrong about the end of the world, maybe she was wrong about Santa too.

I took the problem to my father who told me about another little girl who had posed the very same question many years before. She'd written to the editor of a famous American newspaper to ask him 'Is there a Santa?' and he had assured her there was. 'So there you are,' he announced, closing the matter and returning quickly to his own newspaper.

I just didn't buy an explanation from some editor in a far-off land, who'd been writing, after all, in an entirely different age. Maybe Santa had been real then, but – a terrible new possibility came to mind – what if he had since died? Perhaps that was what the girl in school had meant when she had said he didn't exist.

Since my Nana was the one who was always droning on about the wonders of reason, I thought she should know that, on this occasion, it was failing badly. To my irritation, she did a complete about-turn. 'Reason isn't all it's cracked up to be,' she said. There were some things you couldn't work out, no matter how hard you tried. You just had to believe. 'Don't be a Doubting Thomas,' she warned, but I couldn't help it. Christmas was a mere week away. It was vital to resolve the thing once and for all. 'Seeing is believing' was another of my Nana's sayings and now I decided that I would believe – could only believe – in Santa if I saw him with my own two eyes.

That very week, we were going to town to visit him and I always looked forward to getting on to the train to his grotto. You stepped aboard in the toy department and, as the train rocked back and forth, scenes of flying reindeer and snowstorms flashed by the windows. When you got out at the other side, you were in the North Pole where Santa then lived (I gather he has since moved to Lapland). Some years Santa was thin, other times he was fat. I'd noticed this and had asked my mother why he seemed to have such fluctuating weight. She'd said he sometimes needed to diet to fit down the chimneys. This explanation no longer washed with me. Everyone knew the real Santa could do magic. He didn't *need* to lose weight to fit down a chimney! I was certain that the slimmish Santa chuckling before me in the grotto was an imposter; a mere stand-in for Santa, who was, I was now wretchedly certain, dead.

And yet… there was still one small beacon of hope…

Christmas Eve came and the usual offering of cake and a half pint of Guinness were left on the kitchen table. If only I could defer sleep long enough to sneak down and catch him while he ate! Then I'd know for sure that the rumours had been false.

Night came and excitement kept me awake, as it always did, long beyond my normal bedtime. I could just about hear the sound of 'God Save the Queen' from our newly acquired television, as the BBC closed down for the night. My parents shuffled off to bed. My teenage sister was already asleep in the bed next to mine. I crept downstairs to the kitchen. Light from the street lamp illuminated the room as I peered inside. The cake and Guinness were still there, untouched. Disappointed, I made my shivering way back to bed and waited. And waited. I may have dozed but, some time later, a sound jolted me fully awake.

It was the sound of our bedroom door clicking to. I sat bolt-upright. In the darkness I could just make out the shape of the presents at the end of my bed; the happy bulge of the stocking tied to the post. My heart burst with gratitude. He had brought presents despite my doubts! He was alive and he was real! Nana had been right. Reason wasn't all it was cracked up to be.

I jumped out of bed and dashed to the window, hoping to catch sight of him as he left the house. Pulling back the curtain, I saw in the night sky, an unmistakable flashing light soaring high to the east and, in front of it, the darker shape of a sleigh. I thought I could just make out the forms of the reindeer as they dived into a cloud, Comet and Prancer and the rest and, though I couldn't absolutely swear it, I'm sure I heard the laugh of the man himself as he drove them onwards across the sea to Wales, their next port of call.

THE GREAT FOURPENNY FRAUD
Marian Gormley

Everyone in third class was told to buy an atlas in Coughlan's shop. The nun did not know what the price would be but assured us it wouldn't cost more than one shilling and sixpence. When I asked my father for the money, he gave me a two-shilling piece and told me to bring home the change.

On my way to school the following morning, I met my friend Frances. She was the most popular girl in the school and did not need to buy an atlas for she had inherited one from an older sister and, when she offered to help me buy mine, I felt honoured.

Only the week before, Frances had inveigled me into spending an afternoon sitting in the pitch dark of her coal shed eating chocolates, which she had acquired in highly questionable circumstances. Our absence from school had not been noticed and Frances managed to convince me and our friends that we had had a wonderful time.

Mr Coughlan produced four atlases for my consideration but it was my friend who did the choosing. Definitely the cheapest one at one shilling and fourpence was exactly what the teacher wanted, Frances said, and of course I agreed. Outside the shop, Frances produced a pencil from her school-bag and, taking my new atlas, she crossed out the four of the one shilling and fourpence and scribbled an eight in its place.

'Now we can buy two lucky bags and a sheet of transfers each,' she announced gleefully.

I was shocked into silence and, when I did manage to voice my objections, Frances had all the answers ready. Everyone, including my father, would expect an atlas to be at least one shilling and sixpence. One and eight was still a perfectly reasonable price and I had fourpence change. I had nothing to worry about, and we would be first in class with the butterfly transfers, and you would never know but we might find new pennies in our lucky bags, and if I felt that badly about shortchanging my father I could give him the two new pennies. My lucky bag contained a packet of sherbert and Frances got a green celluloid watch. As soon as my father came home that evening I gave him his four pence change and, when he asked to see the atlas, my stomach did a somersault.

'This only cost one and four,' my father said.

'No,' I lied, 'it was one and eight.'

'You changed the four into an eight.' He pointed to the price on the cover where the alteration was clearly visible.

'I didn't change it.' I was determined not to confess or to betray Frances.

My mother was called upon to give her opinion and she was certain I would never be dishonest. Perhaps, she suggested, Mr Coughlan had put up his prices: she would ask him first thing in the morning. Meanwhile we would drop the subject and have our tea. But I had no appetite and took myself off to bed because I was feeling sick.

After three hours agonising, I made the big decision, put on my dressing gown and went downstairs to unburden myself. I took full responsibility and did not implicate Frances. My father shook his head sadly from side to side and my mother spoke of her bitter disappointment and wondered how could she ever trust me again. The shame of it lived with me for years.

I had almost forgotten the episode, which happened over half a century ago, until recently while I was watching television. A charming silver-haired woman was being fêted for her considerable fundraising abilities. There was something familiar about her and it wasn't until she mentioned the small town in Ireland where she grew up that I recognised her. Frances, a fundraising supremo? I wouldn't doubt it for a minute!

THE WILY TURK

Maureen Keane

Dublin in the late eighteenth century had its share of lively characters, but it is hard to think of one more colourful than Dr Achmet Borumbad. He was lately arrived from Constantinople and he strode the streets in his Turkish robes. A fine figure of a man, he was over six feet tall and his high turban made him even taller. Although much of his face was hidden by a bushy black beard, he was handsome and his manners were exquisite. His English was good and his foreign accent added to his charm.

The doctor had a mission. In his travels in Asia, Africa and Europe, he had noted how frequent bathing in supervised baths improved people's health. What he wanted was to set up an establishment in Dublin where the public could immerse themselves in hot baths, temperate ones, medicated ones and cold ones. There would be a reasonable charge, but the poor would be allowed in free and he himself would treat them for nothing. He convinced the College of Physicians of the merits of his plan and persuaded them to back his application to the Irish parliament for funds. Parliament granted him the money to set up baths in Bachelors' Walk and his successful career was under way.

The baths were instantly popular and the doctor kept his word about treating the poor for free. Society loved him and he was welcome everywhere. The only problem was that he needed more and more money for capital expenditure and the best place to get this was from parliament. To keep his supporters there happy he threw lavish parties for them. This proved to be the doctor's undoing. During one particularly rowdy evening, one of the guests decided he had had enough and left the gathering to go home. The merry, drunken crowd followed him, begging him not to go and clutching at his coat-tails. Unfortunately, he opened the wrong door and fell into a vast cold bath. One by one, those after him fell in too – a scene worthy of the Marx Brothers. Doctor Achmet and his servants fished them out and revived them with brandy and mulled wine, but the experience cooled their enthusiasm for public baths. After that night, the doctor got no more funds from parliament – he could sink or swim on his own. Actually, it did him no harm in the public's eyes and the business continued to be good.

What happened next was an old, old story. Doctor Achmet fell in love with a girl of good family who loved him in return. There was only one problem. Her family insisted that he must convert to Christianity and shave off his heretical beard. He agreed, and on Sunday morning he appeared before her, clean-shaved and in European dress. As she gaped at this newly westernised figure he embraced her and said, 'I'm Patrick Joyce from Kilkenny county, the divil a Turk any more than yourself, my sweet angel.'

Her love survived the revelation and they married. It soon became clear, however, that the public no longer believed in the doctor's skill. It had disappeared along with his beard and his foreign faith. The baths closed down and Patrick Joyce, alias Doctor Achmet Borumbad, vanished from history.

A SHOUTING MATCH

Matthew Byrne

It was a Wednesday morning. One of those soft summer mornings that gives the feeling that life will be just as gentle, with nothing to disturb the even tenor of its way. We had just ended the Holy Communion. The congregation had all gone home, and I was wandering round the church, minding my own business, thinking a few thoughts and murmuring prayers for some folks who needed them.

All was quiet and peaceful, with silence to think in. Till Ruth came bustling in. Ruth was no height at all. Buxum and bubbly with it. Her husband was a 'dumper-driver', as she'd told me the first time we'd met.

'What's a "dumper-driver"?' I asked.

'A dumper-driver, Rector,' she explained, with a kind of smothered disappointment that a grown man could be so ignorant, 'a dumper-driver usually works on a building site. He drives a machine that looks like a tractor with a big scoop in front. He scoops up a great load. Then goes chuff-chuff-chuff to some other part of the site. And he dumps it…!'

You learn something new everyday. Anyway, here she was now, making a grand and bustling entrance. The poor lass had already had three miscarriages. The word in the parish was that she had just had her fourth.

'Ruth,' said I, in welcome to the bustling lady.

'Out o' me way, Rector,' says she, waving me aside. 'Out o' me way. I want to bloody shout at God.'

'And you've come to the right place,' I assured her. 'But let me tell you how best to do it.'

You know the pitying look you get from someone who has decided you've lost whatever bit of sense you had? That's what I got. But she waited.

'What you do, Ruth, is… you go right up to the altar.'

Incredulity! The poor man has lost his wit.

'Go up to the altar. Put your hands like this on the altar. Hold them there. And then, bloody shout at God.'

She's walking up the aisle.

'I'll leave the church for a few minutes,' I tell her. 'Then only God and yourself will know what you're shouting about.'

I went out for five or ten minutes. I came back, and there's Ruth, walking down the aisle with a kind of triumphant air about her.

'Well? Did you bloody shout?'

'Did I bloody shout!'

But, let me tell you the end of the story. About twelve months later, I baptised her first baby. We were walking down the aisle after the baptism, Ruth snuggling her precious, new son into her. And I couldn't resist it.

'Well, Ruth, do you want to bloody shout at God?'

LILY

Frances Cotter

She was known as Lily, but I never saw her as a flower. Her body was gnarled and shrivelled like a wizened nut. And this nut was tough. She was feisty through and through. Large knuckles in her dark-veined hand gripped her walking stick. You would never guess that she was at the mercy of this support. Rather, the stick seemed under her steely command; a wooden slave.

In the nursing home she shared a twin room with a string of elderly victims. None of them could live with the remarks and actions of this six-stone shrew.

The nurses thought that they had hit gold when saintly Mrs Reid offered to share with Lily. Mrs Reid had a halo of snowy hair and wore baby pink. Her demeanour was equally delicate. Yet this gentleness masked a strong woman. Age and wisdom enabled her to live with Lily through a balance of amusement and detachment. All held their breath. Lily seemed to be melting. But then Lily discovered that Mrs Reid was of the other religious persuasion. Amidst a volley of abuse, Lily flung her leather slippers at Mrs Reid. Her keen aim ensured that one missile connected with the lady over her eye. After that Lily lived alone.

Death entered her arena from time to time. Sparring with Lily was not a simple task and, for a long time, the grim reaper returned limping to his corner. Lily could snap out of a coma giving commands. One frightened young intern was seen scurrying from ICU after Lily had returned to life as he borrowed some medical instruments from the bottom of her bed.

'You leave them alone,' she snarled. 'That equipment is for people in intensive care, you young whelp.'

Once she maintained that she saw a light at the end of a tunnel but that an angel told her to go back. Naturally nobody disagreed with her. All secretly sympathised with God who wasn't quite ready to embrace Lily for eternity.

Another time her grandson was at the bedside waiting for death to take her. Other relatives whispered in the corridor. She opened her eyes.

'Michael, will you for God's sake give me a hand up in the bed and pass me that brush till I sort my hair.'

Michael ran from the sickroom like an astonished apostle, announcing, 'She is alive!'

Eventually death won his round and Lily passed away. The young priest who said her funeral mass did not know Lily but he had researched her history well. He gave us a version of her life that seemed vaguely familiar yet it was not quite Lily. He had pushed this tough lady through a pious prism. In fact, his enthusiastic effort to commend Lily caused eruptions of emotion in the church. What most people saw as stubbornness, he extolled as strength and fortitude. Her bluntness was camouflaged as courage. One relative disappeared convulsively into his large hankie. Shoulders shook in every aisle. There wasn't a dry eye.

The evening before, I had seen her for the last time. In the wooden casket she seemed incredibly small. I remembered a story I had heard about her from a time when she lived in her county council bungalow. She had argued with the authorities about rats in the area. They had tried to assure her that the vicinity was pest free. It is said that she found a dead specimen in the garden and parcelled it off in the post to prove her point.

'Now who's right?' was her short accompanying note.

As I looked at her I wondered where that tenacious spirit had gone. She lay now, in her own box, ready for posting.

MAJOR AND MINOR
David Sowby

I attended a school where drill classes and swimming lessons were under the tutelage of a former British army sergeant-major. He was assisted by his son, whom we called 'Sergeant-Minor'. The father was a dapper little man with a red face, white hair and white, waxed moustache. The son was tall, with red hair and a fiery red moustache. Both were always togged out in immaculate white clothes and shoes.

There was a gallery in the school gymnasium where the sergeant-major stood and shouted orders. We used to wait with keen anticipation for him to go into his inevitable routine, about how he'd been in India and China – and up to his waist in snow – but had never seen such a deplorable performance as the one he'd just witnessed. He seldom disappointed us.

Sergeant-Minor cruised around the ranks, waiting for his father to yell: 'Son, bash that boy,' whereupon Sergeant-Minor would lash out with a gym shoe he carried around with him.

For most of us, the best part of drill was vaulting on the exercise horse. The sergeants stood on each side of the horse to receive the vaulter safely, and very effective they were, for I never saw a mishap. The most difficult of the exercises was 'feet inside all the way', in which one had to take a tremendous leap off the springboard so as to bring one's hands to the far end of the horse placed lengthwise, and drag one's feet forward inside both arms. A friend of mine who was especially good at this, and who also did a lot of jumping, both high and long, later developed problems in his lower spine and hips. I have often wondered whether arthritis in ankles, knees and hips is more common in people who did a lot of jumping as children, when the centres of bone formation are still cartilaginous and liable to damage. That could make a good research project.

In addition to gym classes, the two sergeants gave swimming lessons, while those of us who *could* swim went off to the cove at the base of Bray Head. On the way there, we'd see the non-swimmers submitting themselves to the ministrations of the sergeants. The victims assembled on the beach and were rowed to deep water by one of the old salts who hired out boats. The two sergeants sat in the boat holding long poles; a leather loop was attached to the end of each pole. The victim was dragged alongside the boat, suspended from the loop around his chest, being encouraged to swim by the shouts of the two instructors. I doubt whether either of the sergeants were able to swim – I certainly never saw them in the water or out of their clothes.

Swimming lessons went ahead in every sort of weather. One particularly rough day, when the small boat was rocking from side to side, I saw a victim at the end of his pole, one moment dangling in the air and the next disappearing below the waves. Meanwhile, the two sergeants, probably seasick, sat staring ahead in the direction of Wales, seemingly oblivious to the sufferings of their gulping pupils.

Ours wasn't the only school where the sergeants held sway. I have often wondered whether the boys at the other schools were as incompetent as the sergeant-major insisted that *we* were. All the same, boys from our school had a reputation for toughness; perhaps the sergeants had a lot to do with that.

MY PART IN THE CREATION OF A GIANT

Tony Brehony

In the autumn of 1953, the *Cork Examiner* reported that its Christmas edition, 'The Cork Hollybough', would feature short stories by 'Ireland's leading writers, Tony Brehony and John B Keane.'

I had never heard of John B Keane and I'm sure he had never heard of me, but by happy chance, some months later we met in a pub in Doneraile, the Cork village where John was then working. Over a few pints, it didn't take long to establish that we had much more in common that just our literary aspirations. We were both engaged to be married, he to a girl in Listowel and I to a local Doneraile girl. We were also fully agreed on the fact that, on the amount of money we were earning, there was no way we could ever afford such a step. John was getting £2.10s a week as an assistant in the local chemist's shop and I had just been demobbed from the Royal Navy with a war pension which barely topped $3 a week. And despite the *Examiner*'s optimistic suggestion that we were Ireland's leading writers, our literary earnings weren't impressive either – John's first novel had just been rejected and I was suffering from early writer's block.

That's when I told him that I was sick and tired of the poverty-level income that writing short stories was providing and I was going to make a fresh start – I had secured a real job with a company in Dublin paying £12 a week plus a company car, and my already short writing career was going to be put on a very long finger.

'Twelve quid a week!' John B's eyes were alight with his envy. 'And a motor car? Jaysus, boy, you're home and dry! God help me, if I could get something like that I'd be out of this bloody kip in the morning.'

So after much more liquid deliberation on the vagaries of life and of literature, I promised John with boozy confidence that I'd get him a job in the same company in Dublin – I had, I assured him, the right connections. He agreed to hold himself on a twenty-four-hour stand-by for my call and he gave me addresses in Doneraile and Listowel where I could contact him urgently by telegram. We celebrated our new positive approach to life with some more drink and then we went our separate ways.

I never met John B Keane again but, for the next thirty years, I watched him climb the dizzy heights to the very top of the literary ladder. Over the same thirty years, I struggled up my own rickety ladder in the murky world of industry and never once put a creative pen to paper until I retired.

Looking back now at my own meagre contribution to Irish literature since those heady days long ago when the *Examiner* nominated me alongside John B Keane as one of Ireland's leading writers, I can only plead that, unlike John, I peaked too early. On the positive side, however, there is the fact that, by failing to get John B Keane a job in 1953, I didn't deprive the world of literature of his genius. For that, surely I deserve some acclaim. We who are not giants must content ourselves with lesser things.

THE WALKING MACHINE
Peter McCloskey

He always had his silver tin. It came out of his pocket before his backside touched the chair. The tin would open with a flick and he would proceed to roll a cigarette from the tobacco inside. It was like second nature, something as natural as breathing. We always watched in amazement as the cigarette was rolled, and he looked around the room, connecting with the others present. A gentle lick of the sticky part of the paper and then the finished product would be put to his lips and lit. Only then would his throaty voice break the silence.

'A fine night,' he might say, or 'The sea is lumpy tonight.' Everybody would agree and then the conversation would develop its own life, taking on its own unique and individual direction on each separate night. It was as if conversation grew naturally in a wild and uncontrolled way. The silver tin would appear between coughs and another perfect cigarette would be rolled. The only time he was not smoking was when he was rolling a fresh cigarette. The topics of conversation on our nightly gatherings were a marvel to the innocent mind. There was the common bond that drew us together – fishing, but that was no guarantee that it would feature as a topic of conversation on any given night. All the usual suspects would feature from time to time – religion, politics, sex, money and lack of it, and of course drink and the fact that it had the country ruined. The conversation rarely got personal and, as a result, when it did, the subject in question got a great airing.

He rolled a long and slow cigarette one evening in September and something told us that a personal issue was about to be thrown into the arena. It was the way he did the rolling that told us.

'I need a walking machine,' he announced.

'A what?' someone asked.

'Ya know,' he said, 'a walking machine like they do have in them gym places.'

'What do you want with one of them?' another asked.

'I just want one, that's all. Does anyone know where I'd get one?' he replied flatly.

'I do,' said a voice in the corner. 'I'll talk to ya during the week.'

'That'll do,' he replied as he rolled another cigarette. Everyone looked from one to the other in an awkward silence, nobody knowing quite what to say. That night, the conversation never recovered and we all went home early wondering just what the master cigarette-maker wanted with a walking machine.

The winter that year was the windiest we could remember. The trawlers did not go to sea until the New Year was old. Our meetings grew infrequent as the wind howled in from the Atlantic and the warmth of the fireplace was too tempting to leave. It was a battle to open west-facing doors and get safely to the comfort of the car. In the end, over a month passed and the regular group hadn't met. Then Christmas came and the season itself kept us apart while we devoted our time to family and visitors.

Early in the New Year, we were all once again gathered and the cigarette-maker was busy at work rolling his finest, in between imparting the latest gossip or listening to tales from those who had travelled beyond our home. We were burning to ask how he was getting on with his walking machine and maybe ask if he felt he was losing weight.

'Tell us how the machine's going anyway?' one of the lads eventually asked.

'Great altogether. Best thing I ever bought,' came the reply.

'What about the fags though, I mean, don't they affect you?' he asked, getting bolder.

'Why would they? Sure I roll away and smoke away while the machine is on. I don't know myself with the comfort I have.'

'Good God!' our champion exclaimed, 'but you must be the only man in Ireland to roll fags and smoke 'em while walking on a treadmill!'

'What are you talking about, you fool?' the cigarette man snapped. 'Are you mad? What would I be doing walking on a treadmill? I wouldn't walk to the shop. I bought that for the greyhounds.'

THE CONTRAPTION
Hazel McIntyre

The hands of the school clock slowly wound their way towards three o'clock. My mind was far away from the history lesson in progress. Instead of the Battle of Clontarf, I was riding across the prairie with the Lone Ranger and Tonto. It was the day our first television set was to arrive.

Free from school at last, we raced up the lane towards home.

Then I saw it! Perched majestically on the chimney pot, its metal spikes reaching towards the heavens. Little shivers of excitement ran up and down my spine.

'The aerial is up already, I wonder if it's come yet?' my young brother said breathlessly.

'Just think, we won't have to run down the wet fields to McConnell's to see *The Lone Ranger* anymore,' I chipped in.

We burst into the kitchen, throwing our school-bags and coats at our feet. The shelf stood empty to our great disappointment.

'It hasn't come,' my mother said.

'I wouldn't be a bit surprised if it's not smashed to smithereens, the way the railways throw things around,' my father commented from behind his newspaper.

We felt somewhat deflated at this piece of bad news. It was easy to imagine railway porters throwing our precious television on to carriages to get smashed to pieces. 'God, please don't let this happen,' I silently prayed.

Half an hour later, the van arrived in the yard. We ran out excitedly just as the door was opened.

Our fears about the porters throwing it around were soon laid to rest when we caught sight of the huge crate, which must have weighed a ton. It took the might of my father, my oldest brother, Mickey the van driver and Paddy our burly neighbour to lift it off the van.

With the help of a claw hammer, the crate was dismantled. The old rags and straw packing were discarded in endless bundles. Then, at last, the enormous wooden cabinet appeared out of the straw and rags. The small 14-inch screen looked lost in its oak surround, but to us it was the most beautiful sight we had ever seen.

Then began the task of hauling it into the house.

'Now lift when I say... Careful now,' my brother instructed as all helpers shuffled forward under its weight.

At last it was in place, seated on a sturdy table. It was wisely decided by all that the shelf was not strong enough to support its weight.

When finally it was wired up and plugged in, we held our breath in anticipation. A loud hissing sound came from it, then a blizzard appeared on the screen.

'The aerial needs adjusting, that's all,' my big brother said encouragingly. With this, all hands went to the street as he climbed the ladder to the aerial. My father tutted and grumbled as he battled with the mountain of hastily discarded packing.

We formed a human chain from the blizzard on the screen to the yard, while my brother twisted and turned the aerial.

'No, nothing yet, wait, that's a wee bit better. We have the sound now,' I shouted, as hissing strains of Adam Faith singing 'Poor Me' could be faintly heard.

A little more fine-tuning and a picture emerged, to our great relief.

'Let joy be unconfined!' said my father mockingly. We had all settled down to watch *The Beverly Hillbillies* through a light snow flurry when Paddy O'Neill came in. To our amazement he showed no interest in the television whatsoever. Instead he began his usual conversation with my father about the weather and the crops. The only difference from other nights was the raised voices. When he got up to go, he stopped momentarily in front of the TV.

'Them contraptions will never catch on, you know,' he said.

DORMANT ACCOUNTS HOW ARE YA!

Arthur O'Reilly

Not long ago, the Irish government introduced measures to ensure that monies held in bank accounts that had been inactive for some time would be invested for public use. The funds are guaranteed safe for their owners when, or if, they turn up. I forget the amount of money in these dormant accounts, but it would appear to be a drop in the proverbial ocean compared to the funds sitting in a number of African bank accounts just waiting for someone – anyone – to claim them.

During the past twelve months, I reckon I have received, through e-mail, at least thirty different propositions offering me a generous share of, in total, about a US$1,000m. All I have to do to get this windfall is to allow the funds to be transferred from bank accounts in various African countries into my bank account in Ireland. For this simple service, I have been assured that I may keep anything from 15 per cent to 65 per cent of the amounts involved. The sums of money in these different accounts range from a paltry $9m (my share in this particular case would be merely $2m) to a more decent $126m (of which I would receive the not unreasonable sum of $50m).

As I have lately been getting at least one such offer every week, you can see that the culmination of just a few of these proposals would put me at the top of the Irish rich list quicker than my bank manager could think up new banking charges.

The main beneficiaries would, of course, be the generous individuals who are making me these offers. These are (a) bank officials, usually a manager or auditor, who have discovered a large deposit in an account, the holder of which has died leaving no heir, or (b) a diligent public servant who has uncovered sizeable overpayments by contractors as a result of careless over-invoicing by less diligent colleagues in his government department or agency, or (c) the sole heir of an extremely rich,

145

but now extremely deceased, former minister or similar high-ranking official, whose methods of accumulating wealth must have been such as to make a tribunal blush.

To enable my extraordinarily trusting correspondents to transfer this lonely lucre to my bank, I am asked to provide them with details of my account, passport, home and business address, phone and fax numbers.

My head tells me that getting these riches so easily would put winning the national lottery literally in the ha'penny place. My conscience assures me that because the people making these offers are undoubtedly con-artists, any money I would receive would be tax exempt, given the artistic nature of the enterprise. But my heart says, like Chesterton, that to be clever enough to get all that money, one must be stupid enough to want it.

Still, it gives a whole new meaning to foreign aid.

THE HANDS THAT BUILT AMERICA
Carmel Shaw

When I was a child, my father wore a Panama hat and had a belt and braces of plaited leather that he had made himself in a New York factory. Born in a Waterford farmhouse in 1898, he was referred to as 'the Yank' because of a sojourn in the USA in the 1920s and 1930s. In an era when adults did the talking, we children were imprisoned listeners for his reminiscences around the kitchen table.

The Empire State Building, he told us, was the tallest building in the world. The Irish built it and *he* was one of them! The job was finished in just over a year!

'You wouldn't build a chicken house in that time!' my mother commented.

While there, he discovered that a man working on the fifty-second floor had emigrated from a neighbouring townland years before. So, every day he climbed the stairs, stuck his head in the door and shouted 'Up Ballyguirey!', before running for all he was worth. One day, the Ballyguirey man, mad with frustration, managed to grab him 'by the scruff of the neck', as my father put it, shouting, 'What do you know about Ballyguirey, ya little thrawneen?'

'I was at a funeral in New York,' my father said, 'and the like of it you never saw! They came from all over America and every woman there was bawling her eyes out!'

'Who was it?' we'd ask.

'Wan of them film stars. Rudolph Valentino.'

He told us that a hawker who sold knick-knacks on street corners founded Woolworth's and became a millionaire. A relative in

Philadelphia was reputed to have bought buttons from him, when the seat of the hawker's pants was in a questionable condition!

My favourite story was that of the blind man who used to beg outside Bloomingdale's. One day, he dropped dead and the police discovered that, not only had he never been blind, but he owned a mansion in New Jersey and had a million dollars in the bank! My father was outraged, since he had occasionally deposited a few dimes in the man's hat. I took a different view. For weeks, I practised going about with my eyes shut. I became an expert at 'blind man's bluff' and was of the opinion that a white stick and dark glasses were far better career tools that a head full of catechism and Irish. As we grew older, the stories began to lose their appeal. With typical teenage scepticism, we dismissed them as fantasy.

Surfing the net recently, I logged on to the Ellis Island website and, lo and behold, there he was! Matthew O'Brien, Cappagh, County Waterford, on the *SS Regina* out of Queenstown, docked at Ellis Island, 27 March 1923. On a whim I decided to check out the Empire State Building. At almost 1,500 feet, it was the tallest building in the world at the time and built almost entirely with immigrant labour. Work began on St Patrick's Day, 1930, and President Herbert Hoover opened it on 1 May 1931! *Fourteen months*! A few clicks more and I was looking at Rudolph Valentino. Best known for the film *Son of a Sheik*, he died at thirty-one and more than 100,000 people attended his New York funeral in 1926!

So he was right about that too! If only I had believed him, I too might be a dollar millionaire by now, with a white stick in my closet and a big mansion out in New Jersey.

LEAVING THE LAND OF THE EAGLE
Bill Meek

'Don't shoot!'

I didn't actually shout out the words but rather muttered them, hoping that my exhortation *sotto voce* might somehow alleviate what appeared to be a potentially dangerous situation.

It all arose as part of the process of my exiting what is one of the most beautiful countries in the world – sometimes known as 'the land of the eagle', but more generally referred to as the Republic of Guatemala. Actually, the process surrounding my *entry* to that same country was also not without its problems.

The year was 1963. I had been spending time in Mexico engaged in freelance work and, after a while, it had seemed a good idea to head further south. To travel to Guatemala, it was necessary to obtain a visa from its consulate in Mexico City, where I duly presented myself. I would be the last person to condone the practice of transferring animal characteristics to a fellow human being. That said, the official who dealt with me was like a ferret, both in appearance and behaviour. He scrutinised my passport.

'No visa!'

'But why?'

'By the laws of Guatemala no British may enter the Republic.'

At that time, Guatemala and the UK were in what was described as a 'state of belligerency' due to a long-standing dispute as to the constitutional status of what was then known as British Honduras. Exercising considerable patience, I referred Ferret to my green passport, emblazoned with its gold harp with a message from Mr Frank Aiken, Minister for External Affairs, requesting 'all of whom it may concern to allow the bearer, a citizen of Ireland, to pass freely and without hindrance'.

Ferret was not impressed.

'Irish, British – it is all the same.'

This led to a robust debate. Eventually Ferret was prepared to compromise. He would telegram his foreign office for instructions, provided I bear the cost of this communication. I agreed. The following morning I collected my visa and by evening had arrived in Guatemala City on a Mexican Airlines flight.

Leaving was something else. I may have flown in, but the return was by way of a series of bus trips, an adventure in itself, lasting several days. On the last leg, I got chatting with a Mexican who turned out to be of Irish descent. We both alighted at the final stop, which was in fact a remote frontier post – a small corrugated building shimmering in the mid-morning heat. The official within was obviously irritated at being disturbed from a card game with three colleagues. He dealt with the Mexican swiftly but demanded payment from me to perform the same service. My new-found friend was outraged on my behalf and threatened to report him to a higher authority. The official shrugged and gave me a nasty glare but stamped the document. The two of us left the building and proceeded towards the border a hundred yards away.

It was then that I suddenly realised that, under the stress of the situation, I had left my passport behind. I turned around and at the same moment saw that on the roof of the building two men were crouched beside an old-fashioned machine gun, the type with a serrated barrel and a stream of ammunition spilling down from the magazine. In a country much wedded to the wearing of uniforms, it was disturbing to note that these guys were dressed in T-shirts and jeans.

Nervously I re-entered the frontier post. Miraculously my green treasure with its gold harp lay unnoticed on the counter. The officials were once again deeply involved in their card game. I simply picked it up, walked out and for a second time headed down the dirt road in the direction of the frontier. I didn't look back at the men on the roof, but it was then I commenced intoning my muttered mantra: 'Don't shoot. Don't shoot.'

They didn't.

Within a few minutes I stepped over into Mexico to be immediately confronted by an armed bomber guard. But he was clad in a neat olive-green uniform. Somehow, in the light of recent events, this seemed almost reassuring.

BED AND BREAKFASTING IN THE COUNTRY

Melosina Lenox-Conyngham

My wee cot is sited in a glade of trees; a twist of smoke curls from the chimney, honeysuckle entwines the pillars of the porch, a lavender bush grows by the door and roses ramble over the walls, peeping through the windows. The roses also tint my spectacles, blotting out the fact that bindweed is an even more invasive climber and that goose grass, too, is a keen contender for wall space. The lavender bush is but a raggedy specimen and the curl of smoke is from the firelighters that I have thrown in desperation on to the damp wood of the fireplace. But Conrad Hilton said that 'enthusiasm was everything' and, when I nailed a 'bed and breakfast' sign to a tree, I felt that already he must be feeling the cold wind of competition, for soon my name would be synonymous with Ritz and Waldorf.

This was some time ago when there were very few B&Bs, so my optimism was rewarded when an unwary youth on a bicycle fell into my net, or rather into my cobwebs – the olde worlde look is not only on the outside of my house but is also part of the interior décor, as I am no great shakes with a duster. Oh what a great Irish welcome I gave him; I laid before him plum cakes, sponge cakes, three kinds of biscuits and tea out of a huge, brown pot. My friendly conversation was like a waterfall about his ears, and at supper, I was so excited that I practically got on to the plate to see how he was enjoying his food.

He was terrified for, even when he had gone to bed, having locked his door, I carolled through the keyhole enquiries as to whether he needed a hot-water bottle or more blankets – and this was on one of the hottest days of the year.

While I was in the midst of cooking an enormous Irish breakfast for him, he slipped away, leaving the money on the table. I ran after him calling that he had not yet partaken of the devilled kidneys and kedgeree that I had imaginatively added to the menu. But this made him pedal faster than ever.

The next people were treated very differently as their arrival coincided with the disappearance of my horse, an experienced escapologist who the previous month had galloped up High Street and had been caught just about to enter The Monster House, Kilkenny's leading department store.

The guests, a Canadian couple, and their car, were immediately commandeered to take part in the search and capture. And by the time we had successfully accomplished this mission, I was so exhausted we all retired to a pub where they had to sustain me with strong drink. They told me happily that it was just how they had imagined Ireland would be and booked to stay another two nights.

From then on I became more confident and was positively blasé when the Arts Week administrator asked me to put up the quartet that was to play a concert of medieval music and wanted a quiet place where they could practise. It stretched the capacities of my hostelry to the limit, or rather to the walls, and I even had to vacate my own bedroom. The guests arrived in two huge Mercedes that were considerably longer than my house and their musical instruments took up all the space downstairs; a clavichord blocked the fridge door, a couple of viols were laid across the chairs and music stands and cases were strewn over the floor.

At dawn, Professor Ulsamer was in the garden tootling on his *dudelsack* – a herd of cows his entranced audience – while his wife harmonised on her *glockenspiel* in the little wood nearby, but I think it was the *Krummhorn* that brought a neighbour hotfoot to ask if I was in trouble. I emerged sleepily from my lair under the kitchen table to explain.

'How sour sweet music is when time is broke and no proportion kept!'

LIGHT OF MY LIFE
Paul O'Dwyer

'Storm force winds expected later this evening.' The newscaster's voice seemed to betray his disappointment. I turned off the radio and concentrated on my driving. Christmas afternoon 1997. The winds were strong as the setting sun disappeared behind the Galtees. Nenagh town was one hour's drive away. This was a big event: my first Christmas at my girlfriend's home. I was delighted with the invitation from Deirdre's father to visit and stay with the family. I was equally aware of the importance attached to such an invitation. The steering wheel felt clammy and my mouth felt dry.

I had agonised over a suitable Christmas gift to bring to her parents. At the point of purchase each time, devilish thoughts robbed me of resolve. If I bring a bottle of whiskey and/or wine, will Deirdre's dad think me too fond of 'the drop'? And so the bottles were returned and the search resumed. If I bring a 'safe' box of biscuits will Deirdre's mother think I believe her baking to be sub-standard? The biscuits were re-shelved and the search continued. Finally, on Christmas Eve I saw it. The perfect gift! Sitting prettily in the front window of a gift shop on a little mound of fake snow – a candle. A six-inch holly-decorated Irish-made Christmas candle. I wrapped it up in festive paper and placed it carefully in the passenger seat of my mother's Fiesta.

That candle represented my hopes and dreams of a good first impression. I left my home in plenty of time, just to be safe, in case of flat tyres, fallen trees or any other acts of God; those stormy winds really were gusting. As I approached Cashel, those fiendish thoughts started to stray back into my mind. Was a candle a good enough present to bring on Christmas night? Would they think Scrooge was visiting with such a small gift? 'Has this man the "wherewithal" to look after my daughter if all he brings is a candle?' I could almost hear it said.

As I passed Holycross, the doubts were growing like the winds buffeting the car. I prayed for solace. As I reached Borrisoleigh, my doubt was almost certainty. I slowed the car in the vain hope of finding an off-licence open. By now I was going to bring whiskey, wine and biscuits too! However, being Christmas Day, there were no premises open. Doubt gave way to despair. Perhaps if I stop at a house, explain my situation and throw myself at the mercy of the occupants, a bottle of something could be found? My nerve failed me and, with a heavy heart, I found the little Fiesta arriving at the front door of Deirdre's home. The leaves pirouetted in violent circles as the winds grasped at my scarf.

I nervously rang the doorbell, trying to hide my sense of impending doom, candle under arm, ready for the embarrassment. The bell wasn't working. I knocked on the door and presently the lady of the house opened it. She carried a flashlight.

The electricity was out due to the violent storm; the family members were all looking for – you guessed it – candles! The hero of the hour had arrived! My ingenuity in choosing such a present was recalled years later on our wedding day.

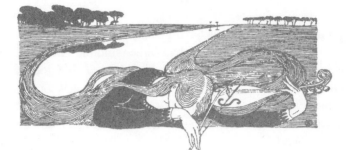

A Sense of a
Presence

BRIDIE HANNA
Sam McAughtry

In the mid-1960s I was having a bad time. I was a clerk in the Ministry of Agriculture, I had three children, and I had been overlooked for promotion after ten years in the job, mostly through my own fault. Round about 1967 a new branch was formed with offices near Belfast City Hall and the personnel division trawled the branches at Stormont for staff to carry out the new work.

For divisional line managers, the formation of a new branch is a God-given opportunity to dump their problem workers, and so it was that I was one of a bunch of head-the-balls and eccentrics who turned up for duty on the first Monday of the new scheme. Dick, beside me, reading the racing page of the *Daily Mirror*, had served as a sergeant in the Palestine police in the run-up to the foundation of the Israeli state in 1948 when Irgun was shooting and bombing police and soldiers. Dick had come out of it with a drink and gambling problem as big as the Golan Heights. Alongside Dick was Tom, a spare-time coal salesman, who spent twice as much time on the phone in the main hall selling Milligan's Coal to farmers as he did working for the ministry. Then there was Alec, a committed communist, who openly read *Pravda* in the original. We were a bit like the Dirty Dozen.

In charge was a lady of middle years, small, with an east Down accent, a nervous smile and fluttering hands. She should have had a senior clerk to help her, but the chap concerned was another problem case who had sent in a long-term sick note. The scheme's launch was a shambles. Hundreds of forms arrived each morning and acknowledgements were miles behind.

For some strange reason I was putting in an eight-hour day for the cause, but I was just about the only one. After about three weeks of Marx Brothers madness, I happened to glance at our supervisor, sitting on her own at the head of the class. She looked close to having a tiny little cry into her hanky.

A woman clerk at the back of the room was knitting a scarf under the table, Dick was picking out horses, Alec was laughing softly at a Russian-language joke and the two women were talking about the new driving test and asking each other questions from the Highway Code. I got up and went over to the junior staff officer.

'Do you want a hand, Miss Hanna?' I asked. I didn't know why I was doing this. I hadn't been this co-operative with a line manager for years, but I thought she was too nice for this brigade.

'How do you mean?' she enquired, a bit suspiciously.

'I know how to help you,' I said. 'You're handing out these forms to us as they come in, so you don't know who's doing how many. Tell them to put their initials on each form when they've acknowledged it and they'll think you're checking on their output.'

Her mouth dropped open. 'How do you know that?' she asked.

'Because I'm one of them,' I said, laughing. She laughed too. We tried it out next morning. It worked, and soon we had a branch that, if it wasn't running like clockwork, at least was running. With Dick I discussed horses at lunch time, with Alec I talked about the work of Donegal writer Patrick Magill, the darling of the Left, and I warned Tom the coalman that there was a system on the switchboard that checked who was making outside calls. The ladies, who were moderate enough cases, responded readily to my suggestion that Miss Hanna was under pressure from her male boss in his plush Royal Avenue office.

One day Miss Hanna asked me to call her Bridie and I sat beside her as she told me about her sister the nun and her happy home at the foot of the Mournes. She looked at me sideways.

'There's a promotion board coming up soon,' she said, 'and I have recommended you.'

I had to warn her that, as the police say, I had form. 'I am a character,' I said, 'I have been on promotion boards before and here I am, none the better for it. You might come under suspicion for recommending me.'

Anyway, still unconvinced, I went before the board to please her and, to my utter astonishment, I got the promotion.

'Bridie Hanna,' I said, 'have you been burning candles or what?' She smiled.

'You'll be all right from here on,' she said.

Well, she was right. I went on up the grades after that. It was Bridie Hanna's doing. She broke the log jam. There are clear and distinct turning points in our lives and this was a major road ahead in mine. My wife and I kept in touch with Bridie Hanna, visiting with our children in her home by the Mournes, and she gave them sweets to the point where they were sick outside later.

She was a lovely lady. I'm glad I turned from poacher to gamekeeper that day.

SUNNY SIDE UP
Hedy Gibbons Lynott

My eye is caught by the notice on the window of the diner. It says 'Irish bacon served here' and a longing for the taste of home propels me in for breakfast. I've just achieved one of my small ambitions in life by ordering Irish bacon, pancakes and two eggs over-easy. 'Two eggs, over-easy.' Ever since I first heard that phrase in my cinema-going youth, it has enthralled – and puzzled – me. Because, not having any 'Yanks' in our family, I had no idea what it meant and nobody to ask. What kind of eggs were over-easy? Were they easy to get? Or left over? And if so, from what? Did it mean, 'I'll only have them if you have them to spare?' Or, that they're easy to cook? And then there was 'sunny-side up'. Were the eggs in America brighter than ours? Or did they, like the best heroes in those long-ago movies, have a 'shady' side?

I don't notice the person sliding into the high stool beside mine, until a gravelly voice says, 'You hungry, or what!' It's a statement, not a question. I smile and continue to give my sunny eggs their due attention. 'You on vacation?' I drag myself away from my Irish bacon and look at her. Arthritic fingers are wrapped around a cup of coffee; hillbilly red nails contrast with the white ceramic. Beady brown eyes demand my attention. 'You on vacation?' I nod. The hillbilly red mouth smiles. 'New York, New York!' And she waves a weary hand towards the street; shakes her grey, frizzy head from side to side. Silence. I take a mouthful of egg. 'Radio City Music Hall!' My eggs are getting cold. 'You heard of the Rockettes?' She gives me a sideways look, bites into her cheese Danish and flicks an imaginary crumb from her skirt.

And then I notice her legs. Wrapped around the stool beside me, their elegant length in 'natural tan' stretches below a royal-blue skirt, its slit reaching just above the knee. I abandon my sunny eggs. Had I heard of the Rockettes? Only yesterday I'd toured the Rockefeller Centre and Radio City Music Hall. Had stood on the enormous empty stage, gazed out at the auditorium and wondered what it was like to high-step it out into the blaze of those footlights. I had seen how the stage was marked off in segments, so that each of the thirty-two dancers would have their own reference point in its vast emptiness. I had even stood on the very place marked out for one of those Rockettes, let myself feel the curve and height of that gigantic Art Deco auditorium, could almost hear the roar of applause across the years.

The stooped shoulders beside me straightened; head high, eyes right, arms extended, one still-slender foot points on the floor. For a moment she could have been the lithe brunette who invited us into the stars' dressing room yesterday. 'I used to be one.' She holds her pose. Is she hearing that long-ago roar of applause for the Rockettes? Feeling the heat of those spotlights? She eases herself off the stool. 'Have a nice day!' And with a wave of her gnarled hand and a flash of hillbilly red she hobbles towards the door.

Outside, on the corner, the traffic lights change. I watch the grizzly head bob across Second Avenue and disappear – on the sunny side of the street, of course.

IMPRESSIONS OF COLOUR
Vincent McDonnell

When I was growing up in the 1960s, the colour of my world could have been described as drab grey. A revolution might have been taking place among the young of London and New York, but it was far removed from the wilds of rural Mayo. The only illumination in my grey world came from books, music and Fr John, my English teacher, who first brought colour into my life.

Such was his influence on me that when I found myself, a teenager, in London in 1970, I didn't head for the Irish haunts of the Gresham Ballroom or the Galtymore. Instead I made my way to Trafalgar Square to the National Gallery. I wanted to see the Impressionist paintings Fr John had introduced me and my fellow students to over the previous five years.

He was a big gentle man who never raised his voice, yet commanded absolute respect. I still picture him in his black suit, smudged with chalk dust, and with his reading glasses perched on the end of his nose. He was never without a bundle of books clutched to his chest or carried precariously beneath an arm. In time, those books were to become a window into another world where light and colour were celebrated.

He was an ideal teacher because he believed in what might be described as a holistic approach to education. He tolerated the prescribed English texts and, like me, would have much preferred to proscribe most of them. He covered enough of the course to ensure that his students were prepared for their exams and spent the remainder of the time on education.

It was during this time that he introduced us to his bundle of beloved books. Here was the poetry of Dylan Thomas, Robert Frost and Emily Dickinson, and the paintings, in glorious colour and light and movement, of a group of artists I'd never heard of – the French Impressionists.

Until then, art for me was Millet's depiction of the Angelus, the ubiquitous Sacred Heart and the dark brooding images of Christ and His saints. They gazed down threateningly, mournfully or accusingly from every wall throughout my home. They hung in the schools and the churches and there seemed to be no escaping them, until the advent of Fr John.

The first painting he ever showed us was Renoir's *Les Parapluies*. As he spoke about the colours, the use of light and the harmony of the composition – the circular umbrellas and child's hoop – I could not mistake his passion. Here was a painting which had no religious significance. It might simply be a photograph of people sheltering from the rain, yet instinctively I knew it was more than that.

Over our years together, Fr John told us of the other Impressionists and showed us colour plates of their paintings. He introduced us to Van Gogh, my own favourite, and to Monet, whose use of light and colour simply dazzled. And we all fell in love with Degas' dancing girls in their white diaphanous dresses.

So it was that at nineteen I found myself face to face with paintings I had only ever seen in books. Here was the original *Les Parapluies*, here were Monet's lilies and Degas' dancers. And here too was Van Gogh's *Cypresses*, not a smooth surface at all but with the paint layered on as Fr John had once explained to us.

Signs forbade touching the pictures but I couldn't resist. Leaning in over the rope barrier, I traced the layers of paint with my finger, following the stroke of Van Gogh's palette knife. In that moment, I heard the echo of Fr John's voice and I knew that we who had known him had been blessed.

He has long gone to his rest, but his legacy remains. And whenever I find myself in London, I visit the National Gallery. I make my way to the Impressionists' gallery and sit there quietly and let the colours wash over me. And as I sit there, I fondly remember the first time I saw Fr John and his bundle of books, and how I never imagined the colour and pleasure they would bring into my life.

INTRODUCING OLYMPIA

Nuala Ní Chonchúir

At the Paris Salon of 1865, Édouard Manet's painting *Olympia* caused a scandal. This luminous nude was referred to as, among other things, 'a female gorilla' and 'a deformity'. Parisians swarmed to the Salon hoping to be outraged. Finally, the painting had to be cordoned off to protect it from the angry hordes. Today, Olympia hangs in the Musée d'Orsay and the painting is acknowledged as Manet's great masterpiece.

I'm not sure when I first thought to myself that *Olympia* was the most beautiful painting in the world. But the first time I saw her in the flesh, so to speak, my stomach flip-flopped and I stood in awe for a long time.

Manet, who was an academic painter, painted *Olympia* as a homage to Titian's *Venus*. But Parisians were horrified because the model he used was considered altogether too brazen. How dare she gaze from the painting with such sensuality, her only clothing a black ribbon around her neck and a dusky blossom pinned to her hair? And why was her hand placed across her leg in such a suggestive way? Who *was* this woman who appeared to be little more than a streetwalker?

The model that caused this uproar was Victorine Meurent, a slender, working-class Parisienne with alabaster skin, who has been portrayed by art historians as a prostitute and a drunkard. Even though she is a central figure in nine of Manet's greatest works, including *Le Dejeuner sur l'Herbe,* like most artists' models she has been written out of the picture. She is seen as a body rather than as a person in her own right.

But Victorine, as it happens, was very much her own person. Although little of the facts of her life remain, it is known that she used to live at 191 Rue du Faubourg-Poissonnière.

This street lies on the edge of Montmartre, just a skipping distance from the shining domes of the Sacré Coeur. By happy coincidence, the hotel I booked for a winter weekend in Paris was situated on that very street. These days, the ground floor of number 191 is a *boulangerie* and *pâtisserie*, its window a carnival of crusty breads and pastry treats. A large wooden doorway opens to the yard that leads to the apartments overhead.

I stood outside the building on a biting January morning and imagined Victorine tripping out through that very door, to spend a few *sous* on hot bread on her way to model for Manet. Or indeed, on her way to buy materials for her own paintings. Because, as it turns out, Victorine Meurent was an artist as well as a model. And what's more, like Manet, she exhibited at the prestigious Paris Salon. Her painting *Bourgeoise de Nuremberg* was exhibited there in 1879 along with two paintings by the man for whom she had previously been a favourite model.

Manet's biographers seem to have been filled with a peculiar distaste for Victorine. They record her as a pathetic figure, poor and dying from alcohol addiction by the 1890s. However, Victorine lived until March 1927. She actually died at the age of 83 in the Parisian suburb of Colombes, where she lived with a female companion.

But what of Victorine's pictures? Although she was a member of the French Society of Artists and she exhibited at least up until 1903, sadly no trace remains of Victorine's paintings. What we *do* have to remember her by is a painting of an assured young woman, who commands attention with her fearless gaze: Manet's magnificent *Olympia*.

A ONE-MAN SHOW ON THE DUBLIN–CORK TRAIN

Des MacHale

What is it about a railway carriage that brings out the selfish beast in some of us? One of my many minor vices is that I like to stretch myself out in a train, spreading my newspapers, shopping, books and food all over the place, in the hope of giving the impression that I am a member of a large group of travellers and that all four seats in my section are taken. Then I can stretch my legs and selfishly avoid the small talk that one often has to suffer on a long train journey. But I assure you that I practise this strategy only on uncrowded trains: if the carriage is full, or even nearly full, I quickly gather up all my belongings and share my seats with all and sundry – honest I do!

I remember sitting in good time on the Dublin–Cork train in Heuston Station early one Sunday morning, blissfully surrounded by all the newspapers I could lay my hands on, my head buried in a sea of newsprint. The carriage, which was virtually empty when I boarded the train, must have been filling up more quickly than I had imagined, because a kindly voice suddenly enquired, 'Is this seat taken?'

'No', I mumbled and quickly began to gather up some of the avalanche of newspapers that surrounded me.

An elderly gentleman removed his tweed overcoat, folded it and sat calmly opposite me. When I looked up to smile and say hello, my heart missed a beat – who was staring me in the face but Eamon Kelly, Ireland's premier storyteller and *seanchaí*, the man who had almost single-handedly restored and perfected the art of the oral yarn. Admittedly he was also a fine stage actor and film star – I had seen him both live on the stage of the Cork Opera House and on the big screen in Brian Friel's moving and funny *Philadelphia, Here I Come* – but it was as a storyteller and *seanchaí* that I most admired him.

For nearly three hours on that train, until we parted company at Mallow where he changed trains for Kerry, I had my own Eamon Kelly one-man show. I listened mostly in silence, just nodding my head, but frequently doubled up in helpless laughter as he wove an incomparable verbal spell over me. He never introduced himself – I knew very well who he was, but he never let on if he knew that I knew who he was, if you follow me. Maybe it didn't matter to him, but I soon realised that he was just as natural, friendly and funny face-to-face as he was on the radio or stage. At times on our journey, he assumed the persona of Old Ned, the *seanchaí*; other times he just philosophised about life and reminisced about his youth and his adventures as a carpenter in north Kerry.

How could I tell this man that when I was a postgraduate student in England in the 1970s, I incessantly played on my record player an Eamon Kelly disc recorded in the United States on the Spoken Arts label, so much so that I thought that the stylus would wear through the groove? I played it often for international audiences, and a Pakistani friend of mine got into the habit of saying 'Things rested so' in a broad Kerry accent. Another friend of Irish ancestry from Glasgow used to demand translations of the record's finer points in Eamon Kelly's own words – 'English that for me'. I played to fellow students – from England, Turkey, Germany, Japan, China and the United States – Eamon Kelly's rendering of the legends of the *Gobán Saor* and his less intelligent son; the astounding saga of the parish priest's umbrella, and the doubtlessly true tale of the goat who regurgitated the red shirt he had eaten and so saved a train from certain disaster. And who can forget his timeless fable of the invention of the looking-glass and its profound effect on interpersonal relationships in a rural Irish community?

To my mind, Eamon Kelly's greatest talent was the way he could spin out a seemingly trivial incident or three-line joke into a twenty-minute story that always held the interest; the side roads he visited were often just as interesting as the main theme. Humour – genuine original folk humour – was always the centrepiece of his stories, and his timing and command of language were unrivalled. As a child, I first heard him on DinJoe's *Take the Floor* on Radio Éireann and from that moment I was a fan and have been so ever since. His many stories have of course been published in book form by Mercier Press, but it is the voice, the accent and the subtlety of language that I miss. For example, in a single sentence he gave the best ever summary of the Irish Civil War when he described one character in 1921 as fighting for the IRAE against the IRAH.

Thank you, Eamon Kelly, for the countless hours of pleasure your stories have given Ireland and the Irish people worldwide; but thank you most of all for that free three-hour one-man show you gave one of your most devoted fans on the Dublin–Cork train all those years ago.

A TRUE ENTREPRENEUR
Virginia Connolly

What makes the entrepreneur? I suppose if we knew the answer to that one we would all be at it.

However much we might ponder the make up of the species, I think it is easy enough to recognise entrepreneurship when we see it in action; this strange knack of identifying a gap in the market at the right time, supplying the goods or services required to fill in – at the right price, of course – and off they go! It seems too easy. The hunch might not work the first time, or the second, but eventually they hit the jackpot.

A very good example of this is Charles Bianconi, who arrived at the tender age of sixteen in Temple Bar in Dublin in the year 1802, apprenticed to an art dealer. At first he worked in town but, later on, he was dispatched to the country, for a week at a time, with a pack on his back. He got tired, he got wet, he even got pleurisy as a result of a bad drenching, and he saw clearly this was not the route to fame and fortune. When his period of apprenticeship was over he opened a shop in Clonmel which offered 'gilding and picture-framing services in the newest style' which was successful, but not successful enough.

He looked around him and spotted the gap in the market. There was no reliable public transport for the ordinary people. Some things do not change! After Napoleon's abdication, Bianconi noticed that the prices of horses and grain had fallen in Clonmel and he reasoned that the demobilisation of the Irish troops would shortly bring an enormous influx of skilled drivers back to Ireland. He decided to risk his meagre savings.

Then catastrophe loomed: Napoleon escaped from Elba, the French welcomed him back joyously, and Louis XVII fled to Belgium. Bianconi's dream was about to turn into a nightmare and then the angels smiled on him. The allied armies under

Wellington put a permanent halt to the Emperor's hundred-day gallop and, after that, it was back to business as usual in Clonmel. Bianconi's first car took the road from Clonmel to Cahir on 6 July 1815, less than a month after the Battle of Waterloo. And after that he never looked back. From then on it was all a case of increasing wealth and honours and friendships of the great and the good.

An exacting and demanding, but fair, employer, he was tough as nails in business but curiously regarded himself as a romantic. He'd had a love affair as a boy in Italy and professed himself astounded that she hadn't waited for him when he made his first trip home – twenty years later! However, he consoled himself by marrying a nineteen-year-old Dublin heiress when he was forty years old and they went straight to Clonmel the day after the wedding so that his manager could join them for supper and bring him up to speed on the business.

His organisational skills must have been incredible. By the 1840s, he had over thirteen hundred horses and one hundred coaches on the roads of Ireland, providing reliable, affordable transport. What a pity he isn't still around.

THOMAS D'ARCY McGEE: IRELAND'S SON AND CANADA'S FATHER

Tony Quinn

I walked around Parliament Hill behind the Federal House of Commons in Ottawa. Passing by monuments to Queen Victoria and many eminent Canadians, I stopped at the imposing statue of a political orator, Thomas D'Arcy McGee. He was called 'Father of the Canadian Confederation' because of his efforts to unite that diverse country in the mid-nineteenth century.

McGee was born in 1825 at Carlingford, County Louth, where he is still commemorated. He grew up in Wexford where, speaking at a young Temperance Society meeting, he impressed Fr Matthew, the crusader against excessive drinking. McGee pledged never to consume alcohol.

At seventeen, McGee left Wexford on a cargo ship for Quebec City. He wrote for Boston newspapers before returning to Dublin as a journalist on the nationalist *Freeman's Journal*. He was associated with Thomas Davis, the Young Ireland Movement and its newspaper, *The Nation*.

After the abortive rising of 1848 he fled to Scotland. There he read a police notice offering a reward for the capture of himself: Thomas D'Arcy McGee, described as twenty-three years old, 5 foot 3 inches in height, with black hair and a dark face; a delicate, thin man, dressed in a black shooting coat, plaid trousers and light jacket.

His wife, Mary, who was expecting their first child, met him briefly in Derry before he furtively embarked on the *SS Shamrock*. Disguised as a priest, he escaped to America.

D'Arcy McGee's organising ability impressed Canadian Catholic leaders, who invited him to settle in Montreal, a city remarkable for long winters and sudden springs. In 1858, McGee was elected to the Union Parliament in Toronto, which linked English and French speakers in an uneasy alliance. An independent liberal with remarkable vision, he proposed a Canadian confederation, a free nation in a British Commonwealth.

When he became Minister for Agriculture and Immigration, political donations financed his Montreal house, which had stone lintels carved with shamrocks. He promised to repay that generous gift from loyal supporters. D'Arcy McGee spent his best hours in that house, relaxing with his family and working in his well-stocked library.

He achieved a lifelong ambition by qualifying as a lawyer at McGill University. As D'Arcy McGee matured, he shed his extreme Irish nationalist views and became a Canadian states-man. But intrigue and sectarianism undermined domestic bliss and political stability. His enemies included both extremes: Orangemen and Fenians. He opposed the Fenian invasion of Canada from the USA and the Irish voters in Montreal deserted him.

McGee resisted Queen Victoria's choice of the new Canadian capital at Ottawa where the Confederate parliament met in 1868. Late on an April night, the forty-three-year-old MP walked from his office to a hotel in Ottawa. A sudden flash and a sharp blast of a shot, apparently from a Fenian assassin, ended his life. The state funeral at St Patrick's, Montreal, was a sad but triumphant homecoming for Thomas D'Arcy McGee.

Relaxing after my quest for his story, I reflected on an irony: The Irish-Canadian statesman, who as a youth espoused the temper-ance anti-drink cause, is remembered now because of the name of Ottawa's popular Irish pub: D'Arcy McGee's.

COMMODORE JOHN BARRY – FATHER OF THE AMERICAN NAVY

Gerry Breen

Few Irishmen have matched the achievements of Commodore John Barry, who died 200 years ago, on 13 September 1803. Indeed, it has been said that, had it not been for Barry, the American Revolution would have been lost.

John Barry was born in a modest thatched cottage in 1745 at Ballysampson, about ten miles from Wexford town. When Barry's father was evicted by his British landlord, the family was forced to relocate to the village of Rosslare. Barry's uncle was captain of a fishing skiff there, and the young man determined to follow his uncle to sea. In the course of the next fifty-eight years, he rose from humble cabin boy to senior commander of the entire United States fleet and became one of the greatest heroes of his adopted country.

An imposing figure of a man, Barry stood close to 6 feet 4 inches in height. He also stood tall in the annals of American naval history and fully deserves the proud title of 'Father of the American Navy' which was bestowed on him by his contemporaries.

The Irishman's contributions to the American War of Independence are unparalleled. He was the first to capture a British war vessel on the high seas; he captured two British ships after being severely wounded in a ferocious sea battle; he quelled three mutinies; he fought on land at the battles of Trenton and Princeton; he captured more than twenty ships, including an armed British schooner in the lower Delaware; he wrote a book that established a set of signals for effective communication between ships; and he fought in the last naval battle of the American Revolution in 1783.

During the War of Independence, the English tried to persuade Barry, who had shown himself to be a wonderfully effective combat commander, to change sides. He was offered a bribe of £20,000, plus full captaincy and a command in the Royal Navy, but he rejected the offer with the words: 'Not the value and command of the whole British fleet can lure me from the cause of my country.'

Following the war, he was instrumental in opening up new trade routes with the Far East and China. When the navy was revived in the 1790s, President Washington summoned Barry to the President's mansion to receive Commission Number One in the navy. As head of the navy, Barry supervised the construction of the first frigates built under the Naval Act. From then on, he held the courtesy title of commodore.

Commodore Barry died at his home at Strawberry Hill, three miles north of Philadelphia, after serving at the head of the United States' navy under presidents Washington, Adams and Jefferson, and he was given a full military funeral. Barry has been honoured in many ways: he is recognised in the Statue of Liberty museum as one of the six foreign-born great leaders of the War of Independence, his statue stands in front of Independence Hall in Philadelphia and four US naval ships have carried his name.

Commodore Barry Bridge, which was opened in 1974, links Pennsylvania and New Jersey across the Delaware River. The 13th of September is recognised as Commodore John Barry Day in at least two states – Pennsylvania and New York. President Dwight D Eisenhower ordered a statue of Commodore Barry to be presented on behalf of the people of the United States to the people of Ireland, and this was unveiled in 1956 at Cresent Quay, Wexford, where it overlooks Wexford Harbour.

FATHER PROUT

Douglas E Mellon

My English teacher made all his pupils learn Father Prout's ingenious poem about the bells of Shandon church, probably because it was written by a Corkman, like himself, rather than for its intrinsic literary merit. We learnt the poem but knew nothing of the poet, who was a truly remarkable man.

Father Prout's real name was Francis Sylvester Mahony. He was born in Cork in 1805. His father owned a prosperous wool business in Blarney and sent him to Clongowes Wood College. He started studying to be a Jesuit there and continued his studies in Paris and Rome.

In 1830, he returned to Clongowes as a teacher. After what was called a 'late night frolic' he lost his job and was expelled from the Jesuits. The frolic could not have been all that serious, for he was accepted by the Irish College at Rome and ordained as a priest in 1832. It was while he was in Rome that he wrote the famous poem. He scribbled its first two lines on the wall of his bedroom. They remained there for years and became a tourist attraction.

He was assigned to a parish in Cork and showed great courage and devotion to his duty as a hospital chaplain when the whole district was struck by an epidemic of cholera.

Two years later, after a sharp disagreement with his bishop, he moved to London and ceased to exercise his priestly functions. Instead he started to write, under the name Father Prout. No one knows why he chose that name. He must have known, or at least heard of, the real Father Prout, who had been a priest at Watergrasshill in County Cork during his childhood.

His articles, which he called the 'Reliques of Father Prout', established his reputation as a writer of great erudition and wit and they opened the doors of literary London to him. He joined a group of gifted writers, which included Dickens and Thackeray, with whom he was soon on friendly terms. More importantly, perhaps, for an aspiring writer, he got to know a publisher called William Maginn. He was another immensely talented Corkman, who had founded a journal called *Fraser's Magazine* and made it the most important literary journal of its day. Father Prout's articles further enhanced its prestige.

Father Prout carried his learning lightly. For his own amusement, he translated most of *Moore's Melodies* into both Greek and Latin and published them as *Moore's Plagiarisms*, much to the annoyance of their original author.

He translated the poems of another Cork poet, Richard Alfred Millikin, who is best remembered for writing 'The Groves of Blarney', although he wrote a number of other poems. Father Prout translated some of them into Greek, Latin and Italian. He also translated many of his own poems into various languages, but I have never come across a translation of his 'The Bells of Shandon'.

After a few years, he got bored with London and started to travel. He wandered through Egypt, Greece, Hungary and Turkey, which must have taken great fortitude and been a severe test of his linguistic ability.

In 1846, he returned to Rome and became the Rome corres- pondent of the *London Daily News*, at the suggestion of Charles Dickens. His articles were thought important enough to be collected and published in book form, under the title *Facts and Figures from Italy* by Don Jeremy Savonarola, a pseudonym of Father Prout's.

Two years later he moved to Paris and became the Paris correspondent of the *London Globe*. While he was living there, a friend who saw him in the street described him as 'trudging the boulevards with his arms clasped behind his back, his nose in the air; and with a quick, clear, deep-seeking eye wandering to the right and left; and sarcasm, not of the sourest kind, playing like a jack-o'-lantern in the corners of his mouth.' This description is confirmed by a picture taken by a Dublin photographer called Lesage.

Father Prout died in Paris in May 1866. His body was brought back to Cork and is buried in the vault of Shandon church, whose bells he has made world famous.

JAMES USSHER
Al Byrne

Last April, the President of Ireland formally opened the new James Ussher library in Trinity College Dublin. This is a brand-new addition to the existing libraries in the college, which include the Berkeley, Lecky, Long Room and Hamilton. Collectively these all make up what is now one of the biggest and most famous libraries in the world.

But what did this James Ussher do to merit having a library named after him? For that matter, who was James Ussher?

Well, for a start, James Ussher was born in 1581 at 3 Fishamble Street in the Liberties in Dublin. The Usshers were Protestants – and one of the oldest and most respected families in Dublin. James went to school in what was officially called 'The Hospital of King Charles' over in Oxmantown Green on the north side of the Liffey. It was a free school and came to be known as 'The Blew-Coat School'.

His school days over, Ussher entered Trinity College at the ripe old age of thirteen. Such was his university career that he was elected a Fellow of Trinity at the incredibly young age of twenty-one. He went on to study theology, philosophy and such like and, at twenty-six years of age, was appointed Professor of Divinity. He was subsequently appointed Vice-Chancellor of Trinity at the age of thirty-four. He was then ordained and, after some parish work in Finglas, he eventually became Protestant Archbishop of Armagh and Primate of All Ireland.

Now you might well assume that all of this was a wonderful achievement for any man. And indeed it was. But not for James Ussher. For it was he who estimated that the date of the creation of the world was 23 October 4004 BC; *and* he produced written evidence in Latin to prove his case. This and other publications earned for him such accolades as 'he who is head and shoulders above his fellow students' and 'the most learned man in the realm'. And, to cap all of that, a man called Charles Richard Elrington, who was Regius Professor of Divinity at Trinity for twenty-one years, published a seventeen-volume edition of the works of James Ussher.

But even that is not the end of the James Ussher story. During his lifetime he had collected a vast quantity of books and, when he died, he left 10,000 volumes to his daughter, Lady Tyrrell. At that point, Oliver Cromwell became interested in acquiring the books for the state. Eventually they were bought by King Charles II for the princely sum of £2,200, and the said Charles II assigned them to Trinity College library. So, in a roundabout way, it can be said that James Ussher bequeathed 10,000 books to Trinity library.

James Ussher died in 1656, aged seventy-five. Cromwell himself ordered that Ussher should be buried in Westminster Abbey. And so he was.

In the Long Room library in Trinity today you will find the busts of fourteen famous men who were (and I quote) 'eminent for genius and learning'. And there amongst Socrates, Homer, Milton, Shakespeare, Newton and Plato, you'll find the bust of James Ussher. And *there* rests the case for calling the new library in Trinity 'The James Ussher library'.

A PERIOD PIECE

Bairbre O'Hogan

Attending a funeral recently in Taney parish church in south County Dublin, I noticed a plaque on the north wall in memory of Francis Stuart Verschoyle and William Arthur Verschoyle, two young local men who died in World War I, in Ypres and Arras respectively. Their surname immediately brought to mind my late mother's great friend, Mrs Verschoyle, or Mrs V as we called her. I wondered if they were related to her husband and thought I might be able to trace a family connection, possibly through the internet.

Mrs V may be better known to you as W M Letts, the author, playwright and poet whose work is sometimes featured on Ciarán Mac Mathúna's *Mo Cheol Thú*. My memory of Mrs V is as a small, slightly stooped, white-haired lady who walked with a stick and treated me to a glass of orange juice and Viennese fingers in Johnson, Mooney & O'Brien's café in Dún Laoghaire each Friday morning when my mother took her shopping. She was such a gentle lady that a lame robin, whom she named Steptoe, used to hop in through her open kitchen window to feed from the crumbs left for him on the sill. Her back garden – the front door of her cottage opened directly on to the road – was enclosed by a high stone wall, which sheltered a colourful array of old-fashioned flowers that she delighted in showing to her many visitors. Naturally, her little sitting room was full of treasures – her own work and that of her contemporaries and friends such as Padraic Colum, Monk Gibbon, Patricia Lynch, Lady Gregory and Jack B Yeats, who was her neighbour when she lived as a young married woman in Fitzwilliam Square.

Modest about her achievements, in 1957 she described herself to an *Irish Times* interviewer as 'a period piece, a has-been, totally unknown to this generation'. She told Maeve Binchy, in a 1969 interview in the same paper, that the only reason she was interesting was because she knew so many of the people Ireland then cared about. Mrs V could never have imagined that, by means of the internet, her writings would be accessible to, and accessed by, billions of people.

But none of the internet sites can ever catch the essence of Mrs V. They can't echo her chuckle as she recalled how her husband had told her, soon after their marriage, that there were two things Miss Letts could do which Mrs Verschoyle shouldn't do – attend the Arts Club in St Stephen's Green and swim in Seapoint. Nor can they portray her delight in the devilment and joy of the 'bold unbiddable child', nor her empathy with those who did not have children. No site can ever capture my mother's pride in her family featuring in 'Demeter's Children', in the book *Knockmaroon*. Mrs V's trick of showing visitors who had outstayed their welcome something of interest in her hall while opening the door to let them out goes unrecorded on the web. Only so much can be recorded – names and dates, facts and figures, publications and editions. The rest of her story – the real story – was known only to her friends and relatives.

Did I manage to trace the relationship between those two soldiers and Mrs V? No, but I learned a salutary lesson. All those lovely stories about her that I was told by my mother, all the background knowledge that she had as a friend of Mrs V, all the inside information she had on what had inspired her to write – I have let them slip away. I have lost them forever.

THE TWO FACES OF EVA GORE-BOOTH
Phil O'Keeffe

She was a name in a primary-school English reader – sixty years ago. Thirty years later, as I stood at the head of the staircase in Lissadell House, I remembered the little poem and the words came winging back.

> The grand road from the mountain goes shining to the sea
> And there is traffic in it and many a horse and cart,
> But the little roads of Cloonagh are dearer far to me,
> And the little roads of Cloonagh go rambling through my heart.
>
> The great waves of the Atlantic sweep storming on their way,
> Shining green and silver with the hidden herring shoal,
> But the little waves of Breffny have drenched my heart in spray
> And the little waves of Breffny go stumbling through my soul.

This poem, 'The Little Waves of Breffny', was the only claim to fame in Ireland of Eva Selena Gore-Booth. Born the third child of Sir Henry Gore-Booth at Lissadell House in Sligo on 22 May 1870, she was two years younger than her more famous sister, Constance. The two were very close, sharing many happy childhood days, as they raced their carts up the long drawing-room and through the doors of the library at Lissadell House.

I found it easy to picture the old house with its gaiety, singsongs, quiet evenings and bubbling girlish laughter. I found it easy to picture W B Yeats, Maud Gonne, George Russell and others of that time, and, in the midst of the literary readings, the frail and delicate figure of Eva Gore-Booth.

She was a prolific writer and, at the age of twenty-eight, published her first book of poems, to be followed six years later by two more volumes. 'The Little Waves of Breffny' was included in the third book, described by Katherine Tynan as a small masterpiece. George Russell, writing as Æ, said: 'Poems like that sing themselves into one's being and have a dear place in memory.' In Ireland her work was virtually unknown. She published over 400 poems – some only four lines in length. The poetry was full of gentleness and quiet moments. Reading them, one might fail to see the other face of Eva Gore-Booth – the defender and champion of women's rights. The family owned land in Salford in England, and in 1897, having travelled in India and America, Eva went to live in Manchester, where she worked strenuously for women's rights. Writing was her first love, and she took up her pen in defence of the mill and factory worker. She wrote brilliantly on political and economic subjects.

But the pen was not enough. She threw herself wholeheartedly into the cause. She spoke at election meetings, organised rallies, and her frail figure was a familiar one at the mill gate and the coal pits. This did not come easy, and ill-health dogged her steps, but she braved the elements, the taunts and the threats. Her poem 'The Street Orator' reveals some of her feelings at the time.

> *At Clitheroe from the Market Square*
> *I saw rose-lit the mountain's gleam.*
> *I stood before the people there*
> *And spake as in a dream.*
>
> *At Oldham of the many mills*
> *The weavers are of gentle mind.*
> *At Haslingden one flouted me,*
> *At Burnleigh all the folk were kind.*
>
> *At Clitheroe through the sunset hour*
> *My soul was very far away.*
> *I saw Ben Bulben's rose and fire*
> *Shining afar o'er Sligo Bay.*

Exhausted by her activities and writings, which now included some published plays, in 1913 illness forced her to rest. The following year, at the outbreak of World War I, she threw herself into the Women's Peace Crusade.

Always a pacifist, she found it hard to be in sympathy with her sister Constance back in Ireland. She was aware of her sister's activities. She also knew many of the leaders of the 1916 Rising, but she could never sympathise with their militant methods. When the leaders were executed, she returned immediately to Ireland to be with their families, most of whom she knew well. She was a source of strength to them in their darkest hour. Of this period she wrote:

> *Grief for the noble dead*
> *Of one who did not share their strife*
> *And mourned that any blood was shed*
> *Yet felt the broken glory of their state*
> *Their strange heroic questioning of Fate*
> *Ribbon with gold the rags of this our life.*

Lissadell House is where I found Eva Gore-Booth, and at Lissadell House we leave her. There her spirit still lives. W B Yeats immortalised Eva and Constance Gore-Booth and their home in his famous lines:

> *The light of evening, Lissadell,*
> *Great windows open to the South,*
> *Two girls in silk kimonos, both*
> *Beautiful – one a gazelle.*

THE NUN OF KENMARE

Gerry O'Malley

Granuaile, Ann Devlin, Countess Markievicz... Irish history has produced only a handful of remarkable women. That is not to say that remarkable women didn't exist, only that they are not mentioned in the history books, which were written, in the main, by men.

In her day, Margaret Anna Cusack was the best-known living Irish woman. Her writing and her activities were reported in the newspapers of England, the United States, Canada and Australia as well as at home. She wrote some forty books, several musical works and poetry. Two popes praised her work. A cardinal called her 'the Irish Joan of Arc'. She was the country's first campaigner for the rights of women, particularly poor, uneducated working girls. The peculiar thing was that her fight was conducted for the most part from inside the walls of a convent, and an enclosed order at that. The name by which she was known all over the world was 'The Nun of Kenmare'.

She was born in Dublin in 1829 of strong Protestant upper-class stock. While attending a posh boarding school in England, she read Thomas Carlyle and developed a social conscience. She decided to spend her life working for the underprivileged. The problem was: how to go about it? Charitable work was only permitted as a pastime for rich married ladies. She became an Anglican nun and worked for a time among the poor in London's East End. After a few years, she returned to Ireland, became a Catholic and started her life as a Sister in the Poor Clares. She was thirty years old.

When a Poor Clare convent was established in Kenmare, Sr Mary Francis Clare, born Margaret Anna Cusack, became its most famous resident. She started writing about history and was known to her readers as 'M F Cusack', but in 1872, her first work on social reform was published in New York under the name 'The Nun of Kenmare'.

For the next ten years she waged a paper war for the liberation of the underprivileged and the righting of injustice. She took on the influential Landsdowne Estate and all absentee landlords. She supported the Land League of Davitt and Parnell and Home Rule. Her words were described as 'violent, incendiary and seditious', and not just by landowners and politicians, but by ecclesiastics as well. It was the policy of *all* authority to deny that distress and poverty existed.

The Famine Relief Fund she set up collected today's equivalent of €1m. The name of the Nun of Kenmare was enough to evoke horror at the dinner tables of the great – so she must have been doing something right! Accusations began to pour in. It was said she diverted famine-relief money to help the Land League and finance boycotts. Her life was threatened. Her parish priest denounced her. The Archbishop of Dublin, Dr – later Cardinal – McCabe, pro-English and pro-landlord, forbade women to engage in politics. The Nun of Kenmare said: 'What use are my rights when those in power are determined to violate them?' Defeated, she left Kenmare where, for ten years, her writings had been the convent's sole financial support.

In Rome, she asked to be relieved of her vows as a Poor Clare. Pope Leo XIII, with whom she conversed in Italian, encouraged her to continue writing and gave her permission to found her own order. In spite of papal approval, when she went to New York to fundraise for the new order, the archbishop of that city denounced her and hounded her out of his diocese.

In her last years, in poor health, she reverted to Anglicanism. She died in her seventieth year and is buried at Leamington in Warwickshire.

THE MAN WHO CAME BACK FROM THE DEAD

Joseph O'Neill

Once he was the most feared man in Britain. Today he is forgotten. The Che Guevara of his day, men spoke his name with awe or dread. He founded the most potent revolutionary organisation of the age and inspired Clarke and Pearse. He even came back from the dead.

James Stephens was born in Kilkenny in 1825. His first job was as an engineer with the Limerick and Waterford Railway. But his passion was nationalist politics. He joined the Young Ireland movement and was in the thick of the fighting in Ballingarry, County Tipperary, during the 1848 rising. Wounded, he escaped to France after shaking off the police by staging his own funeral. This ruse was so successful that, when Stephens later returned, his friends insisted he was an imposter.

Paris in the 1850s was a revolutionary's haven. There Stephens rubbed shoulders with the most advanced thinkers of the age, including Karl Marx. Living in abject poverty in the Latin Quarter, he eked out an existence translating Dickens into French.

He and John O'Mahony, an Irish scholar, honed their plans for a revolutionary party dedicated to an independent Irish republic. They called themselves Fenians, after Fionn Mac Cumhaill's legendary warriors.

What was novel about Stephens' plan was that it drew on the strength of the Irish diaspora, particularly Irish-Americans. While O'Mahony crossed the Atlantic to mobilise American sentiment, Stephens slipped back into Ireland.

In the guise of a beggar, Stephens set out to walk the length and breadth of Ireland. With typical thoroughness, he aimed to contact every potential supporter in the country and inspire them to join his movement.

By the time he reached Dublin in 1858 he had planted the organisation in every county in Ireland. And it was in Dublin, on St Patrick's Day, in Peter Lanagan's timber yard in Lombard Street, that he established the Irish branch of the Fenians, the Irish Republican Brotherhood.

In the years that fòllowed, Stephens extended his organisation everywhere Irish exiles made their homes – Australia, South Africa and Canada – and in Manchester, London, Glasgow, Liverpool and every centre of Irish population on mainland Britain.

Stephens was a workaholic who shunned no hardship. He raised and trained 80,000 men. He claimed to have infiltrated every regiment in the British army. His newspaper, *The Irish People*, enraged Dublin Castle and bombarded the British authorities with jibes and insults. By 1865, world events were turning in his favour.

Relations between the USA and Britain were so bad that war seemed imminent – a perfect opportunity for Ireland to strike for independence. More important still was the end of the American Civil War. Thousands of battle-hardened Irishmen, intoxicated by Stephens' talk of an Irish republic, were anxious to return to Ireland, desperate to play their part in the struggle for independence. As the pressure for action became irresistible, Stephens promised a rising before 1865 was out.

At the last minute, with everything in place, Stephens wavered. While he was vacillating, Dublin Castle struck. Swooping on the offices of *The Irish People*, they arrested Stephens and his lieutenants. Undaunted, Stephens challenged the court: 'I despise and defy any punishment you can impose on me.' Their immediate punishment was to lock him in Dublin's impregnable Richmond Gaol.

But just as British spies had penetrated the Fenian movement, Fenians had infiltrated the Dublin Metropolitan Police and Richmond Gaol. With the aid of police officers and gaolers, and a ladder and tables from the prison dining room, Stephens scaled two 18-foot walls and escaped to the South Circular Road. Not until Éamon de Valera walked out of Lincoln Prison was the British government more embarrassed.

But Stephens' decision to delay the rising cost him the leadership of the movement. He spent the last thirty years of his life in impoverished exile, first in France and then in Switzerland. As a result of Parnell's intervention, the British government allowed him to return home in 1886. He spent his final years anonymously in Booterstown Avenue, Blackrock, where he died on 2 April 1901. This time he did not come back from the dead.

THE DEATH OF MARAT

Jackie Morrissey

Those of you who have ever wondered what exactly one should wear for an assassination have much to learn from Marie-Anne-Charlotte Corday, murderer of one of the leading, and most bloodthirsty, figures of the French Revolution, Jean-Paul Marat.

Marat was a strange character, probably paranoid, famous for his battlecry of 'we are betrayed'. His fondness for demanding the death penalty made him a dangerous character, hated and feared by many, despite his title of 'friend of the people'.

Enter citizeness Charlotte Corday. Inspired by her reading of Plutarch, she decided that it was her duty to assassinate Marat, and so made her way to Paris for that purpose. Her first attempt failed, as Marat's mistress refused to admit her to the house. With a true understanding of the man's bloody enthusiasms, Charlotte returned to her hotel and wrote him a letter promising to reveal details of a plot against the revolution. She then settled down to await a reply.

Historian Anita Brookner describes how Charlotte whiled away the time. She summoned a hairdresser, then dressed carefully in a spotted muslin dress with a pink shawl. She completed the ensemble with a tall black hat with a green cockade and black tassels. Thus suitably attired, she set out in a cab for Marat's house.

Once there, she slipped in and confronted Marat. Marat was in the bath, a place where he spent much time trying to alleviate the effects of a disfiguring, uncomfortable skin disease, reputedly acquired while hiding in the Paris sewers to evade his enemies. He was wrapped in a sheet, to avoid contact with the copper tub, and his head was wrapped in a turban soaked in vinegar, a supposed cure. He often worked from his bathtub, using a makeshift desk. The walls of the room were decked in ornate and expensive wallpaper – a strange choice for this austere advocate of the common man. On one wall hung crossed pistols with the sinister slogan 'La Mort' ('Death') underneath.

Charlotte Corday made an initial pretence of writing down the names of plotters, then she pulled out a knife and stabbed Marat. He rapidly lost consciousness and died and Charlotte was arrested. Marat was embalmed and buried quickly because of the heat and the supposed unhealthy state of his blood.

A famous painting by Jacques Louis David entitled *The Death of Marat* commemorates this moment. David, a fellow revolutionary and friend, created a powerful image. Marat lies half out of the bath, leaning towards the viewer, his hand still holding the quill with which he had been writing. He is draped in sheeting, his body, idealised in the convention of heroic nudity, displays little sign of the disfiguring skin disease which we know to have been present. The austere, plain background shows no sign of fancy wallpaper or crossed pistols. In his hand, he clutches Charlotte Corday's letter – not, as in reality, a list of plotters for execution, but a plea: 'My misfortune commends me to your kindness.' Another paper on his packing-case desk shows an order for a money gift to be sent to a poor soldier's widow. His sheet is patched, a nobility of spirit is reflected in his serene dying face. Altogether, it is a picture of a secular Christ, a martyr dying for his people. This is particularly ironic, since both artist and subject heartily disapproved of religion.

It is a powerful picture, proving, perhaps, that a work of propaganda can also be great art. Most of all, though, it demonstrates that the death of Marat makes a fascinating story, whether told in words or in paint. Philosophy, fashion, art and revolution – a very *French* assassination tale.

GENESIS OF A FOOTBALL FAN
Leo Cullen

They are romances in themselves, the stories of why those among us who watch cross-Channel football support the sides we do. Recently I had cause to reflect upon this phenomenon in the case of my own chosen team. I had cause to reflect back to the origins of my passion.

Growing up in the middle of Ireland, I knew very little about 'the beautiful game'. Then I went to boarding school in the soccer city of Waterford and all that changed. My Uncle Michael, a city man, rescued me from college each Sunday and took me to Kilcohan Park to watch his team, the Waterford 'Blues', play against all the teams of the League: Drums, Hibs, Bohs, Shels, The Hoops, Dundalk. I loved it at Kilcohan Park, a gusty raucous place. My uncle loved to have me as a companion and, as we walked home to tea at my aunt's house in the onset of winter evenings, we criticised and praised our team like knowledgeable football scribes. It was mostly criticism: 'Donkeys!' my uncle said. 'That is not "the beautiful game".'

One day a wizard appeared along the sideline of Kilcohan Park. He lined out against Waterford, on a Cork Hibernian side. He was old, or looked old to me. But he was a class apart. He had a different touch, the touch of a professional. When he got the ball, he spun along the wing with it and never got caught in a tackle but crossed it clean as a whistle. He had a way of remaining aloof from the hoofing and sod-flying that went on about him.

I was taking in all this when my uncle leaned down to me and said: 'See him. He's the great Tommy Eglington who scored bagfuls of goals as a winger for Everton.'

Let me say here that I had made one little connection with soccer before going to that soccer-mad town of Waterford. Around the age of nine or so, I had been very taken by a headline in the sports pages of the *Sunday Independent*, 'Everton tame Wolves', it read: a hair-bristling headline, a trigger to any young imagination.

Now here was that name again. The name my imagination had already fed off without my knowing: Everton. Only, now I fastened it into that place in the heart where loyalty resides.

I learned all about Tommy Eglington. Back in 1946, fifteen years previous to that day on which I watched him waltz up the Kilcohan wing, he had crossed the Irish Sea from Dublin, with his skills and his kitbag, to play for Everton in the city of Liverpool. He had returned to Ireland after a successful career in English football. Far from being able to retire on his laurels, he was soon prevailed upon to play for Cork Hibs. I learned about other Goodison legends: Dixie Dean, greatest of them all, who scored sixty goals for Everton in one season. The only difference – I had seen Tommy Eglington.

Then one night recently, forty years into a long and oftentimes frustrating relationship, Everton – 'The Toffees' as we fans affectionately call them – came to Bray to play a friendly. I was ill – not feeling at all well – but I went along; loyalty knows no sickbed!

It was a calm and dry night on the Carlisle Grounds. Before kick-off, the announcer asked for a minute's silence: 'To mark the death of 'Toffees' hero, Tommy Eglington.' His voice brought an instant hush to the stadium. All rose. You could hear the bucket seats hit back on their springs.

A minute's silence. And in that minute, as I looked at twenty-two players standing motionless on a bone-dry pitch, my mind's eye beheld a mature yet still youthful figure dancing down a wing. And a lifetime as a football fan reeled like a film before me. And I heard the water lapping on the beach of Bray, water that had come all the way across the Irish Sea from Birkenhead.

PADDY THE PIGEON

Gail Seekamp

When news broke of the D-Day landings – sixty years ago – an elderly gentleman in County Antrim was surely listening to his radio with particular interest. He was Mr Andrew Hughes of Carnlough: A World War I veteran and a well-travelled and educated man. But he was also a pigeon breeder of some repute.

A quarter of a million carrier pigeons served with British and US forces in World War II. Of these, just a few hundred took part in the Normandy campaign that began on D-Day – 6 June 1944. They included a pigeon called Paddy, bred by Mr Hughes.

Paddy was a black-and-white dappled pigeon, described as 'highly intelligent' by his RAF handlers. But when he was hatched in spring 1943, he looked as unpromising as all pigeon chicks do – blind and helpless with damp scraggy feathers. When Paddy was a week old, Mr Hughes slipped a ring on his leg. It bore Paddy's National Pigeon Service number: NPS 43-9451.

That May, Paddy left Mr Hughes' loft for his first posting. It was at RAF Ballykelly, a Royal Air Force base near Derry. Paddy began training and was assigned to Air/Sea Rescue missions.

At that time, RAF planes and supply boats were still at risk from marauding German U-boats and stray bombers. Even lack of fuel or bad weather could bring down a plane, so the RAF equipped crews with metal pigeon carriers. Each held two birds, placed beak to tail. The containers floated. If a plane ditched into the sea, a crewman would try to scribble its co-ordinates on wafer-thin paper. With luck, he might stuff the message into a cigarette-sized tube strapped to a pigeon's leg. Once released, the bird would 'home' to its RAF loft, bearing the vital SOS.

In this way, RAF pigeons saved hundreds of lives, braving storms, injury and exhaustion to deliver their messages. Perhaps

Paddy rescued such a crew. For in March 1944 he was sent to an RAF base near Portsmouth. By then, preparations for the Allied invasion of France were at fever pitch. Men and materials were being secreted into camps all over Britain's south coast. Soon, they would cross the English Channel and strike at Hitler's forces.

Early on 6 June, almost 5,000 vessels of all shapes and sizes surged through a chilly grey sea towards Normandy. There, thousands of soldiers would meet their destiny on five beaches, code-named: Sword, Juno, Gold, Omaha and Utah.

It seems Paddy came ashore on Omaha on 9 June, a beach which had seen the bloodiest combat of D-Day. Even now, the sector was still in turmoil. Tanks from crack German divisions were pouring into Normandy, clashing with Allied troops in countryside that was ribbed with ancient hedgerows. It was ideal defensive terrain. Somewhere, against this chaotic backdrop, Paddy was released.

We do not know what his mission was. Nor his message. But we do know he was liberated on 12 June, at 8.14 a.m. He flew from Normandy back to his RAF base near Portsmouth in four hours fifty minutes. It was the fastest crossing by a carrier pigeon in the Normandy landings.

For this achievement, Paddy was awarded a Dickin Medal for bravery on 1 September 1944. This is the animal equivalent of the Victoria Cross. Paddy was the only Irish animal to be thus honoured for service in World War II.

Imagine the feelings of Mr Hughes as he hunched over his wireless on 6 June and in the heady days that followed. And how he felt, a few months later, to learn that Paddy would return to Carnlough a hero. Perhaps glad. Bemused. And proud. Mr Hughes' own days of military service were long over. It was left to his pigeon, winging furiously across the Channel in June 1944, to play a part – however small – in those momentous Normandy landings and earn them *both* a place in history.

A Sense of
Poignancy

DOGS AND DEATH
Enda Wyley

The hand accidentally lets go of the lead and the young dog seizes its chance to escape. A half-crazed little creature now, the dog is a ball of white fur and ecstatic leaps bounding across the curved road. A van – whiter than the dog and a hundred times its size – rounds the bend. There is no stopping it. The driver hits the dog and keeps going. The little terrier, only a second ago playful and free, is now a whimpering, fast-breathing dog close to death – panicked, eyes darting, but still alive.

I have no blanket to keep him warm. A man who had been sipping coffee in a nearby café runs to help; he wraps the dog so professionally in his jumper that I think he must be a doctor.

I have no car. A waitress races across the road and is urging me to lift the quivering dog into my arms and come with her. She'll drive me to the vet's surgery. I ease myself into her back seat.

The road along the canal is congested with early evening traffic. My dog is panting faster now and a trickle of blood trails like a red petal from his mouth. He is dying but fighting to live. I coo soft sounds into his ear and rub his shattered body in sympathy, urging him to fight on. I am heartbroken but admiring of his brave heart.

Ironically, in my bag is the book *The Lives of Animals* by J M Coetzee. I have only had my dog for a short time and I wanted to read what one of my favourite writers has to say about animals. Just last night I read these words:

> Anyone who says that life matters less to animals than it does to us has not held in his hands an animal fighting for his life. The whole of the being of the animal is thrown into that fight without reserve. When you say that the fight lacks a dimension of intellectual or imaginative horror, I agree. It

is not the mode of being of animals to have an intellectual horror; their whole being is in the living flesh.

This passage races through my mind now as I hold my dying dog on my lap. Dogs may not possess a reflective awareness of mortality, but they do have a practical awareness of death, as demonstrated by my little dog fighting for his life.

At the animal hospital, there are long hours of waiting. The vet speaks of funeral arrangements. He says, go home and rest. It's been an ordeal. Have a whiskey.

Walking back alone along the South Circular Road, I begin to cry. Aristotle said there can be no friendship between adults and children because they are not equals – and I scorn myself for being so emotionally attached to a dog. But then I think, why shouldn't my dog and I be bonded? In less than a month he has become a joyful, complex part of my family. On more walks than we have ever had before, we are forced to slow down, notice every bush, plant, gate post, street lamp in the city, we get to know every dog and cat nearby, to be aware of every bird and how they scatter at his pounce and bark. He is praised, smiled at and commented on by every passer-by. People in our neighbourhood know his name, not ours. We have not had one unobserved meal since he arrived.

I am home. It is late now and I decide to sleep. Did you know that some aborigines measure the cold of the night by the number of dogs they need for warmth? A very cold night might be a four to five. I calculate that this night is a two. But I have no dog to comfort me.

I settle down, wait for the morning, for the phone to ring – and for the vet to say everything is OK after all.

SOCRATES THE SEA MONSTER

James Cotter

In the mid-1980s I stopped believing in God. I remember the moment well: I was lying in bed listening – and this is true – to *Sunday Miscellany*. A woman was talking about how she had decided to become an atheist at the age of eleven. I was ten and thought this seemed like a pretty good idea. After the Tooth Fairy, the Easter Bunny and finally Santa Claus, it just seemed like the obvious thing to do. But unlike most things I decided to do when I was ten, such as living forever and inventing the world's first rocket-powered dog, I kept not believing in God.

I was fourteen before I started refusing to go to mass. I made my Confirmation, of course. I stood in church in my itchy new suit, resolutely not taking oaths and not swearing allegiance and then feeling guilty as aged relatives cooed over me and slipped me tenners. Even though I am an atheist, I have always done Catholic guilt well.

As a teenager in my good Catholic school, it was strange to be the only one who stayed seated at the start of every class as the kids around me rose to pray, to be the one who stayed at the back of the church when all the other boys went up to take Communion. But it was grand, it was modern Ireland, and the worst the priests could do was glower at me and mutter, rather than hitting me with a big stick to convince me of the goodness of their divine message.

But times have changed. Now I'm just one of the silent majority who don't worship, who don't go to mass anymore. It's still deeply uncool to be an atheist. To have anything so strong as an opinion on religious matters is viewed as a quaint, almost old-fashioned, interest in something that just doesn't matter anymore. Modern Irish spirituality seems to consist of a vague consensual notion that there might be something out there – probably is – and, sure, isn't it as well to get married and buried in the church just in case? And if I want to learn more, sure there's night courses on the latest spiritual theory that's existed in India since time began, and that'll give me some simple bullet points for the meaning of Life, The Universe and Everything. I'll have my spirituality with a sprinkle of Catholicism, some Reiki on the side. Oh, and I'll have a coke to go, please.

But just because religion isn't the centre of our society any more, does that mean we shouldn't have a spiritual side? Socrates said that an unexamined life is not worth living, and he should know, as he spent so much time with his head in the clouds considering the meaning of life. He'd often accidentally crush cities underfoot because he was thirty storeys high. Or was that Godzilla?

Anyway, whether Socrates was a giant sea-dwelling monster or just a guy with a really long beard, he had a point, and just because the answers our grandparents and their grandparents believed in don't always work for us, it doesn't mean we shouldn't be trying to find the answers ourselves, does it?

Even though it's been more than a decade since I went to mass, there are still things I miss. I miss the togetherness and contemplation of church, the ceremonies that drag us all – young and old, rich and poor – into a unified people that care and feel for each other. Every Easter, the church I went to held a midnight mass. At the start, the congregation would stand in complete darkness, each of us holding a single unlit candle. The priest would appear at the back of the church. Above his head he would hold a single, stout candle. As he began to walk up the centre of the church, parishioners on each side would light their candles from it and then pass the flame to their neighbours. So, as the priest walked towards the altar, the sea of darkness would be slowly engulfed in a massive swelling tide of brightness until the whole church would glow from the hundreds of candles and the sparkling reflections in our eyes, as we brought light to darkness – together – as the Eucharist returned to the tabernacle and Christ rose again.

And I miss the tunes. The multi-harmonic blast of pure uplifting joy that can happen, without fanfare, in thousands of churches all around the world at the same time every Sunday morning. We atheists haven't quite cracked that yet. Of course, that's why the devil invented rock 'n' roll.

MARRIAGE BY CANDLELIGHT

Sinéad McCoole

In another time and place it would have been a society wedding – a ceremony conducted with joy, as befitted the union of two upper-class Irish families – a marriage of the daughter of a successful solicitor from Temple Villas, Rathmines, with the son of the Director of the Museum of Science and Art, Dublin. His family's wealth came from his mother's side. She was an heiress with a considerable fortune, and owned a number of properties in the city, including Larkfield in Kimmage.

The couple were not young by the standards of the day: the bride was twenty-eight years old while the groom was twenty-nine. They could have been described as somewhat bohemian. The groom was addicted to wearing large rings and bracelets. He was a poet and a writer and had spent much of his youth travelling to Italy, Sicily, France, Malta and Algeria. He had always had poor health, and now he was dying of glandular TB. She was an artist who had been a student at the Slade in London and was critically acclaimed for her work as a caricaturist. While she was at the Slade, she had her portrait painted by William Orpen. The work was entitled *Young Ireland*, a prophetic title, as the sitter would one day be seen as a symbol of a new Ireland. It was the couple's wedding that would ensure that her name would be remembered for generations to come.

The story of the marriage ceremony would be forever imprinted on the minds of those who heard it because the wedding took place just hours before his execution. Joseph Mary Plunkett, one of those executed for his part in the 1916 Rising, married Grace Evelyn Vandeleur Gifford in the prison chapel of Kilmainham Gaol just before midnight on 3 May. He was shot at 3.30 a.m. in one of the prison yards.

The couple had arranged to marry on Easter Sunday, 23 April 1916. However, this plan had been thwarted, partly because of a confused message and partly because of the upheaval of the Rising, which commenced on 24 April.

When he knew he was to be executed, Joseph requested permission to be married, and he was granted this request. Grace entered Kilmainham Gaol on 3 May at 6 p.m. She paced up and down... waiting... until finally, at about 11.30 p.m., she was brought to the prison chapel. She did not see her fiancé until she entered the chapel, which had been lit by candlelight because the gas supply to the gaol had been cut off during the Rising.

There were no friends in attendance, although Grace's sister Nellie, who had taken part in the Rising and was stationed in the College of Surgeons, was a prisoner in the gaol. The marriage certificate records that witnesses to the wedding were two soldiers, John Smith and John Carberry of the 3rd Battalion of the Royal Irish Regiment. A number of armed soldiers were in the chapel and those soldiers who assisted at the ceremony did so by shifting their rifles from hand to hand.

During the marriage ceremony, the couple were not allowed to speak, except to recite the words of their wedding vows. Immediately afterwards, Joseph was taken back to his cell and Grace left the gaol. Nearby lodgings were found for the new bride by the priest who had married them. As she was now Joe's next of kin, she would be permitted to see him before his execution. At 2 a.m., Grace received a letter granting her permission to return to Kilmainham Gaol. Later, she recalled their last meeting: 'I saw my husband in his cell for ten minutes. During the interview the cell was packed with officers and a sergeant who kept a watch in his hand and closed the interview by saying, "Your ten minutes is now up".' She later said: 'We who had never had enough time to say what we wanted to each other found that in that last ten minutes we couldn't talk at all.'

Balladeers sang of the tragic story of the woman who was maid, wife and widow all in one night. A ballad recorded by Jim McCann has the words, 'Oh Grace, just hold me in your arms and let this moment linger'. Knowing that the reality of the experience was less intimate makes it seem more poignant. But what is important is that the story remains in the folk memory of the people. As her nephew Donagh MacDonagh wrote, Grace had entered what he considered to be the 'most secure of all National Pantheons, the world of the ballad'. And so the story of the wedding ceremony of Joseph Plunkett and Grace Gifford lives on.

MY WILD IRISH ROSE

Jean Darling

O n that particular day, all five years old of me was perched cross-legged in the bowl of a candy floss machine, covered up to my neck in the sweet sticky stuff, having publicity stills taken by Stax Graves, the *Our Gang* photographer, when I noticed that my costume was being nibbled away at the back by a small boy who had strayed from his family who were standing on the sidelines talking to our director, Robert McGowan.

Beside the nibbler there was a pretty little girl named Rose McGowan, whose dark curls were caught back with a blue ribbon that matched the colour of her eyes. I liked Rose the moment I met her, which was when she joined the nibbler, and the three of us dissolved into sticky sugar-coated giggles. When finally cleaned up, we girls spent the rest of the day together. It was as though I had suddenly found a sister.

The McGowan family had come from Ireland and they planned to spend a month in Hollywood and, as Rose and I were inseparable, our director said she could come to the studio every day as long as she promised to stay on the sidelines and be as quiet as a mouse while the Gang was filming.

Being younger than the other Gang kids, and a girl, I was as welcome in their circle as a boil on your nose. Only Fatty Cobb was kind during school hours: he taught me to read properly and write in joined-up letters. Rose taught me things, too, like how to crochet, and some Irish skipping rhymes. I taught her to chew balsawood and took her up to the wardrobe department to string long ropes of beads that I had found in a giant boxful of treasures that had been salvaged from scrapped costumes over the years.

But best of all, Rose liked me as a person. Then, there was another reason I loved her so much. We shared the same birthday, 23 August, which made us birthday twins, even though she was two years older.

Too soon Rose was gone, after rounds of tears and hugs and kisses. Promises of an early return blended with the choo-choo-chooing of the train as it pulled out of Union Station.

Alone once more, my whole being ached with missing my friend until a letter arrived from Dublin enclosing a snapshot of herself in her school uniform. This snapshot became a sort of security blanket, accompanying me to the studio every day, and from then on we exchanged letters on a weekly basis. When I left the Gang, Rose was sent my vaudeville itinerary, so the exchange of letters continued, even though I was hard-pressed for time, with five shows a day, autograph sessions, personal appearances and doing correspondence schoolwork.

Months gathered themselves into years and, when I was almost twelve, word came that the McGowans were coming to Hollywood for the whole month of August. Though it was only April, excitement reached fever pitch and letters went back and forth every other day, filled with plans about all the things we would do and the wonderful birthday party we would have.

Early in June, the letters stopped. I kept writing, getting more worried with each day that passed with no word from Rose. Something had to be terribly wrong for her to stop writing after almost seven years.

Over a month passed before a letter arrived from Dublin. But this time the writing on the envelope was unfamiliar – grown-up – not at all like the ones written by my friend. My heart grew cold.

The letter was from Rose's mother. It was friendly, kind and gentle, but just how gently can you tell a child that her only real friend had died of diphtheria?

BRIGID

Michael Harding

When Brigid was a child, her father, long dead, appeared to her in the bedroom to advise her that a cow was calving. Out she got, and down she went to the barn. And sure enough, she was there in time to assist at the delivery.

She fell in love with a man on a bike. Because no one else had a bike at the time. But he also played in a band. She used to go out with him, the accordion and trumpet strapped to the rear seat, her on the bar. Wheeling through the night to far off dancehalls.

She married him. And her life was full of music. Sixty years later he still made her smile. How he used to straighten his dickie bow before he entered the dancehall. That was the moment she fell in love with him.

She told me all this when I was driving her from the nursing home where her husband was dying. I drove her up the winding mountain path to the cottage she lived in. And I waited as she took a large key out of her pocket and turned it in the rusty lock. And we went in, and she proceeded with matches to light the lamp, pumping the little handle as she held the flame to the paraffin wick.

'Do you know,' she said, 'I only used his bike once. It was in winter, and the land was waterlogged, but I cycled seven miles to get a tooth pulled.'

She admired dentistry.

'And we were poor. I saw a man used to come in here in the evenings,' she said, 'to listen to the music, and he would light his pipe with coal from the fire, and then he'd leave the house an hour later with that same coal in this pocket. But,' she said, smiling at the cat that rubbed itself against her feet, 'the bike was the makings of us.' She showed me a picture of her husband, standing erect with his comrades, all musical weapons at hand, and her elbow moved across the surface of the glass, taking a little grime from it so that I could see more clearly the gallant musician in his bicycle clips and dickie bow.

And I left her there. The comrade of her life dying in his sleep fifty miles away. Yet, as she closed the door on me, I felt she was not in the slightest bit lonely in her cottage of paraffin lamps and old photographs. It struck me that she was glad to see the back of me so that she could be alone. And feed the cat.

Over the years, she sometimes manifests in my dreams as a wise old woman. And sometimes I travel past where she used to live – up the winding roads and laneways of her musical life, the townlands they cycled through long ago – and I see such enormous houses now, with patio doors and wrought iron gates, and cut-stone walls and sleek black cars. But I sometimes wonder. Where is Brigid now?

DADDY, I HARDLY KNEW YOU
Nicola Lindsay

I remember thinking how blue his eyes were. I remember feeling that he came to the house too often. I remember how filled with resentment I was that, when he was there, my mother's attention was on him and not me. I rejected my future stepfather's friendly advances, backing away unsmiling, silently retreating to another room – any room – as long as it wasn't filled with his presence, his voice, his smell. I was five and I wanted my world to remain unchanged.

I didn't miss my father. He would have to have done all the things a father does and *then* gone away for me to have missed him. He was always more absent than present, my mother told me in later years. Apparently, he'd preferred his London club, racing at Newmarket, gambling for high stakes and dining and dancing with pretty women who didn't want domesticity any more than he did.

When I was much older, I realised that I didn't have one single memory of him before his final leave-taking. There must have been rows, upsets, happy as well as sad times with him at home, but I seemed to have managed to blank out every detail of every event that included him.

I do remember the lady who came to help my mother during the week: Mrs Underhill, with her tired, pale face and smiling eyes, who seemed to carry around her a faint aura of lavender and carbolic soap. I thought I had never seen anyone so tall and thin. She used to let me put the clothes through the mangle in the scullery and water the bulbs in the window boxes. She would lift me up, holding me firmly around the waist as I leaned out with the small copper watering can, my arms wobbling with the effort of reaching the far side of the boxes.

'Careful now!' she'd say each time. 'Don't drown the poor things.'

I remember how our wire-haired terrier would rush in circles, round and round, barking dementedly until old Uncle Nick stopped trying to read his paper and got up from his deckchair muttering 'Shut up, you bloody fool' and waving his walking stick at the delighted dog, who would then circle him from behind and leap up with both paws on to the back of the old man's jacket. Uncle Nick would spin round with a roar and Scammel would be off like a small, furry torpedo, straight to the giant chestnut tree at the bottom of the garden, where he would sink down on all fours, his sides heaving, eyes gleaming and pink tongue lolling from his mouth like a slice of ham protruding from a badly made sandwich.

I remember how Uncle Nick would remove me from the line of fire when I had been impossible and my mother was ready to strangle me. He would take me for a walk through the lime-tree-lined square outside our house to the small corner shop where humbugs and lemon sherberts glowed inside tall glass jars.

I remember the ambulance coming to collect him when he was dying of pneumonia. Of course, being only five, I didn't know that he was dying, but I can still see the ambulance men carefully carrying him out through the gate – and feel the anguish of his going. I know I cried myself to sleep that night and many nights afterwards.

The first time my father and I met and talked was when I was twenty-one and married and about to leave England for Africa. We were polite, contained, careful with each other. We were complete strangers. There were no points of reference, no shared experiences, no affectionate memories.

It wasn't until many years later, when my own children were small, that I realised what a terrible loss it had been not to have known and been known by my father and that the tears I shed when Uncle Nick died weren't just tears for a beloved uncle but grief for a surrogate father who had so gently and constantly shored up the gap that was left by my missing parent.

THE FATHER

Tony Watson

He was a nice man really – my father.

A tall man, over six foot in fact, a slender build, and he still had a full head of hair when he died at the age of eighty-three, unlike his sons, whose hair started to recede in their twenties.

'Sure, I have more hair myself,' he said, after he was presented with his first follicly challenged son-in-law.

Like a bad actor, he did not know what to do with his hands; always rubbing them together, or holding them behind his back as he walked the acres of his small farm. A man of few words, a shy man, but to a stranger he appeared aloof.

He married late in life – he was forty-four and she was eighteen. It was probably an arranged marriage. Their honeymoon consisted of a one-day visit to Athlone; they never went away together again. He went to Galway for a day each summer. He rose early, put on his suit, shirt and tie, cycled to Athlone and got the train to Galway. There, he went to Salthill, rolled up the legs of his trousers and, still with his hat on, waded up to his knees in the Atlantic until it was time to come home.

Sometimes of an evening and for no apparent reason, he would break into song; always the same song, the only one he knew, 'The Rose of Tralee'. We would do our best to try to keep from laughing out loud. He would continue, despite our sniggering, until the end of the song, staring all the while at the back of the fire or staring out the window at a distant point on the horizon.

Saying the rosary was a mandatory chore in our house, but he had a wonderful solution: as my mother commenced the Hail Mary, he immediately started the response, thereby cutting the time by half.

He ruled his family of five sons and four daughters with a firm hand and had difficulty accepting that the eldest ones wanted to make their own decisions, wanted to go their own way in the world. All of us were expected – no, ordered – to work on the farm, particularly at the weekends when hay and turf had to be saved. 'Whatever rest you need you can take in the evenings,' he would say, as we broke our backs turning over wet sods on the turf bank.

I remember the first challenge to his authority. It was a Sunday evening and my eldest brother wanted to go to the movies, or the 'pictures' as it was called then, but my father was having none of it.

'Sure, it might rain tomorrow and the hay would be ruined. We'll finish it tonight.'

My brother stood upright, looked him squarely in the eye, and threw his pitchfork in the ground. He then left the field and walked purposefully back to the house. He was followed by the second eldest and then by the third. That morning my brothers had entered that field as boys and they left it now as men. I can still see the pitchfork quivering in the ground – a symbol of defiance, of an old order changing to a new one. We younger ones stayed put – it would be much later before we challenged him, and by then it would be much easier.

When his eldest children started coming home late – like midnight – they were met at the door by an irate apparition in grandfather shirt and longjohns enquiring loftily if they thought they were staying in a guest house. 'A guest house,' he would repeat for emphasis, with all the aloofness of a President Hillery. But his power was broken. Naturally it was all my mother's fault – she had raised a bunch of 'corner boys'. He watched in awe and incomprehension as his little girls locked themselves in the bedroom and emerged hours later in a cloud of perfume, their hair backcombed into huge beehives, and mini-skirts concealed underneath more sensible skirts that would be discarded in the garage after they had left the house. He never sang for us again.

As he lost control of his older children, he also ceded control of the house to my mother, who had changed, by necessity, from a slip of an eighteen-year-old girl to a formidable matriarch. In the evenings he paced his farm, debating with himself the relative merits of cattle farming versus tillage, should he sell cattle now or in the spring? I can still see him pacing back and forth across the field that was called 'the half-acre', a stooped black figure silhouetted against the dark blue of the night sky.

One Saturday evening, when I was about twenty, we met in town by accident. After a strained silence, he awkwardly asked me to have a pint with him in the Palace Bar. I refused, saying that I had something else on. Only later did I realise to my shame and horror that this was his invitation to me to enter the adult world, to drink with him man-to-man. But the moment had passed.

I worked in different parts of Ireland and England and, from time to time, went back to visit the family. The genuine welcome was in his eyes that his words could not convey. And when I left he would walk me to the car in silence – there was always something unspoken between us.

As my life progressed, bringing as it did a little prosperity and with it the holidays, the trips abroad, the designer labels, the fancy restaurants, all the things that meant so much – and mean so little – I tried to get away from where I came from, and from what he was. But yet – isn't it strange – isn't it strange how I have grown to be like him, tall, reasonably well built, now feeling in my back the arthritis that made his old age so painful, and my shyness that is often perceived as aloofness by others? Now I, too, can be seen pacing back and forth as I try to work out life's vicissitudes. I, too, who never can express in words the tumult of feelings that beats within.

I did not mourn him enough when he passed away in 1972. If I didn't mourn him properly then, maybe that's what I'm doing now?

He was a really nice man – my father.

JUST US GIRLS

Mary Mullen

So there we were, my five-year-old daughter Lily and I, in Alaska for the summer to visit Grandma. We spent five weeks in the forty-ninth state. We ate fresh salmon from the Kenai River, which flows in front of my mother's house. We walked in the woods of birch and aspen trees. We played with the neighbours' children. We walked down the footpath to the lake. The sun shone every day. Flowers wore electric-bright colours and the vegetables were huge and tasty from all the extra daylight in the land of the midnight sun.

But mostly we did the shopping and laundry and cooked for my eighty-three-year-old-mother, a lively Chicago-Irish woman with roots in counties Clare and Tipperary who homesteaded in Alaska fifty-eight years ago with my father. She was recovering from a hip replacement operation. Seeing her Galway girl, Lily, who was born with Down's Syndrome five years ago, would make her feel better. We three generations would walk down to the bridge so Lily could throw stones into Soldotna Creek, where I used to play as a child.

On our last day in Alaska, we went to our favourite beach for a picnic. We took sausages and built a fire in the sand. Aunt Peggy took vegetarian sausages for our neighbour's girl, Meera.

'We're Hindu. We don't eat meat,' said Meera proudly.

Time passed slowly as we roasted our sausages. The girls got more small sticks of wood for the fire. Every pore of my body soaked up the scene. There was my ageing mother, sitting with her titanium hip on the silver sand, drinking a beer. There were my darling daughter Lily and lovely Meera and cousin Claire at the fire learning the fine art of roasting sausages from my oldest sister, Peggy. The beach stretched for miles to our left and miles to our right. We were the only humans around. The tide was slowly going out. No waves. Although the day was ending, the air was still warm. Driftwood logs decorated the bank behind us. In front of us, twenty miles across the now quiet waters of Cook Inlet, lay the magnificent Alaska Range mountains. Mount Spur, Mount Redoubt, Mount Illiamma (all Indian names) turned from denim blue to delicate pink as the sun meandered lazily towards the horizon.

Claire, aged fifteen, and Lily held hands and walked towards the water. My mother and my sister Peggy looked at each other with grave concern. Claire harmed herself last year and has scars on her wrist to prove it. She spent time in a children's psychiatric hospital and has received counselling since. Our family is still a bit jumpy about her. I watched with fascination as the tall, broad-shouldered Claire held Lily's tiny hand. Claire's head bent down towards Lily. They were chatting, but we were too far away to hear the conversation.

'Will I run after them?' asked Peggy.

'No,' I replied. 'Let them go, let them bring out the best in each other.'

It was nine at night and the silty water of Cook Inlet was still warm. Claire and Lily swam and frolicked for a long time. They came back to the fire and shivered. We have to go, it's late and tomorrow we will start our two-day journey back to Galway.

After quenching the fire, we walk silently in the sand, each of us wishing that this night would last forever. Just as we start to trudge up the steep hill to the car, the three girls notice a yellow rowing boat. It is nestled in a small eddy created by a stream which pours into Cook Inlet. The eddy is flat calm. The rowing boat is tethered to a net rack which holds gill nets used by commercial fishers to catch salmon. The girls jump into the boat, Claire at the oars. I untie the line and off they go up the stream, Meera in the stern, Lily in the bow, sitting like princesses. Claire's suicide attempt, Lily's Down's Syndrome and Meera's inexperience in the wild are forgotten. They are just Alaskan girls rowing along, forgetting about their three admirers on the shore. Mom, Peggy and I shout encouragement and delight into the eddy. Then we are silent. Claire carefully lets Meera and Lily have a go at rowing.

'Never stand up in a boat,' she says. 'Crawl.'

They do what she says.

No one remembered to bring a camera.

THE STORY OF A BOX

Peter Jankovsky

And now it's my turn to be the guardian of the book, the book that was kept in a prominent position in our family for as long as I can remember, first in my grandmother's little flat, then in ours, and now my mother has given it to me for safe-keeping. It is the size of an old copy of the Bible, the kind of book you would hold against your chest when carrying it around, which I sometimes do. Just look at its warm golden polish – ah, and now you see that it isn't a book at all, but a box, a book-shaped box, a lady's work-box, beautifully, lovingly crafted in every detail of its simple but tasteful inlay work. On its top you can see the outline of a heart and, within it, in elegant curves, the initials H and C. And though the box is not a book, it still contains a story, the story of HC, of Hedwig Christen.

Hedwig came from Silesia, a rural part of former Prussia. In her late teens, at the beginning of the last century, she went to Berlin and eventually found a position as a housemaid and cook with a wealthy but kind family where, due to her pleasant character and complete reliability, she soon became a valued member of the household. That could have gone on indefinitely. But, on one of the free afternoons she had every second Sunday, Hedwig met Paul, a young cabinet maker, and fell in love.

After a while of going out together, Paul made her a work box for her sewing things as a token of his love and a quasi engagement present. Then she found herself pregnant – a disaster in her situation – but she had trust in Paul. She told him, but at their next meeting he told her that he thought there was something wrong with the timing. In other words, he expressed doubt that she had told him the truth. Without even arguing her case, she turned around, walked away and never saw him or spoke to him again. She gave birth to the child and brought her up all on her own, refusing any support from Paul. From her meagre earnings as an ironer, she managed to give her daughter a sound education, so that she could rise in the world and work in an office. And when her daughter found herself a war widow with one child after only a few days of the last war, Hedwig moved in with her to look after the child. And that's why I spent the first twenty years of my life with Hedwig Christen, my grandmother. I received nothing but love from her, gentle but firm, and as, after Paul, she never had another relationship with a man, you could say that all the loving potential she had in her for the other gender was bestowed on me.

I said that she never saw Paul again, and that is true in a particularly poignant way. In one sense, though, she saw him every day: she saw there was always a photograph of him in their room, at child's eye-level, so that she at least had an image of her father. My mother also remembers seeing him once or twice in person, the last time in hospital when she was six years old. He had contracted TB and she remembers playing with the rings on his bony fingers. When she left, he pleaded with her to bring her mother along the next time. But Hedwig remained hard. Only when he was close to death did she yield and go to the hospital, but when she entered his room the nurses were putting new sheets on his bed. He had died a few hours before.

What had caused these two people to inflict such pain on each other? They were fond of each other, I have no doubt. I only need to look at the box to see the love that went into its making and to imagine the joy it gave her. Paul may have been influenced by his own mother, who seemed to have had ambitious plans for him. And Hedwig had nothing in this world but her honour and integrity, both of which Paul had put in question with his most unfortunate remark. Within the bounds of her lifelong humility, I knew my grandmother to be a proud and incorruptible person, but who wouldn't sympathise with my grandfather dying alone, remorseful but unforgiven? I'm sure this is not the whole story. The key to it is lost, as is the key to the box. Otherwise, it is in pristine condition. It is the only object of any value and beauty that my grandmother ever possessed.

And now I realise that I haven't given its full description; I've only talked about its outside appearance. The inside of the lid is its most striking part: Paul used five different shades of wood there. In the middle of a golden-glowing rectangular field there is a geometrical design which vaguely resembles an abstract eye. And in the dead centre of it, the prescient maker of the box inlaid a small, round piece of mother-of-pearl, perfectly fitted. It shimmers greyly, and looks for all the world like a single, arrested, unquenchable tear.

BRUISED GRASS

Joe Kearney

It is said that our sense of smell is the sense most conducive to recollection. I believe this to be so, because each spring I react to a scent that achingly reawakens within me memories of a time almost forty years past. This memory is so vividly real that it never fails to bring me up short and returns me to a time and place of brightness and innocence when the world was huge and everything seemed possible. The smell in question is that of the first cut grass of the season. The sharp green aroma released by the cutting and bruising of grass leaves unfailingly opens the floodgates of recollection.

To trace the origin of the memory, I have to go back to rural Kilkenny in the early 1960s and to the lush redolent summer meadows of that time. During one of those particular summers, I fell in love with and courted a wonderful dark-haired girl who lived in a neighbouring village. We were both then enjoying the seemingly unending days of a school summer holiday and, like all young lovers, lived only for the time when we could be with one another. However, the dilemma was: where could we meet? There were no cinemas or coffee shops. Strict social etiquette dictated that we could not meet in one another's houses and, anyway, keeping our courtship secret added a certain danger and piquancy to the relationship that was hugely exciting. But, as they say, love conquers all and we eventually discovered the luxuriant privacy of the uncut meadows.

These were wonderful places. In a time before silage, selective herbicides and factory farming, the meadows were allowed to develop into verdant grasslands. We would carefully make our way to the centre of one of these fields, leaving as little evidence of our passage as possible, and select a suitable area to create a fragrant love nest, far removed from the public gaze. Similar to ourselves, our bicycles were also hidden from view, in a deep ditch under the shelter of an overhanging ash tree. Both cycles were abandoned in a clumsy confusion of spokes, pedals and handlebars, not at all dissimilar to our own awkward and innocent entanglements.

Mary's mother owned a sweetshop and, whereas our hearts and spirits were sustained by young love, our corporeal side had to be content with 'borrowed' toffees, flash-bars and cigarettes. Looking skywards, side by side, and with Mary's hair fanned behind her and tangled within the bent stalks of ripening grass, we talked, dreamed and planned the future. Meadow larks and swallows soared and swooped above us, framed within the circle of bruised grass. With ears filled with birdsong, crickets' chirpings and drowsy bees and nostrils filled with the scent of crushed herbs, our lives, like the warm summer days, stretched before us with boundless possibilities.

But summer days won't linger forever, not even when they smile their blessings down upon young lovers, and eventually the meadow grass was cut. All too soon those drowsy days evaporated like the smoke from our 'borrowed' cigarettes. Our thoughts reluctantly turned to school when the evenings shortened and when wood smoke and a chill in the evening air reminded us of autumn's approaching breath. Soon other preoccupations were present to concern us. Mary returned to her convent boarding school and I to the local secondary school. A couple of half-hearted letters later, we drifted apart.

I'm sure that if we passed one another in the street today, it is unlikely that Mary would recognise me or I her. I know our lives have taken totally divergent paths since that summer. Nevertheless, at least once a year I am transported back by the smell of bruised grass to those summer meadows. I can see a ladybird climbing within the confusion of Mary's hair, the seed heads of grass stalks waving gracefully above us and, once again, I am instantly uplifted upon memory's wing to a time of hope, beauty and innocence.

SERENDIPITY
Valerie Murphy

'Serendipity' – a word whose syllables I loved to trip off my tongue long before I understood its true meaning: 'the faculty of making unexpected discoveries by accident'. Let me tell you how I experienced such an occasion many years ago on a beach in Donegal. My sister and I rented a house on the Fanad Peninsula and brought our respective children with us on a nostalgic trip to the beaches of our youth. Our kids looked rather bemused at these 'thirty-something' specimens of womanhood racing along the sand to check if their favourite rocks and sand dunes were still there. They were, and they had withstood the test of time better than we had. Our offspring, however, were not impressed by the endless rain that week. It didn't help, being incarcerated in a Spartan house without a Play Station, miles from civilisation as they knew it.

My sister and I took turns at escaping from the asylum to walk along the craggy strand, revelling in the crashing Atlantic waves, lost in a mist of tangy, salty air and vivid memories. On one such trek, I saw the figure of a man pencilled in the distance – his coat scrunched up against the biting wind, just like mine. You cannot avoid stopping to exchange pleasantries when you have been the blur on someone's horizon for a considerable time. Anyway, the friendly air of Donegal seeps into everyone's psyche.

We chatted about mundane things at first: the weather, holiday plans, etc. He was from Derry and had experienced many personal traumas during The Troubles of the 1970s and 1980s. I listened to his lilting voice reminiscing over the horrors he had witnessed and we mused over the clanging fears of those times in comparison with the relative tranquillity of Donegal. I found myself talking of minor tragedies in my own life, which somehow paled into insignificance when placed alongside his ordeals. We laughed then at the absurdity of two total strangers standing in rapt conversation, while the sleet lashed down around us.

It reminded me of a time when I was heading to Wexford with two toddlers some years earlier. Suddenly, a sign appeared on the roadside advertising a craft shop. As I was looking for an unusual wedding gift for an American couple, I decided this might be a golden opportunity, so I turned down the rickety lane to an old farmhouse. The showroom, tucked away discreetly in a former stone barn, was an Aladdin's cave of treasure. The artist and owner proudly showed me her work. It was a rainy day then too and we chatted like old friends, exchanging family details and outlining our hopes and dreams for the future. When one of my little sons bumped his head on a table, she ran through the rain to her kitchen to find some chocolate to calm him down. I left reluctantly an hour later, clutching a well-wrapped present and warmed by our cosy chat.

I relayed this similar story to my new-found friend many years on and, encouraged by the empathy in his eyes, elaborated my account of this lady, who, I had heard, died suddenly some months after our encounter.

'I know,' said my Derry companion wistfully.

'You do?' I stopped in my tracks. 'How?'

'She was my sister,' he replied quietly.

He then proceeded to fill me in on the other pieces of the jigsaw – their lives as children, her marriage and moving south to raise a family.

Somehow the poignancy of his story brought us back to the reality of the stony beach. I felt embarrassed at having evoked some painful memories for him, however unwittingly. He, for his part, was touched that a stranger could bring two strands of his life together in such an unexpected way.

There was really nothing left to say at this point, so we just shook hands and parted. As I trudged along to outpace the incoming tide, I reflected on the quirky fate in life that catches you wherever you may be, whether in the lush countryside of the south-east or the rolling mists of Donegal.

INISHEER
John H F Campbell

In the 1950s, only a small number of people left the motor vessel *Dun Aengus,* anchored briefly off the island's small beach, to holiday in Inisheer. A retired Welsh schoolmaster, a warden from Portlaoise prison and myself were among the regulars. Brendan Behan and the artist Seán Keating were more colourful visitors.

In those days, when foreign holidays were taken by a comparative few, the Aran Islands were an exotic destination. Inishmore was a day tripper's paradise, with its jaunting cars setting off for the great fort of Dun Aengus high over the Atlantic. Inishmaan, dark and brooding, was the most mysterious of the islands; Inisheer, the smallest of the three, the sweetest and most vulnerable.

Ostensibly, I was in Inisheer to improve my Irish. *Bail ó Dhia ar an obair*, I would say hesitantly as I passed an old man digging a patch of potatoes. He would begin a slow trickle of speech and I would edge along the side of the road nodding my head and blurting out occasional *tá fhios agam*s till I was out of earshot. The intelligibility of the mainlander took a severe knock from my efforts at communication.

I could walk for hours on the western side of the island without seeing a soul. Paths led in all directions, ending, as often as not, in a clump of nettles and a drystone wall. In the tiny fields on a sunny day, it was as hot as the Mediterranean. Out on the rock ledges, the waves curled in slow arcs of green and foam-white light.

My host took a lively interest in my social life.

'Máire's a grand girl,' he would say. 'Why don't we go up to her house and pass the time of day with her?' I had less confidence in these jaunts, but went along with them to keep him happy.

One night he left me outside a house on the edge of the village. A dog barked distantly against the rise and fall of the sea. I went up to the door and knocked softly.

'Tar isteach,' a voice said. A woman sat in the inglenook carding wool, her daughter a dim presence in the shadows behind the curtained window.

'Coilín asked me to see whether you'd need any fish tomorrow,' I blurted out.

There was a silence. The woman got up and took a kettle from the hob.

'Will you have a cup of tea?' she said.

I sat on a chair near the fire and held the warm cup in my hands. A clock ticked on the dresser. There was a big case filled with clothes in the far corner and a small, worn carrier bag beside it. I thought of asking whether someone was planning a journey but didn't. We talked of this and that, my reasons for coming to the island, the hardness of the islanders' lives, the vagaries of the weather. The girl did not speak. After a while, I got up and took my leave. Clouds had gathered over the island and a chill wind was blowing. I made my way in the darkness along the track between the stone walls towards the distant light of Coilín's house.

The next morning the boat was due in at eleven o'clock. The sea was rough and the beach was darkened by blustery rain showers. I walked down and stood by the water, a little apart from the knot of islanders waiting for the *Dun Aengus*. The girl – wearing a red skirt – and her mother, were among them.

The boat came in and anchored off the shore. Currachs were brought down to the water's edge. The girl turned to her mother. For a long moment they looked at each other, saying nothing.

Then, blindly, she picked up her case and the carrier bag, stumbled into one of the currachs and it pulled away. Her mother turned and walked slowly back up the beach. I asked Coilín later about this scene.

'Ah,' he said, and he sounded embarrassed, 'she's gone to America. The father went off five years ago. They heard nothing from him. God help the poor woman now, she's on her own.'

I've thought often since about that time. Why did Coilín leave me outside that house? Did he expect something of me? Did I fail him? The woman in the red skirt remains hauntingly in my memory – a burning symbol of leaving and loss.

NO FRONTIERS

Michael Timms

Political changes of the last few decades have rendered many frontiers and borders invisible. The barriers are coming down all over Europe. So it's easy to miss the boundaries. Language is about the only border guard left in some places, and most of the time you can slip past him quite easily. Even France, renowned for its haughty disdain of other tongues – particularly English – can surprise. And I am truly thankful, since my attempts at the French language are more comedy than communication. I have enjoyed campsite holidays with my family – spending hot days on the beach and slow nights with good food and plenty of wine – never having to speak a word of French.

It amazes me how far we can travel in a foreign country without speaking at all. I re-discovered this when I arrived in the south of France for the holiday where I was going to 'get away from it all'. I was *en route* to a house in a small hillside village above Carcassonne, just north of the Pyrenees.

Passing through immigration, all I have to do is flash my passport and I'm a part of this different world. I collect my bags and head for the car-hire desk. I present my booking reference, credit card and licence, without needing to understand any of the words said to me. And, *voilà* – that's a word I do know – I have the keys and I'm walking to the car park.

A visit to the supermarket requires no more than another production of the credit card to ensure I am stocked up with the basics to feed myself. I head for the hills and my first evening 'at home' in France – without having had to say a word to anyone.

Maps guide me to the village and then a street plan to the house. These are provided by the landlord, who has also left brief notes on the dining-room table. Guess what – they're in English! So now I know where and when to put my rubbish out. I also learn that the only shop in town is just across the road, an *épicerie* – a sort of corner shop, except it isn't open all hours, just two hours in the morning and three in the evening. And if I want croissants and baguettes for breakfast, I'd better get a move on, because loaves have to be ordered the night before.

I leave the house in high spirits. I'm part of the community now, doing what all the locals do at this time of day. By the time I've crossed the street, the blood has drained to my boots: what else do all the locals do? Speak French.

Inside the shop there's a small queue. I take my place – and as I get closer to the counter I am heartened that no one else has come in behind me. Then, just as I am about to be served, in comes a woman with her young son. Embarrassed by the audience, I nevertheless go through my performance, which is more pantomime than linguistic panache. In so doing, I believe I have secured my breakfast for the next morning. I move to leave, and the young boy stands aside.

'After you, please.'

'Thank you,' I reply.

I don't turn to see it, but I imagine a faint smile of pride on his mother's face. And, as I cross the warm sunlit street, I realise this boy has just flashed *his* passport. The one that will take him away from this place.

CAMEO IN DANGER OF SINKING
June Considine

Mizen Head and Farranfore – southeasterly backing northerly four or five. Tyne, Dogger – cyclonic becoming northwesterly three or four. My childhood resonated with such nautical warnings and when, in the evenings, my mother twisted the dials on the wireless, we listened to an echoing voice uttering names like Plymouth, Biscay, Shannon, Rockall, Fair Isle, Malin, Hebrides. The shipping forecast was relatively easy to pick up, but our wireless really crackled when she tuned into the shortwave band that connected the fleet of small ships plying between Ireland and the Continent.

My father worked on one such ship, cooking for a crew of hungry seamen, and, through the radio communications between the ships, she knew when she could expect him home or when there might be an unexpected delay. Sometimes he arrived at night when we were sleeping – but his arrival during the day was flagged in advance by my mother standing before the mirror applying lipstick and perfume. Her smiles, her happiness, triggered our own excitement and we would wait by the number 35 bus stop and escort him home to her like a prized possession. We knew that, as soon as they had kissed – which sometimes took an interminable length of time but had to be endured – he would get down to the real business in hand by opening his travel bag and presenting us with our presents.

Some memories will always remain indelible and so I remember an evening when the newspaper was delivered through our letterbox and the sound my mother made as she glanced down at the front-page headline. She trembled with shock and lifted her hands to her eyes. It was August 1950 and the headline read: '*Cameo* in Danger of Sinking'. Sailing up the Wicklow coast, the ship my father worked in had hit the Arklow sandbank. The *Cameo* had tried to escape the clutches of the sand but, when my mother read that terrifying headline, the ship was stranded like a beached whale, shuddering, straining, pitched in a battle of survival against the elements. It was a time of waiting, of hoping she could be refloated on the incoming tide.

By the second day, a storm had blown up and the *Cameo*, battered by the force of the gale, was holed. The ship began to take water. A lifeboat was called and the crew were ordered to jump into the arms of the lifeboat men. They had to leave everything behind, clothes, personal possessions, gifts. As the waves crashed fiercely against the sinking ship, my father stuffed a rag doll with a china face into the back pocket of his trousers, and, when he jumped deep into the night, she came with him. Each member of the crew was rescued. This would be a sea tragedy without human victims. Our long vigil was finally over.

On his arrival home there was no travel bag to be unpacked, but he handed me the doll and told me a story about angry seahorses and singing winds, and a brave crew of lifeboat men urging sailors downwards into their arms.

'We'll call your doll Cameo,' my mother said. 'She is the most precious gift you will ever receive.'

Of course, I did not understand. At five years of age, danger is an incomprehensible force that cannot touch the mind of a small child. All I understood was that I had a new doll with a special name. But I can still remember how our wireless crackled with static as my mother twisted dials and how, for some reason, she was crying instead of laughing when she opened the front door and found my father standing on the doorstep.

GOING HOME, COMING HOME
Theo Dorgan

I met Kevin in Grogan's, home for the Christmas from Moscow where he has a small building business.

'C'mere,' he said, half-way down a pint, 'd'you remember Sasha, the plasterer I had over here to do that gallery job last year? Did I ever tell you about him going home last Christmas?'

This is the story he told me, though I've told it in my own way here, because a story is never the same from one telling to the next.

'Angels, get your lovely angels!' Sasha was shouldering his way down Moore Street when the high voice snagged him. Strings of bright angels hung from a frame above the battered stall, connected to a battery and transformer.

'How much?' He bought a box, shoved it awkwardly into the green carrier bag, gave the woman her money. A strong woman, broad shouldered, her heavy coat, her fleece cap and shrewd small eyes more than familiar. Sasha choked up for a second, remembering Moscow. He was frowning, turning away, when the woman grabbed at his wrist, looked up into his eyes and said, 'Here's some wrapping paper for ya. Safe home, love, and a Happy Christmas to ya.'

That night in the airport, a large whiskey before him in the raucous bar, Sasha remembered her words, the smile she gave him.

Sergei clapped him on the back. 'Soon be home now, eh? I bet Tatiana will be glad to see you, eh?' Sasha just looked at him. 'Oh, sorry, I didn't know. Sorry. Still, never mind, eh? Plenty more where that came from.'

At Sheremetyevo they shared a taxi with two other men from their construction gang, all four in a state of befuddlement, half-jokes and snatches of song, all they had left as luggage. Sasha got out first, near the towering flats where he lived, off the outer-ring road. The lifts were broken, as usual. He walked up the seven flights, out along the snow-whipped balcony to the door of his flat. Darkness everywhere at this hour of the morning. Still clutching his paper-wrapped package, he stepped into the endless cold and silence of his few rooms. It felt as if everything inside him was running down. It felt as if some dangerous edge was very near.

He shook himself hard, stormed into his bedroom, grabbed a few wire coat-hangers from the closet. Twisting and mangling the brittle wire, he made a rough triangular frame. He swept back the grey net curtains from his front window and hung the frame there. Suddenly, he was sweating. He struggled out of his heavy coat, dropped it on the floor. He went through to the kitchen and switched on the radio, filled a kettle, banged it down on the spluttering gas flame. Then he went back and retrieved the package, removed the carefully sellotaped paper, opened the box, shook out the tangled skein of angels.

Music was beginning to warm him now as he hunted for a screwdriver, took the plug off a bedside lamp and fitted it to the lights. With gentle hands he arranged the string of angels on the wire frame in the window, reached down and almost reluctantly shoved the plug into the socket.

The white angels began to pulse and glow, his breathing beginning to settle to the same pulse as he went through in a trance to lift off the kettle, switch off the gas, find the tea and teapot. The music began to swell again as he scraped a chair across towards the table, feeling suddenly empty. He was looking at the lights reflected on the wall of the hallway when there was a knock at the door.

Impassive, beyond curiosity, he opened the door.

'I saw your lights,' Tatiana said, 'your lovely lights. From down there. I was wrong. I'm glad you're safe home, can I come in?'

He looked at her breath, hanging like a cloud around her. He looked beyond at her at the heavy sky full of snow. He opened his great arms wide. He said, 'Come in.'

GOING HOME FOR CHRISTMAS
COMING HOME FOR CHRISTMAS
Deirdre Purcell

Going home for Christmas, coming home for Christmas – two of the most evocative phrases in the English language. They encompass a pocket dictionary of others: joy, excitement, hope… filial duty, guilt, paying dues…

I was thirteen when I first came home for Christmas.

A scholarship girl from Dublin, I had spent my first term, a long, *long* fifteen weeks, in a boarding school by the shores of Lough Conn.

No visits, no outings. Envy of other girls' ease with one another, not to speak of scrumptious Sunday sponge cakes brought in weekly by their mothers.

It's a dismal, foggy weekday morning in late December and we serious travellers – four girls from Dublin and one from Cork – chug away from Ballina railway station. We change trains at Manulla, where the platform is even greyer. Wetter. Colder. We care little. We're going home for Christmas.

The big Dublin train pulls in and we find a compartment to ourselves. We chat quietly as the drowned fields and small towns glide past our window. It is 1958, when people are still conscious of electricity bills, so the outward manifestations of the Christmas spirit are confined to glimpses of paperchains, an occasional Christmas tree or crib, a modest star on a church spire.

We take out the sandwiches the nuns have given us. I can't eat mine. I'm going home for Christmas.

Athlone. People getting on, people getting off. The chat dies away. Just seventy miles to Dublin.

Outside the train window, streaked with grime, darkness falls. Nothing to see now. We chunter through a blind landscape as, like keys on a piano, the swishing telegraph poles count out the miles…

Mullingar. Bustle. Lights. People embracing on the platform. Only fifty miles to Dublin.

At Maynooth, we tidy away our debris like the well-trained convent girls we are. We button coats, check shoelaces, put on our berets.

Butterflies.

We're nearly home for Christmas.

The train squeals slowly into Westland Row. The others pull bags from the overhead nets, stand impatiently in the aisle. I cannot follow.

Because, as we slid along the platform, I caught sight of my family: Mamma, Dadda, my seven-year-old brother in beret and good coat, his hands up, holding theirs.

All three were scanning the windows of the train.

They were looking for me.

I am felled by tears of purest joy.

I bid the others a muffled 'Happy Christmas' from under my seat as I pretend to be searching for something I have dropped; I scuffle and scrabble around the floor until I gain control.

Somehow it had not occurred to me before that my family loves me.

I had not known that I love them.

I am the last to leave that carriage, probably the train – although I don't remember that. I do remember that, as I walk towards my small family, they are as controlled as I am. Delighted to see me but mostly – and jovially – relieved.

'We thought you weren't on it! We were nearly sending out a search party!'

The chat on the way out of the station is about tiredness and train journeys, the Dinky crane my brother wants from Santa and the new house they had moved into while I was away –

But joy, like a brilliant fish in deep water, glistens underneath.

There was a Christmas tree in Westland Row that year, or maybe memory has added it to my picture. There was certainly cloudy breath on cold air, and gloves and scarves and great clatter and chatter.

And on the way home to Ballymun, we made a detour, up one side of O'Connell Street and down the other, to look at the Christmas lights in the trees, in Clery's window, Madame Nora's, and then, at O'Connell Bridge – the *pièce de resistance* – the moving neon Santa, his reindeer and his sleigh on the façade of McBirney's.

My parents are dead now and my brother and I are home at different places for Christmas, but, since that first homecoming to the echoing, clanking, steaming platform at Westland Row, I have known that, no matter what, we four knew what we knew.

A Sense of the Past

AN AMAZING ENCOUNTER AT
ARDEA CASTLE

Sean Steele

Perched precariously on a cliff-top eight miles south-west of Kenmare in the parish of Tuosist is Ardea Castle. Apart from a stunning view over Kenmare Bay, there is little to show that a great fortress once stood there. A few standing walls, arched doorways and piles of cut stone are all that remain. It has been like this since 1652, when Ardea was bombarded by an English warship and much of it fell into the sea.

Prior to this, the castle had belonged to the O'Sullivan Beare clan, who had occupied it for centuries and had managed to hold on to their lands after the Tudor conquest. However, during the Cromwellian wars, they had supported the Royalist cause and had paid the price. Not only was the castle destroyed, but their lands also were confiscated by William Petty and passed on to his descendants, the Earls of Shelbourne.

In 1802, some one 150 years after the bombardment, George Beltz, an English visitor to Tuosist, encountered an elderly man called Kerry O'Sullivan who, although living in great poverty, claimed direct descent from the O'Sullivan Beare family. At a prearranged meeting at Ardea, O'Sullivan produced a set of crumbling documents which he claimed were title deeds granted by the English Crown to his family. But, as he was illiterate, he was unable to read them, nor was he entirely sure of their content. They had, he said, been passed down from father to son for generations but had been damaged by decades spent in smoky and damp cabins.

To assure himself of the man's authenticity, a somewhat sceptical Beltz put several questions to O'Sullivan, who proceeded to give a detailed account of his family history and genealogy. Beltz then checked the crumbling documents laid out on the grass before him. As a man of letters, he had little difficulty translating the Latin text of the parchments and was astonished by what he found, and by the accuracy of Kerry O'Sullivan's answers, much to the delight of the assembled crowd.

To his amazement, he found the original title deeds in which Elizabeth I granted title of Ardea and its lands to Kerry's ancestor, Philip O'Sullivan Beare, after he pledged loyalty to the Crown. Astonished by this find, Beltz looked further. Among the ancient documents were agreements with Spain concerning port facilities in the area. Revenues from Spanish boats were an important source of income for the local chieftain. Beltz was further shocked to find himself holding what seemed to be another document – from James I, dated 1612, together with a wax impression of the great seal of that monarch – confirming Philip O'Sullivan Beare's ownership of Ardea.

When Beltz visited Ardea, it was in little better condition than it is today. But its importance was still recognised by local people. Descendants of the castle's rulers continued to live locally, where the local people held them in high esteem despite their much-reduced circumstances. In a situation that must have been a source of shame and humiliation, they were forced by circumstances to lease land at nearby Cloonee Lake from the Earls of Shelbourne.

Their last descendant, Maria O'Sullivan, who lived at Cloonee, died in 1922.

On further questioning, Beltz discovered that Kerry O'Sullivan was not, however, the rightful holder of the ancient O'Sullivan Beare title; that belonged to his eldest brother, John, who had emigrated to America in 1731, settled in New Hampshire and had become a teacher.

He died in 1795, having outlived by some months his fifty-four-year-old son John, who had achieved fame as a general during America's War of Independence and earned considerable praise from George Washington. Beltz established that General

Sullivan's father, John senior, was seventh in descent from Philip O'Sullivan Beare, who had lived 200 years previously.

What happened to the precious documents in Kerry O'Sullivan's possession is not recorded. After the encounter at Ardea, they disappeared from the historical record. Years of being kept in harsh conditions probably took their toll and they simply crumbled to dust, lost forever.

In 1807, after meeting Beltz and hearing about this encounter, the Dublin-born travel writer, Isaac Weld, wrote: 'That writings of such a nature should be preserved for almost two centuries, and that an illiterate man whose family for generations had not enjoyed a condition above that of peasants, should be able to give such a detailed account of his genealogy, is a circumstance to which a parallel would not be readily found, except among the Irish.'

THE WATERFORD WARRIOR OF THE
MONSIPI RED-INDIAN TRIBE
Helen Hegarty

Recently, leafing through tomes in the National Library, I came upon Tom Barry drilling and training his men for hand-to-hand combat against a vastly superior army. Naturally enough, I thought I had stumbled on an account of the Crossbarry ambush, where, in 1921, Barry and a handful of Volunteers decimated a company of the Essex Regiment.

Not so. I knew I was on the wrong battlefield when Red-Indian arrows came whistling through the account. This Tom Barry was born in 1772 to a Waterford merchant and his wife.

1790 saw the seventeen-year-old Tom sailing out of Waterford, in response to a partnership offer from his uncle in Carolina. His mother's tears and a queasy stomach were forgotten when a shipboard romance beckoned. Having danced his way across the Atlantic, young Tom visited Violet Hill, Charlestown, where he courted Elisa, proposed and was accepted.

Run-of-the-mill stuff, certainly, but, even as he swore eternal constancy to his blue-eyed sweetheart, Indian knives were being sharpened for his scalp. Tom's uncle traded with the Wianadon Indians, which led to his nephew riding out on a misty morning in 1797 to do business. Dallying, on horseback, he found himself surrounded by braves of the Monsipi tribe. He was stunned by a blow, and his forehead was cut diagonally in preparation for scalping.

Being contrary to the Monsipi's code to scalp a living man, they dragged him to their village, where women bound the unfortunate young man to a tree-trunk to be burned alive. He pleaded for his life, and a female lifted her tomahawk and cut him free, washed his festering wounds and tucked him up in a deerskin bed.

This chief's daughter had a say in tribal matters. Normally, prisoners taken in war were offered to the war widows. If rejected, they were tortured to death. However, an exception was made for Oneida and she was allowed to keep the Waterford man. Though she cosseted him with venison and fruits and taught him her language, Tom – seeing her more as a sister – still sought to escape. That's men for you. Treasuring Elisa in his heart, he asked Oneida to help him, but she was having none of it. Three days later he was married, and joining in the wild wigwam winter dancing.

A spring ambush by the Ooromins drove the Monsipis to war. Barry, commanding 300 warriors, said: 'I taught them to march and wheel in regular order and convinced them of the necessity of keeping closely embodied when engaged with the enemy.' His plan was to feign retreat by the archers and draw the enemy to open ground where impatient spearmen waited. Tom Barry's army lost twenty men to the enemy's two hundred.

Barry, who was still obsessed with Elisa, again begged Oneida to help him escape. Dressed in her richest furs, carrying her tiny baby and avoiding hissing serpents, Oneida and her husband covered many miles before reaching a friendly village. When they arrived in Charlestown three days later, the Waterford uncle was very taken with his niece-in-law, who became the object of small-town curiosity.

Meanwhile Elisa waited. Her mother wrote: 'Initially, my poor Elisa was enchanted but, alas, when she heard you were married, sorrow took possession of her. Now dangerously ill, she wishes to see you.' Oneida was tactfully dissuaded from accompanying the erstwhile lover to the deathbed.

Europe beckoned. The couple refused to leave their son with his doting grand-uncle, but accepted his gift of £4,000, which took them to London in 1799. Given the stir caused by Lord Edward Fitzgerald's redskin bodyguard earlier, Tom Barry, with his scarred forehead, his squaw and papoose, must have been a celebrity of his time.

What of Waterford? Our hero's diary suggested a return during 1800. Did he reach his *urbs intacta*? Did he show off his papoose to the quayside merchants? Did he stroll with his russet-skinned wife over the cobbles to Reginald's Tower and mention that other Waterford couple, Strongbow and Aoife? Did he? I don't know. You tell me.

FAMILY FORTUNES
Dympna Murray

Jimmy would have been on the *Titanic* – if he could have raised the fare to travel. But in 1912, his job as a pork butcher's apprentice in Cork did not pay very well, so he began to look elsewhere for better prospects. When the recruiting officer for the Royal Irish Rifles was in town, Jimmy gladly signed on. A year later, he was in India. It was to be a short visit, as the clash between King and Kaiser called for his presence in Flanders. Maybe he regretted leaving the job in Cork when he experienced the butchery and bloodshed on the Western Front, but at least he survived the carnage.

Back in rebel Cork, the welcome home was lukewarm – Jimmy was in the wrong uniform. Even the family did not receive him with open arms. But there were arms back in Picardy – a *petite mademoiselle* called Marguerite – and soon French wedding bells replaced the bells of Shandon…

Three-quarters of a century later, I stood by the graves of Jimmy and Marguerite for the burial of their son, Jacques, and mused on the chance happenings that shape individual and family lives. Surrounded by the heavy marble statuary in the traditional deep purple of French cemeteries, Jimmy's descendants gathered from all parts of France, together with a handful of Irish cousins. From Marseilles, there was now Sebastian, a rugby player with a shock of red hair and a physique like a Munster forward. Chatting with him was Michel, an athletic *gendarme* from Grenoble. He was renowned in family circles for his liquor, made from alpine plants – a French version of poteen but perfectly legitimate, since he had 'married into' a farming family which had the right to distil their own spirits.

Apart from them stood Philippe, the Parisian grandson – Charvet-shirted and suited, exuding success and urbanity. He winced, just a little, on hearing the broad vowels of the cousins from Languedoc and looked slightly pained at the determined efforts of the few Irish relatives to bridge the linguistic gap. His handsome face froze when confronted with an olive-skinned in-law from North Africa. Fortunately, someone from his own world rescued him from that embarrassment: cousin Patrick – wasn't he banking in Lille? But no, Patrick had taken up painting and, like Gaugin, had left the bank and was now working on his art in a village in Brittany. He was planning to move to west Cork – if he could afford it – and immerse himself in Celtic mists and imagery.

I wondered how long it had taken Jimmy to learn French when he settled in Boulogne in 1918. Certainly his family had little trace of their father's mother-tongue. I remember the time I first visited Jacques' home and the champagne was opened; he confused 'cheers' with 'cheerio' and, for a moment, I thought it was a parting glass rather than a welcoming toast! But he had just enough English to deal with the tourists at his stall in Boulogne market, where he was a consummate salesman. I watched him handle three or four customers at once, advising one on the best *saucisson*, passing a sample of Camembert to another, identifying a potential new customer with a special 'Bonjour, Madame' – a real Bill Clinton at charming his audience. He was a connoisseur of food and wine and knew where to find the best, whether simple croissants or top-class *foie gras*. One taste survived from his father's homeland, and that was an appreciation of well-aged Irish whiskey. After his funeral I watched his old friends savour tots of fifteen-year-old Jameson as they reminisced about the 'good old days' of their youth and complained about the youth of today. *Plus ça change*!

I wondered what Jimmy from Cork would have made of the whole thing. I think he would have been rather amazed, and maybe a little amused.

LIEUTENANT O'SULLIVAN
Jack Fallon

On the front wall of a house in the main street of Boyle is an oval plaque to the once-famous film actress, Maureen O'Sullivan. It marks the birthplace of the glamorous girl who carved a niche for herself in the role of Jane in the popular *Tarzan* films. The street has a Georgian look, with a vista of fine doorways and tall windows running straight as an arrow to the mighty gates of the building once known as Boyle Military Barracks. Seldom is the famous actress spoken of without mention of her father, Lieutenant Charles O'Sullivan, born in Cork in 1878, an officer in the Connacht Rangers, a plucky regiment of recruits from the west. Those were the palmy days of the garrison towns: the officers were bluebloods, drawn from the Ascendancy, products of the public schools and greatly in demand for the eligible daughters of the Big House. Charles O'Sullivan, a handsome, blonde officer and son of a titled merchant prince in Cork, had already served in South Africa and in India during the time of the Raj. He was in every respect a suitable boy.

In a scene well described by Elizabeth Bowen in her novel *The Last September*, the young lieutenant and the beautiful Mary Fraser of Riversdale House met on the exclusive tennis court across the river that flows through the town. Well-groomed matrons sat on green slatted seats watching tennis balls hurtling across a net while keeping eyes peeled for budding romances. The young couple was drawn for the mixed doubles. Cupid's arrow was straight and true: they were married within a year. Their eldest daughter, Maureen, was born to the sound of the reveille on 17 May 1911. Army life for Charles O'Sullivan, the adjutant of the garrison, was happy, leisurely and privileged during those early years of marriage. There were the dances, regattas on the Shannon, numerous tea parties in the Ascendancy houses, like Woodbrook, Rockingham and the Fraser home in

Riversdale. But the idyll was soon to come to an abrupt end, when the fatal shots that killed Archduke Ferdinand and his Serb wife plunged Europe into World War I. Men of the Connacht Rangers were put on a war footing and there were tearful partings. No one could anticipate the carnage of the next four years as officers and men set forth for a war that so famously failed to end all wars. It was a war that touched the lives of many homesteads waiting in dread of that fatal telegram.

Nobody visits the war cemeteries of France and Belgium without inhaling the sense of grief, the sacrifice, the human loss; the loss on bitter loss that crowded brave men to an early grave in Ypres or Passchendaele. For O'Sullivan, active service at the front was to come to an early end. On 14 September, in a farm outside the French village of Soupir, he was caught in enemy fire while leading his men. His right arm was shattered, a war wound that would torment him for the rest of his life. A worse tragedy befell his brother-in-law, Jack Fraser, who was cut down while dragging him to safety. Men fell thick as the autumn leaves. For the bereaved families of the town, there are the memories and the memorabilia: on the mantelpiece the uniformed man photographed with his company, the war medals with their coloured ribbons stored away, the letters written from the front bound in ribbon and occasionally read with curiosity by a younger member of the family.

When Maureen O'Sullivan unveiled the plaque in her honour in 1988, she said: 'My life has come full circle. I am home again, where I was born and where I spent my happiest years.' A pleasant memory of a changed town. The old barracks today is also just a memory; it is now a heritage building. Outside on the wall is a plaque to the famous Connacht Rangers where each November on Remembrance Day the men who departed for distant graves are remembered. Like the Greek heroes returning from Troy, those who survived were so traumatised they would never again feel at home. One of those was Major Charles O'Sullivan, who died in Dublin in 1950 and is buried in his native Cork.

ORANGE SONGS

Kevin Casey

I am holding a book that is, at first sight, unremarkable. It has a ring mark on its faded blue cover, because someone must have once placed a damp glass there. It's called A Collection of Orange and Protestant Songs, compiled and arranged by William Peake, and was published under the authority of the Grand Orange Lodge of Ireland and the Grand Black Chapter of Ireland in 1907.

The quality of the songs in the book varies – some are fine ballads and some are not – but most have two things in common. They suspect or dislike or loathe all things 'Popish' or 'Papist' or 'Roman' and they celebrate the glorious achievements of King William.

Here are just two typical verses from a typical song:

> *In time of tribulation*
> *God raised a warrior bold;*
> *'Twas William Prince of Orange*
> *Whose memory dear we hold.*
> *He fought the foe with courage*
> *The Popish hosts o'erthrew,*
> *He is the joy and pattern*
> *Of all good men and true.*
>
> *He stood before all nations*
> *Truth's champion to be.*
> *'Twas he who saved our country*
> *From Priest and Popery.*
> *The blessings that he left us*
> *Our Church and Liberty,*
> *From Rome and Ritualism*
> *For ever we'll keep free.*

This gives a flavour of the tone of these songs. All of them are well worth reading, if only for the insight that they provide into popular Orange culture of the time – just as nationalist and republican song-books provide equivalent insights.

I have said that, in itself, this book is unremarkable, but perhaps there is an aspect to it that provides considerable added interest. This is the record of some – or perhaps all – of its previous owners. One of these was the Reverend W Harper of Dalkey House, Dalkey, who has inscribed his name and address in pencil just inside the back cover. Another, whose signature I simply cannot decipher, wrote on the flyleaf: 'Was Ireland worth losing to the Empire for this?' That's an interesting question, though almost certainly too simplistic.

Most interesting of all is the inscription just inside the front cover, which reads: 'J C Bowen-Colthurst, Capt, 2/RI Rifles, Downpatrick.' That's a name that I expect many of you will recognise as infamous.

In 1916, in Portobello Barracks, on the day after he had murdered an unarmed seventeen-year-old boy who was simply returning from church, an out-of-control Bowen-Colthurst ordered, without the benefit of any charge or any trial, the summary execution of three Irish journalists he had arrested the previous day. They were Patrick McIntyre, the editor of a paper called *Searchlight*; Thomas Dickson, the editor of a magazine called *Eye-Opener*; and the celebrated journalist and pacifist, Francis Sheehy-Skeffington, who was out and about only because he was attempting to prevent the widespread looting of goods from shops.

On Bowen-Colthurst's orders, they were forced to stand against a wall in Portobello Barracks and were shot so quickly that it has been suggested that they would not even have known what was about to happen.

And so the name of Bowen-Colthurst, a previous owner of this book, entered into Irish history.

How can I be certain that the signature is genuine? That's the final surprise of this book. A handwritten letter has been somewhat crudely gummed inside its back-cover. It was written by Frederick W Shaw – a first cousin of George Bernard – and the paper is headed by the printed address of his residence: Bushy Park, Terenure. It is dated '22.3.09' and reads as follows:

> Dear Colthurst,
>
> I got that book of Songs and did not know who had sent it, certainly it is a most – [here there is a word that I cannot decipher] production and whoever compiled it ought to be set-upon but gently. Remember I told you that there are many extremists in the Orange Society whose style and views I never did approve of but it is the same in all secret societies. Please do not imagine that the tone of those songs with their willing to swagger reflect the views of the Orangemen in general. I am glad that you called my attention to it as I may be able to do something to check such effusion,
>
> Frederick W Shaw

This remarkable letter, so moderate in its tone, suggests something about Bowen-Colthurst that may not have been generally known. In 1909, when he was stationed in Downpatrick and acquired this book, he was obviously concerned by the extremism of the songs that it contained. Yet, a mere seven years later, when he was stationed very close to Shaw's house in Bushy Park – where he may or may not have been a visitor – he was responsible for acts infinitely more barbaric than anything even hinted at in the most extreme of these songs.

I wonder why.

LIGHT THE FIRE
Michael Massey

Early each winter morning there's a dull thud as the central heating kicks in. Like an athlete's efficient heart, it pumps warm liquid through the arteries of the house. It pings through the pipes, gurgles in the radiators and, when we rise, we rise into a fog of heat.

As a child the first thing I noticed when waking on winter mornings was my nose, my very cold nose. The nose was the only thing protruding from the covers. It was a thermometer. On frosty mornings penguins and polar bears would have felt quite at home in my childhood bedroom. Even the inside windowpane had a coat of frost. The beauty of those fascinating whorls of ice covering the glass was totally lost on me.

I was a reluctant riser. Because of the cold, I resisted all attempts to prise me from the cocoon of heat. As cajoling graduated to threats, I'd raise my knees to my chin, rock from side to side, tucking the clothes tightly under me, trapping every ounce of heat, eliminating all draughts. I was a butterfly waiting for spring sunshine.

Besides, I could hardly move beneath the weight of clothes. Sheets, blankets, eiderdowns, overcoats. Yes. Overcoats. On the coldest nights overcoats descended on the bed like a heavy fall of snow. I was trapped beneath layers upon layers.

'Light the fire,' was my reply to entreaties and threats. It was a mantra. *Light the fire.* The fire in question was an open one in the kitchen. Eventually, the scrape of a shovel, the clatter of a coal-bucket and the waft of fried bread rising up the narrow stairs sent the polar bears and penguins scurrying from the bedroom and sprung this caterpillar from its chrysalis.

Times change. We light the fire in the evening now. Just for atmosphere. That's posh. Still, waking up in an Arctic bedroom was probably a lot healthier than the internally heated, double-glazed vacuums we've created. Carpet-mites, bed-mites, dust-mites proliferate in our hothouse environment. We're in danger of creating a nation of asthmatics.

When the central heating thumps on now, warm memories of cold-nose mornings flood back. Flicking aside the ridiculously light duvet, I rise into desert heat, and, now and then, for old times' sake, I shout back down the years to the ghosts of childhood: *light the fire*.

SUMMERS AT ROSSLARE
RAILWAY STATION
Terence Corish

L ike most people who were children in the 1960s, I think that the sun always shone during those summers, but I'm certain that Irish mothers were obsessed with dosing their children's skins with sun unhindered by considerations of depleted ozone and skin cancer. Just a bit of lotion on your shoulders would do. To an eleven-year-old Dublin boy, sunbathing was a pursuit of boring adults with laughable physiques. To hang around a railway station, indefinitely, by the grace of gentle and bemused stationmasters was what made my summer holidays at Rosslare magical.

Why did adults describe trains to children as 'choo-choos'? Parents today who have never seen a steam engine are still doing it. These anthropomorphic engines had swept back faces and serious eyes – Metropolitan Vickers, Manchester, 1950s… General Electric, Detroit… thousands of horsepower! Looking over them; checking out their works… four- and six-wheel bogies.

There was only one staff member on any shift in the station and he resided in the nerve centre, the signal box. This was a perfectly proportioned little timber building with a steep slated roof and windows along three sides and, inside, it was *exquisite*. Everything was crafted with pride. Big steel levers sliding on racks: green, red, blue, black, handles, shiny from hard use. Distant signals, upfacing and downfacing home signals, points. There were big green stacks holding the brass staffs – like battens in a relay race; these were passports for trains on a single lane. Hand-turned generators. 'Whirr-ur-ur-ur-ur' up the line to Wexford… 'drdrdrdrdring' – he's heard and replies. Pull out the brass staff, fasten it in its leather holder with a wire lasso, three

257

or four signal levers to pull, grab the lasso and let's go – it's coming.

One summer Sunday a dream came true. I talked a driver into taking me in a cab for the afternoon's seaside shuttle between Rosslare Harbour and North Wexford, as it was when the town had two stations. My God, I've died and gone to heaven.

The driver, Joe, asked me, 'What do you want to do when you grow up?'

'I was thinking of being an engineer... but I might like to be a train driver.'

'Don't be stupid,' he replied. I was speechless.

In the evenings, after my tea in the guesthouse, of boiled egg, diaphanous ham, lettuce and sliced pan, I'd slip down to the station. Some evenings, Johnny would be on duty. He was a soft-spoken Corkman exiled in Wexford, probably in his late fifties. He didn't walk up and down the platform to do his duties; he cycled. Johnny was tolerant of me and, on chilly August nights, we sat in the box by a little stove leeching smoke of standard issue sod turf, with me in a short-sleeved shirt and short pants. Most evenings, we would say nothing. Sometimes, as if in a Flann O'Brien novel, we'd exchange gems of knowledge. Once I explained nuclear fission to him, as I understood it anyway, using the stove as a model. He nodded at every revelation. He once told me that Jeyes' fluid killed weeds. The nights were broken by at least one course of treacle-black tea and thickly buttered currant bread and they were ended by the passing of the late express from Cork to the harbour.

By the time I was twelve years of age, such comings and goings interested me less, but Johnny's company was still valued and I'd visit him occasionally.

In the mid-1970s, Johnny retired to his small farm on the edge of the Sloblands. My model railways were neglected and my holidays at Rosslare had to entertain me in the atrocious teen age. Trains and stations were barely remembered. Discos and girls were more interesting now and, introspective and moody, I'd even taken to lying on the beach.

I didn't see Johnny at all during those years until a chance meeting when I was about nineteen. He leant over his farm gate and asked what I was doing with myself. Soft-spoken and listening keenly, he was older, though still alert, but the warmth between us was lost. I was just a young adult and he, just an old one. A few years later, he passed on.

I recall all of this now, nearly thirty years later, on a train from Nice to Paris cutting through soft countryside at nearly 160 miles per hour. All I hear is a soft hum and all I feel is a gentle swaying in my ample plush seat. Outside, it is a clear warm September day and, on the edge of a little village, a young woman in a red summer dress is cycling; indifferent to the sleek hi-tech tube passing her in a couple of seconds. This *Train de Grand Vitesse*, the state-of-the-art in 'choo-choos', interests me, pleases me, but I do not feel the joy of involvement in important things, in the exciting work of grown-ups. For a moment I can taste strong tea and curranty bread taken in the signal box and I want to stick my head out of the window to grab the hoop.

ON THE RADIO
Aidan Dowling

A few years ago, in a farmhouse in County Limerick, I came across an old Marconi radio – the standard 'valve' radio found in many Irish kitchens from the 1940s on. Although the walnut-effect casing was mildewed and peppered with woodworm, the radio itself worked perfectly. It was tuned to Athlone and, out of curiosity, I turned the dial to see what other stations it would pick up. To my surprise, the dial spun freely, but the tuning needle stayed firmly on Athlone. The exotic delights of Prague, Hilversum and Kiev must have held no attraction, because the radio had never been tuned to anywhere else and, over time, the mechanism had given in to decay and simply given up.

In our own home, we had a radiogram – an enormous, mahogany affair housing a record player and, to my endless fascination, an eight-channel, shortwave radio. Here, Prague, Oslo and Hilversum boomed out loud and clear, especially in the summer, when pressure is high and radio signals carry further. Being a valve set, the sound was rich and warm, with bass tones that no transistor or three-in-one stereo could match. After switching it on, you had to wait for the valves to warm up and a little green light would start to glow, which only added to the mystique.

The stations were jumbled together in a way that made no geographical sense – Rome, Kiev, Stockholm and Bratislava all lived side by side – unlike the countries from which they broadcast, which were divided at the time by the 'iron curtain'. Back then, the superpowers of east and west used radio to broadcast official state news – also known as propaganda – with Radio Moscow and the Voice of America battling it out in their respective corners.

For a schoolboy immersed in the spy novels of Ian Fleming and John le Carré, tuning in to these stations felt as if you were entering the forbidden world of espionage. Because, in spy novels, one of the ways to let agents know that 'the microfilm had been seized', or that someone had made it over the Berlin Wall, was to use a prearranged and seemingly innocuous phrase – a phrase like 'joyous occasion' – in the main news bulletin. Thus, the mention of a 'joyous occasion' on Radio Moscow would signal to all concerned that the eagle, so to speak, had landed.

So there I sat, trying to spot phrases that sounded in any way out of context. Instead, the presenters droned on endlessly about agriculture in the Ukraine and advances in space technology, in broadcasts that were full of innocuous phrases – any of which could have been a coded message.

In time, I realised that the east was unlikely to ever invade the west and, like the old Marconi, I eventually gave up. After all, no long-range missiles had shown up on the Irish radar; no Russian subs had popped up off the coast. All was quiet on the western front – except in my room, where Led Zep Four now shook the walls with all the force of an underground nuclear test.

By the time we moved house in the 1980s, the radiogram had been consigned to the garage, but, before we left, I tuned in for one last time. The reception was poor and the broadcasts were, frankly, dull, but the familiar voices were all still there. On Radio Moscow, a newsreader spoke of the annual May Day parade in the Soviet capital.

'Workers travelled from all over the Soviet Union to enjoy the spectacle,' she announced cheerfully. 'It was, indeed,' she added, 'a joyous occasion.'

AS GOOD AS BRASS
Patrick McCusker

When I was a young fellow, at an age when wasps in jam jars were important, our house had a strip of brass along the bottom of the hall door. This was the 'kicker-strip'. An odd name, since no one that I could recall had ever kicked any of the doors on our road. Not only was the kicker made of brass, but so also were the doorknocker and the letterbox. These displays of dull gold were on every door up and down the road. Each oozed brightness and competed in the unspoken competition for 'best gleam'.

This was fine, except that brass had one drawback – tarnish. If left unattended, all brass things, like small fires, lose their glow and go out. It was this maddening quality of brass that each Monday morning had the women out on their doorsteps with Brasso and polishing rags in hand. Mondays, for no discernible reason that a boy with a jam jar of wasps could understand, seemed to be the preferred day to attend to hall-door flash. And by noontime all was again as good as gold – as brass should be.

But now and then, sometimes not all was as it should be. The occasional door might not have been attended to. Like a dull tooth in a mouthful of perfection, it would stand out in contrast. Evidence enough, a thing like that, of a lapsed housewife. Indeed it was a tough woman who could withstand for long the unsaid in this regard. It might be Wednesday, or, if she was exceptionally headstrong, Thursday, at the latest, and she'd be out in the apologetic fade of evening with the smell of Brasso drifting on the air. By next morning all doors, without exception, would be gleaming once more for the early milkman genuflecting in front of each brass display.

We no longer have brass kickers, nor do we have Monday-morning attentiveness at hall doors. For the most part, brass has yielded its authority to aluminium or has retreated before high-gloss paints. And it has to be acknowledged that the new look to doors has a certain appeal. But, for all that, something has gone with the going of brass.

The atmosphere on the road has changed. It is Monday mornings that are different. They no longer carry their shoulders as days of particular distinction. No longer do the doors open to the smell of Brasso and the swish of polishing cloths. There is something lost in that. One more opportunity for neighbours to share news is gone. Such exchanges helped bind the road together into a community. But now, with the grooming of brass gone into another time, the Monday-morning doors remain closed. The road is still a nice road, but it has lost something that had been there in the time when wasps in jam jars were important to a boy.

THE GHOSTLY TENNIS BALL
Tomás O'Beirne

There was something weird about finding a tennis ball there in the gutter. It was weird because there were no tennis courts nearby anymore. Neither were there the once-familiar sounds of ball on racket or the cries of 'forty-thirty'. These belonged to another era.

You see, I was looking at what had once been the site of Mount Temple Lawn Tennis Club in Sunbury Gardens off the Dartry Road, which had been closed back in 1960 and which I hadn't visited since. In days gone by, we spent almost the entire long summer holidays up at the club and, as I had nothing much to do that day, I decided to go and see what it looked like now.

Weather permitting, and, of course, memory suggests that it usually did, we played tennis morning, noon and night, or else we just loafed about in deckchairs and talked. In Mount Temple and, I suppose, in many other clubs at the time, generations of boys discovered girls and lost, among other things, their interest in stamp collecting and making model aeroplanes. I suppose girls had a similar experience.

Mount Temple sported some of the best grass courts in Dublin. Some said they were as good as those in Fitzwilliam, which was then in Lad Lane. The pavilion was of the usual timber construction, painted green with a red, corrugated-iron roof, and there was a veranda. Apart from two changing rooms and a tiny bar, there was also the main room, which was used for teas when a league match or a tournament took place, for table tennis and for hops. Hops were a feature of the tennis clubs of the day and every club had regular ones – Leinster, Bective, Percy, Mount Pleasant and Templeogue – and at the end of the summer each had its 'At Home'.

In Mount Temple, the first tangible evidence of the 'At Home' was the arrival on the Friday of the men with a giant marquee. On the Saturday, the finals of the club championships were fought out in front of a substantial gallery and the provision of umpires on raised chairs and line judges gave the event a sense of great importance.

In the evening, the 'At Home' dance was held in the marquee and it was at these that many romances began. Some ended in marriage and some ended the next week. On Sunday, the finals of the junior championships were played, and that night something called a 'scrap dance' took place in the marquee.

Mount Temple/Kenilworth, as it had become, closed for economic reasons and its passing was greatly lamented by those with fond memories of it. Houses were built on the once-pristine courts, but, on that day so many years later, what I saw was not the houses, which seemed nice enough, but the old pavilion and, of course, the many faces that were once so familiar. I wondered if the people in the houses knew about the tennis club they had replaced.

The utter stillness of the afternoon, together with that incongruous tennis ball in the gutter, gave me the eerie feeling that things were somehow ghostly. Was I, unknowingly, participating in some sort of ghost story? Was I a ghost? I certainly felt like one, so I went home leaving the past in peace.

PARISH MISSIONS
Liz Carty

Last year we had a parish retreat, where, to a background of a softly playing organ in a church lit by candlelight, we were invited by mild-mannered, charismatic clerics to relax and reflect and pray.

It was a long way from the pomp and ceremony of the Parish Missions of my childhood, marathon events that lifted us above the humdrum of everyday activity, looked forward to for months and remembered for years afterwards. The Mission was held in June, but the ceremonies began months earlier, when every house in the parish was whitewashed, and every good front room – hardly ever used except for funerals and the arrival of American visitors – had to be wallpapered and polished, the best china washed and freshly starched lace hung at the windows. For the two weeks of the Mission itself we lived a life of unfamiliar, ceremonial graciousness. There must be no unwashed cup on the table, no newspaper left folded untidily on a chair. For we knew that, no matter how remote the dwelling, the missionaries, devoted shepherds that they were, would seek us out, determined that none of us should escape their attentions. They visited the sick and the strong, encouraged the virtuous and rooted out the transgressors who had fallen from their religious attendance, with equal zealousness. Dispensing fear and awe in equal quantities as, ceremoniously attired in Passionist black or brown Franciscan robes or girdled around with rosaries, they swept in and out of our lives, regardless of the havoc they sometimes left behind them.

Bearded like the prophets, travelling in pairs like exotic migrant birds, the missionariers used their pulpit as a stage as, in splendid vestments that were heavy with gold embroidery, they delivered their sermons in sonorous, beautiful voices. Terrifying and entrancing us in turn with their parables of wicked sinners who had neglected their prayers – consummate actors – they could be fierce or gentle, wise or bullying, but they could never be ignored and their message was simple: heaven was beautiful beyond telling, but hell, they grimly assured us, was hotter and deeper than our worst imaginings.

The Mission was our television and radio, theatre and circus, all rolled into one, and the sombre Sunday-morning worshippers, dressed decorously in their good suits, were somehow transformed by the glamour of gold vestments, shining monstrance, banked flowers and the tall stained-glass windows that were only ever seen in their true glory in the full rays of a setting summer sun.

I can still recall the smell of incense and the choir singing Latin hymns, with everybody joining in with more enthusiasm than harmony and the local diva's voice soaring above the rest, piercing in its clarity, like an out-of-tune blackbird.

And afterwards, on the pavement outside the church, we would jostle and push in front of stalls that we called 'stannins' and, bedazzled by the glittering display of holy-water fonts, ornamental plates inscribed with prayers in gold lettering and crystal rosaries sparkling like ropes of diamonds, we children eagerly parted with our carefully hoarded pocket money in exchange for the most fabulous treasures, which would, on the closing night of the Mission, be ceremoniously blessed. Small leather pouches embossed with silver crosses, doll-sized blue medals to be worn on a watchstrap, bizarre little gadgets shaped like toy guns or cameras which, when viewed with one eye closed, showed pictures of saints, shrines, or guardian angels with feathered, outspread wings. For those two weeks, it was as if our ordinary, humdrum lives had been suspended as – farmwork neglected, houses left unguarded – we sat, ringed around by the ceremony of incense and organ music and candlelight, to be reminded of transgressions we would rather forget and truths we had altogether forgotten.

IF I SURVIVE I WILL HAVE FIVE
Marion Maxwell

Castle Rackrent looked out on Allyballycarricko'shaughlin. Sure, it was a bog, but Sir Kit had put a lot of improving thought into landscaping it with trees. So he was not impressed when his new English bride derided the vista as a black swamp. Further tensions arose when, in defiance of his wife's Jewish sensibilities, Sir Kit insisted on having pork sausages for breakfast. Lurking in the background, need you guess, was some unresolved business: Sir Kit's new lady had declined to contribute her fortune in jewels to the needy family kitty. So he locked her up for seven years.

The storyline comes from Maria Edgeworth's satirical novel, *Castle Rackrent*, but her inspiration was a set of real events involving the incumbent of Castle Nugent, not far from the Edgeworth's home in County Longford.

Colonel Hugh Maguire, the real-life Sir Kit, had inherited Castle Nugent from his mother, but it was in one of the Maguire ancestral properties in Fermanagh that the hapless bride's imprisonment began. And it lasted not for seven years but for almost twenty.

In 1745, Colonel Hugh Maguire married Lady Elizabeth Cathcart of Tewin Hall, Hertfordshire. A brewer's daughter, she was already thrice widowed, later reflecting that, of her three childless marriages, number one had been to please her parents, number two had been for fortune, number three had been for rank. That left love, and so it was as a menopausal ma'am of fifty-three that she finally admitted to tying the knot with stars in her eyes.

Her thirty-five year old Irish beau, lately returned to England from a term as a soldier of fortune in Austria, was joint heir to the heavily mortgaged Maguire estates in Fermanagh, but what this dashing émigré lacked in collateral, he made up for in roguish charm; he had already sweet-talked the merry widow into buying him a commission in the British army.

At their marriage ceremony, Lady Cathcart's specially commissioned ring bore the legend: 'If I survive I will have five'.

Lady Elizabeth endowed her new husband with half the income from her properties, but, when he discovered that she was far more wealthy than he had been told, Hugh demanded her jewels and the deeds to her properties at pistol point. She refused to hand them over, so he smuggled her away to Ireland and locked her up.

There, like the fictional Sir Kit, Colonel Hugh entertained the neighbouring gentry with lavish parties and balls. Far from seeking to hide his prisoner's presence upstairs, he would ask the assembled company to drink her ladyship's health, and a servant dispatched to deliver his compliments would duly return conveying her ladyship's thanks.

Lady Cathcart's obituary, published later in the *Gentlemen's Magazine*, gives the true picture of her ordeal. Apart from her jewels, which she had hidden in her wig and her petticoats, her possessions consisted of a prayer book and one old newspaper. Locked in a sparsely furnished attic with one small window, she struggled to retain her sanity by recording remembered conversations, pricking them on the wallpaper with a pin.

After yet another of Hugh's threatening visits, Elizabeth climbed on to the bed and managed to bundle her jewels out of the window to a woman passer-by for safekeeping.

Hugh eventually wore her down and established that the deeds to her properties were hidden behind a panel in Tewin Hall. Setting off post-haste for Hertfordshire, he located the hiding place of the coveted documents. Impatiently taking a jackknife to the rusty lock, he cut his hand. Blood-poisoning set in and he died of lockjaw.

Eyewitnesses recorded that, at her release, his prisoner 'had scarcely clothes sufficient to cover her; she wore a red wig, looked scared and her understanding seemed stupified'. She was now seventy-five.

Lady Cathcart returned to Hertfordshire. She never did take husband number five, but at eighty she was still enjoying dancing. She died in 1789, in her ninety-eighth year, and was buried with husband number one. Almost a quarter of a century had passed since husband number four had found his eternal rest back in Fermanagh, in the Maguire burial ground on Devenish Island.

WHAT IT SAID IN
THE FREEMAN'S JOURNAL
Vivienne Igoe

Thursday 16 June 1904 was an ordinary summer's day in the Irish capital. *The Freeman's Journal* reported in the 'Dublin Money Market' column that there was a rise in the price of government funds. Breweries were flat, however, with Guinness stock moving to lower values. Railways fared better, with the Great Southern and Western recording a rise of 1¼, but the Tramway shares tended to fall. Bank of Ireland stock did not attract buyers.

Kellet's of South Great George's Street, and Todd, Burns and Co Ltd both had great summer sales with bargains in every department.

The report on 'fairs' on that auspicious day showed that there was little demand for store cattle, as most large cattle farmers already had full supplies. Unfavourable weather conditions during the spring and early summer months had cattle in a backward condition.

The 'Shipping News' reported a number of arrivals and departures the previous day. Many of the ships to Dublin were carrying cargoes of coal. *Breeze* from Preston with coal; *SS Captain McClure* from Cardiff with coal; and the wind-driven, masted *Rosevean* from Bridgewater with bricks.

In the Proteus episode in *Ulysses*, Stephen Dedalus sees the *Rosevean* from Sandymount Strand.

It was a weekday and a working day for most people. As the day wore on, the Dublin pubs began to fill with groups of people discussing everything from the weather to the horses running at the various meetings. The official starting prices at Ascot were quoted. There was an abundance of runners that day in the seven races. There were twelve runners in the Gold Cup run at 3 p.m. over 2½ miles. Among the runners were Mr M J de Bremond's Maximum the Second, and Mr F Alexander's Throwaway.

Around the city there were five theatres, with plenty of entertainment to cater for all tastes. Eugene Stratton, the world-renowned comedian, was performing at the Theatre Royal – in a series of recitals from his celebrated repertoire. The Theatre Royal was good value that night, as Mr Russell Wallett and Mr W Smith & Co were also performing in the new musical comedy version of *Fun at the Bristol*.

The Elster-Grime Grand Opera Company was engaged at the Queen's Royal Theatre with their tremendous success, the three-act opera *The Lily of Killarney*, whilst the Gaiety Theatre staged *Leah*, with Mrs Bandman-Palmer, supported by her specially selected London Company. Leopold Bloom considers going to it.

Piggotts and Co advertised *Famous Irish Songs*, which cost one and sixpence each, post-free. Included in the collection was 'The Croppy Boy', which James Joyce sang at the Antient Concert Rooms, when he shared the platform with John McCormack and J C Doyle at a concert held on the last night of the Horse Show Week on 27 August 1904. In *Ulysses*, it was the favourite song of Ben Dollard, Simon Dedalus and Tom Kernan.

The American disaster of the steamer *General Slocum* near Hell Gate in New York Harbour, which Tom Kernan in *Ulysses* reflects on, is covered extensively. Appalling American Disaster – Excursion Steamer on Fire – 500 Lives Lost – Wild Scenes of Panic – Children Thrown Overboard – Women Trampled to Death.

The weather forecast reported southerly fresh or strong winds, later veering westerly and moderating; unsettled with rain generally, some fair intervals. It turned out to be a fresh sort of evening for a walk.

A young man accompanied by a striking auburn-haired girl walked to Ringsend on 16 June, on what was their first date. The man was James Joyce and his companion the Galway-born Nora Barnacle, whom he had met a few days previously walking down Nassau Street. She was employed in nearby Finn's Hotel in Leinster Street.

Joyce subsequently immortalised the day and the enigmatic earthy girl in his novel *Ulysses*. He chose the 16 June 1904 for the action of his novel. This was the first Bloomsday.

THE FALLACY OF MAYERLING
Anne Frehill

On a snowy day in his hunting lodge at Mayerling, a short ride from the city of Vienna, Crown Prince Rudolf, the only son of Emperor Franz Josef, took his own gun and killed first his seventeen-year-old mistress, Baroness Marie Vetsera, and then himself. Ever since, around the world, much has been written – all erroneous – about this so-called 'romantic tragedy'. The Prince, who was trapped in an unhappy marriage to Princess Stephanie of Belgium, was said to have been so devastated by the refusal of the Pope to grant him an annulment that he decided to end it all, taking his beloved Marie with him for all eternity. Even the famous film entitled *Mayerling*, starring a young and handsome Omar Sharif, got it all wrong. Yet the definitive account of what actually led to the events of that awful day may never be written because, in an attempt to suppress scandal at the time of their deaths, many crucial papers relating to the Prince were destroyed or hidden on the orders of the Emperor Franz Josef.

Judging by the most recent historical evidence, it would appear that the real story of Mayerling is an extremely complex one, involving a lethal mixture of political intrigue, rivalry between the Emperor and his son and, of course, the Prince's own rapidly declining physical and mental health. Despite the romantic spin put on the story, Marie Vetsera was merely used as a pawn by the Crown Prince. Yes, they had been having an illicit relationship for some time and, for the young, impressionable Marie, it became an all-consuming love, but the Prince, on the other hand, would seem to have merely been trifling with her affections. While evidence shows that, long before their death, Marie had agreed to throw in her lot with the Prince, believing him to be equally besotted with her, opinion is still divided as to *his* motives.

Some commentators say that he was within months of death anyway, his body riddled with syphilis. Others attribute it to Prince Rudolf's pro-Hungarian political leanings. He had spent much of his youth in Hungary and was widely known to hold different views to those of his father, the Emperor. It is alleged that, in one final attempt to bring disgrace and possible ruin on the Empire, he took the decision to take Marie Vetsera to the grave with him.

Yet another bizarre twist has been added to the tale in recent years, following the discovery of some more of the Prince's private letters. It would seem possible that Rudolf was hopelessly in love after all, with an unnamed third woman who was, like him, trapped in a loveless marriage. Surrounded on every side by insurmountable obstacles, he succumbed to despair and took what he saw to be the only escape from his desperate situation – death. That he chose, cold-heartedly, to encourage the young and gullible Marie Vetsera to accept her death at his hand is what makes this tragedy even more poignant.

After their deaths, the Emperor Franz Josef, in an attempt to atone for the awful events which had unfolded at Mayerling, ordered that the original hunting lodge be destroyed and replaced with a new church and convent. But what of the two so-called lovers? They were not, as desired by Maria Vetsera, buried together. Instead, the Crown Prince was laid to rest in the imperial tomb below the Capuchin church in Vienna. In an effort to avoid further scandal, the Baroness's body was propped up between two uncles in a carriage and, in this way, smuggled back into the city of Vienna, where she was hastily buried at Heiligenkreuz Cemetery.

TOM DOOLEY
Padraig McGinn

Hang down your head, Tom Dooley,
Hang down your head and cry.
Hang down your head, Tom Dooley,
Poor boy, you're bound to die.

And die he did, hanged by Sheriff Grayson for the murder of Laura Foster in January 1866. But was Tom Dooley guilty of murder and did he deserve to die? Many of his neighbours had their doubts and the later conduct of one of them lent substance to these doubts.

The song 'Tom Dooley' was popularised by the Kingston Trio in 1958. They sang of a love triangle in which Tom Dooley, Sheriff Grayson and Laura Foster, the girl who was stabbed to death on the mountain, were the three people involved. But this was not a love triangle but a quadrangle, in which Annie Melton also played a part, perhaps the major one.

Tom Dooley was a handsome young man in his early twenties when Laura Foster was murdered. As a teenager, he had fought in the American Civil War and returned a hero. He had dated two local beauties, Laura Foster and Annie Melton, both of whom were said to be in love with him. Laura Foster was said to be 'very beautiful... with chestnut curls and merry blue eyes... wild as a buck'. Sheriff Grayson had also courted both girls. When Laura's body was found buried on the mountain, Tom Dooley was linked with her murder, as he had been seen coming from that direction with digging tools.

Annie Melton accompanied Tom to Laura's burial. Afterwards, Sheriff Grayson arrested him, and it was Grayson who drove the horses from beneath Tom when he was hanged from 'a white oak tree'. Annie was later arrested. While in jail, she bragged that she would never hang, as her neck was too pretty for a rope. Two years after the murder, she was tried and acquitted by an all-male jury. She later married Sheriff Grayson.

Many years after the event, when she was very ill, Annie said to a neighbouring woman: 'If I knew I would never get well again, there is something I would tell you about Tom's hanging.' But she said nothing more. Then, on her deathbed, she told Grayson something that seemed to crush his spirits and, after her death, he moved their remaining family from North Carolina to Tennessee.

What was it Annie told him that so upset him? Nobody knows, but the locals surmised that Annie had confessed to Laura's murder and told her husband that Tom was innocent. After all, Tom had no motive to kill Laura, for she was mad about him. The neighbours believed that Annie Melton stabbed Laura out of jealousy. Tom Dooley helped Annie by burying Laura's body and so became an accomplice. She saved herself by letting Tom go to his death without saying a word to save him, and he did not implicate her because he loved her. Local people said that, had there been any women on the jury, Annie Melton would have been found guilty. Perhaps... and then we would have had a different song, or no song at all.

THE PRIEST'S LEAP

Sean Fitzgerald

Some few hundred yards west of the town of Bantry, a large recess is cut into the public footpath. Enclosed within this niche lies a sizeable rock. Common sense dictates that this stone should have been removed years ago, but its continued retention is attributed to the observation of an old and gripping legend. And, like all good legends, time and retelling have suitably exaggerated the 'grain-of-truth' from which the story grew.

It occurred during Ireland's Penal days, as a priest on a sick call made his way across the mountain bordering Cork and Kerry. Learning of his intended and illegal administrations, a group of mounted English soldiers set out in pursuit. But they reckoned without the loyalty of the mountain folk.

A humble peasant followed the priest on horseback and warned him of the danger. He urged the hunted man to mount the horse and make all haste across the rugged mountain. But haste was difficult to achieve on the malnourished animal. Soon the soldiers were gaining on the priest, their strategic pursuit directing the fleeing horse towards a cliff on the mountain.

All means of escape thwarted, the horse skidded to a halt at the edge of the precipice. The priest resigned himself to his fate, knowing not to expect mercy. The sunlight reflected on their raised swords as the military closed in. Suddenly, the horse leaped from the cliff edge. The soldiers gazed in amazement as the horse and rider soared into the air and crossed over Bantry Bay, to land on the miraculously softened rock on the road six miles away.

Close scrutiny of the rock today, plus a moderately receptive imagination, will reveal markings synonymous with a horse's forced landing.

This daring flight is attributed to an equally daring man, Father James Archer, a Jesuit. A Kilkenny man, he was one of the founders of the Irish College in Salamanca, Spain. When the Spanish fleet sailed to assist O'Neill and O'Donnell at Kinsale, Father Archer sailed with it. After the ill-fated Battle of Kinsale, Archer and some survivors retreated to Dunboy Castle, stronghold of the west Cork chieftain, O'Sullivan Beare.

The English pursued, but Father Archer escaped before Dunboy Castle was besieged. In the ensuing battle, the castle was destroyed and most of the inhabitants were slain. A wanted man, Archer led a 'will-o'-the-wisp-like' existence around the remote areas of west Cork, administering to the religious needs of the people and encouraging the local chieftains to remain steadfast in their opposition to English domination.

English troops made numerous attempts to capture the priest, but each time they thought they had him in their grasp he managed to evade arrest. Sir George Carew, President of Munster under Queen Elizabeth, was so infuriated by the priest's courageous and evasive exploits that he nicknamed Archer 'Archdevil'. Sir George wrote to Robert Cecil, Secretary to Queen Elizabeth, claiming that Archer had supernatural powers.

'The county of Beare is full of witches,' Carew wrote. 'Between them and Archer, I do believe the devil hath been raised to serve their turn.'

A less diabolic explanation was, of course, Archer's knowledge of the terrain and the wily stratagems employed by the natives in achieving his virtual disappearance during military searches. After many failed attempts to apprehend Father Archer, Carew claimed that the priest 'could walk on sea and fly through the air'.

In a vain attempt to gain further Spanish assistance, Father Archer sailed for Spain in July 1602, never to return. However, Carew's cry of exasperation had already instigated a lasting legend.

THE DOLOCHER: AN URBAN LEGEND
Nigel Quinlan

The origins of the Dolocher are obscure and confusing, and have so far defied verification. According to the most complete account, which can be found in the *Old Dublin Journal*, it was towards the end of the eighteenth century when a man named James Olocher, condemned to die for the murder of a young woman, cut his own throat on the eve of his hanging. No weapon was recovered. On the same night, a guard at the prison, a notorious pit of corruption known as the Black Dog, was attacked. When discovered, the left side of his body was completely paralysed and he claimed he had been attacked by a giant pig.

The following night, another guard vanished completely, leaving only his uniform draped over his gun, which was leaning against the wall at his post. The consensus was that the vengeful spirit of James Olocher had returned from the dead to inflict a terrible retribution on his gaolers.

There followed a series of late-night attacks on women in the Christchurch area. One woman reported having a bundle of clothes torn out of her hands. She described her attacker as having the appearance of a giant pig. This was the creature that became known as the Dolocher.

As the attacks continued, a spirit of fear and hysteria settled over Dublin. One night, a drunken mob, apparently whipped into a violent frenzy, set out from one of the many dram houses in the area, determined to put an end to the Dolocher once and for all. They went out on to the streets and killed every pig they found. It was a long and fearsome night. The honest people of Dublin huddled indoors, while outside the roaring and squealing and screaming went on and on and on. The next morning, there was ample evidence of the night's violence everywhere: pools of blood and scraps of skin and bone. But not a single swinish corpse. They had all been spirited away to hell by the Dolocher, the people said.

The reign of terror was finally brought to an end by a blacksmith up from the country on business. Having spent the night drinking with friends, he set out late for home. It was a cold night and, for a joke, his friends dressed him in a woman's shawl and a woman's bonnet before sending him out with a warning to 'Mind out for the Dolocher!'

He was going through the passageway, known as Hell, at Christchurch when a figure lunged at him from out of the shadows. They struggled and the blacksmith raised a mighty fist and slammed it down on the head of his assailant. As a crowd gathered around him, he was heard to yell: 'I've killed the Dolocher!'

But the Dolocher was not dead. Carried to the prison infirmary, he was discovered to be a man draped in the skin of a pig and crowned with a pig's head. He was immediately recognised as the prison guard who had so mysteriously vanished.

In his confession, the guard admitted to smuggling in and later spiriting away the knife which James Olocher had turned on himself. Also, it was he, the Dolocher, who had incited and led the mob that massacred the pigs. He had arranged for all the bodies to be carried away and hidden in the cellar of a nearby house.

He died shortly thereafter of a fractured skull.

What prompted this bizarre behaviour remains a mystery. Was he a mugger with a macabre sense of humour? Was he a deranged psychopath? Perhaps he was a criminal genius – reports suggest that he was part of a gang and incited fear 'for the purpose of robbery'. Even if this makes him sound like a villain straight out of *Scooby Doo*, it does not detract from the potency of his story. His legend persists, told with ghoulish relish on tourist tours of Dublin city centre, though the days when mothers warned their children to be home before dark 'or the Dolocher will get you' are long gone.

FROM BEDTIME TALES

Catherine Ann Cullen

Morning is wiser than evening, say the Russian fairytales. And rightly so, for how many of our fears are nocturnal – succubi, nightmares, monsters under the bed, vampires – yet vanish at first light. Little wonder that our traditional bedtime stories, the fairytales which give our collective fears shape and form, so often feature beds themselves, and strange bedfellows too.

There's the story of the Frog Prince, where the young princess is understandably loath to take a slimy amphibian under her silken sheets, whatever bargain she might have struck with the creature in broad daylight. Where there's muck there may be brass, but what comes from the river's murky bed is not desirable in the brass one – at least, not until it is transformed into a handsome prince. Princesses are very attached to their fine feather beds, with the sheets turned down so bravely oh.

There's Red Riding Hood, where the wolf hones his cross-dressing skills in Granny's nightgown and nightcap, and hops into her bed – all the better to eat a tasty mortal morsel. What big eyes he has, and what a big stomach full of Granny, and what a big stomach-ache when the woodcutter cuts him open and saves the day. The message from such tales seems not to be 'beware of letting undesirables in your bed' but rather that, if they do get in, either they'll turn into princes with a kiss, or they'll just be turned on their heels by a woodcutter in shining armour who will happen by just as you scream.

There's the Princess and the Pea, where the possibility of an imposter in the four-poster is so intolerable to the queen that she gives the self-proclaimed princess the ultimate pulse test. Twenty-seven feather mattresses are piled up on one pea, yet the poor princess gets not a wink of sleep all night. She is black and blue with the effort, and next morning the queen is pea-green with envy.

Then there are the Twelve Dancing Princesses, who slip out of the dormitory through a secret trapdoor to dance the night away at an underground party. Bolsters in their beds may give the impression that they are dreaming peacefully, but their worn-out slippers give the lie to their pretence of lying down.

And then there are those who really are asleep, those deep sleepers who wait only to be woken – the Sleeping Beauties and the Snow Whites – lovely and lifeless until they are kissed awake by a prince bending over their glass coffin or their century-old silken bed. Be not afraid, the stories tell us, even of death, for what looks like death is only a long, long sleep.

The strangest of all the 'beds at bedtime' tales is the story of Goldilocks. Perhaps this is the story that bear parents tell to baby bears, because it is Goldilocks the human, and not Daddy or Mammy Bear, who is the monstrous intruder here, breaking furniture, stealing food and terrifying the law-abiding citizens of the wood. It is really not fair at all that she leaps out of the window and gets away scot-free.

My sister and I used to leap from the open bedroom doorway on to our bed to avoid having our ankles grabbed by monsters or intruders. Once on the bed, we had sanctuary from all enemies, as if every wick of the candlewick bedspread was a little nightlight for our protection.

Sometimes there was safety in numbers, especially in large numbers of visiting cousins. Topping and tailing in our house was not confined to fruit, it was what my father called the practice of putting as many children as possible into a bed, by putting heads at each end – and pillows, if you were lucky. Your best hope was that your opposite number would be a small child – tall ones meant you got their feet in your mouth and were sure to dream of something unpleasant.

But whether we lay side by side or top to tail, we prayed the same prayer – 'Four corners on my bed, four angels at my head'. And before we closed our eyes, by the light of a nightlight or the crack of light from the door, we identified suspected monsters as a coat draped over a chair or the shadow thrown by a streetlamp.

Then, bolstered by our incantations and our nightlights, we drifted into dreamland. We took comfort in our fine feather beds, courage from the sheets turned down so bravely oh, and consolation from the Russian fairytales, which say that morning is wiser than evening.

MOTHER'S LETTER
David Norris

My mother loved Christmas with an almost Dickensian intensity. Even though she died shortly after Christmas nearly forty years ago when I was just twenty-one, I still vividly recall the Yuletide flurry of activity, starting with Stir-Up Sunday when we were given the rare privilege of being allowed into the kitchen to stir the cake in its mixing bowl, afterwards giving a guilty lick to the wooden spoon, and ending up with the slightly panicky glory of the great day itself.

This year, while foraging for Christmas-tree decorations, some even dating back to my mother's regime, out from a drawer fell a neatly folded letter. It bore her beautiful copperplate handwriting and was dated 26 December 1944. My very first Christmas. I was six months old, my brother John (J R in the letter, to distinguish him from my father, also called John) was five and we were in the Congo. It was there that my mother spent the happiest decades of her life, teaching herself the intricacies of ever more refined areas of *haute cuisine* from volume after volume of beautifully illustrated French cookbooks, and collecting animals which she coaxed from the bush and brought back to Europe in her state room for her friend Sir Julian Huxley of the London Zoo. The Congo was a far cry from snow bells jingling, or an ermine-trimmed scarlet-clad Santa Claus disappearing down the chimney, but still my mother managed to recreate the special atmosphere of Christmas even on the Equator. Here is part of her Christmas letter of 1944 to my grandmother back in the Queen's County:

> You ask what David is like. Well, he's exactly what John Richard was at that age only fatter and more placid. He's always smiling.
>
> We had a quiet Christmas. There was nothing to give John Richard but I had been keeping a drawing book, a Kipling

storybook and the story of Pinocchio and I found a little ebony walking stick with ivory top and bought that. With a tin of biscuits and a jar of homemade fudge, that was everything Santa Claus brought, with one exception! Seeing that his Christmas was going to be on the mean side, I begged a donkey colt belonging to the Company and a friend, M Bosquet, who is a good horseman, had a saddle and bridle made and got a little native boy to ride it to *break it in*!???

It arrived in state early on Christmas morning just after Santa Claus had been disposed of! John was most excited but it never entered his head that it might just be bringing a message or anything. He said, 'Mummy, Mummy, there's a horse with long ears and a thing for me to sit on when I ride him!' He had to have a ride at once. I can't say that the 'breaking-in' had been very successful. The impression I had was that it had never had anyone on its back before! It escaped three times on Christmas Day and had to be chased by the cook, houseboys, waterboys, gardener, chauffeur, sentries, etc., each time. They were all terrified of it so when I go near it I feel as if I were a lion-tamer giving an exhibition! John loves it, talks to it, brushes it and scratches its head. Yesterday afternoon I yoked it up and got the chauffeur to come and help me give John a ride. The famous 'Cooper's ass' wasn't in it! I had to call the cook as well to push its hind quarters down as it kept 'histing' them. John enjoyed it but I'm sure I lost several pounds of fat!

I put all the decorations Mrs Pugh gave me and arranged Santa Claus on the sideboard complete with snow, pine trees, and sleigh full of parcels. I thought the 'parcels' were just empty but J R opened them and we found a cracker which made a marvellous bang when J R pulled it with Daddy, some little birds, a compass, a gollywog and (shades of Brock's Crystal Palace Fireworks!) some magic serpents, two of which I lit for J R and the boys, who really thought it *was* magic! Actually I think it was the best Christmas we've had out here but one thinks that every year. It certainly makes a great difference having the children.

I've just sent off all the Christmas decorations to Yalemba as they are having their Christmas/New Year party next weekend because they have a new missionary arriving by the mail boat.

We enjoyed the carols at Christmas and thought of you all when we listened to the King.

By the next Christmas (1946) we had crossed the U-boat-infested Atlantic and were safely ensconced in my grandfather's house in Laois, where no doubt there was a more traditional celebration complete with Christmas tree, Santa Claus and succulent crispy-skinned goose.

CHRISTMAS MEMORIES

Patricia Scanlan

I love Christmas. For me it's always been a time for family and, if I could go back and live part of my childhood again, I'd choose Christmas.

I've got four brothers and a sister and my parents made Christmas the most magical time for us. Christmas started with the trip to town to see the Christmas lights and to gaze in awe at the shop windows. Shop windows didn't have shutters in those days and Dublin was a safe, friendly city.

'Five for ten, the Christmas wrappin',' cried the traders in Moore Street. The lights laced along Henry Street and North Earl Street, the trees along O'Connell Street sparkling like Tiffany's window.

The six of us would have emptied our moneyboxes and had many uproarious meetings as arguments raged about what Christmas presents to buy. Woolworths' or Roches' were the best for Christmas shopping.

We'd be in a fever of excitement. Any boldness on our part – and there was plenty – was met with the threat, 'Santa's listening.'

By Christmas Eve our excitement knew no bounds as we sat around the kitchen table, with the fire roaring up the chimney. My mother was making the stuffing. All ears would be tuned to the wireless as Santa's helper Aidan read out the letters from children around the country. We'd listen with mounting excitement as Aidan led us to the countdown to Santa's departure. When the magic words 'He's off' came, it was time for baths, tea and bed.

We always had turkey necks for tea on Christmas Eve, with chunky slices of Vienna roll. Those necks were always thick and meaty, unlike the scrawny little offerings you get today, if you're lucky. We would troop upstairs in a tizzy of anticipation to hang up our Christmas stockings.

'Where is he now, Daddy?'

'Greenland, I'd say, lads. Into bed now, quick.'

I still remember the sight of those limp grey stockings dangling from the bedposts.

'Now where is he, Daddy?'

'Heading for Iceland now.'

Giddy chat would fly back and forth between the bedrooms, while downstairs mouth-watering smells wafted from the kitchen.

In those days, there was no such thing as putting up your tree a month in advance. Our crib, tree and decorations went up on Christmas Eve when we were all in bed. My parents worked like Trojans to create a magical wonderland for us.

Exhausted from excitement, we would drift off to sleep, half-fearful of waking and finding Santa in the room or hearing the reindeers' hooves on the roof. I can't describe to you the heart-in-mouth experience of waking in the dark to feel a heavy weight on your feet. 'Has he come?' you'd wonder and give an experimental wiggle. Yes, definitely something heavy.

'He's come. He's come,' someone would shout and we'd all race into our parents' bedroom. Exploring stockings with their treasure-trove of satsumas, a white hanky, toffee sweets and a shiny new penny. We'd tumble downstairs and close our eyes until my father plugged in the lights of the Christmas tree. We'd stand in awe and wonder. Then to the crib, where Baby Jesus lay in his manger, ivy trailing over black papier-mâché mountains that the Three Wise Men had just traversed. An old silver sheriff's badge atop the crib shone more brightly than any star of

Bethlehem. We still have that star and crib and all the figurines, although one of the sheep has lost a leg.

And then to early mass, freezing breath white in the dark and the choir singing 'Oh Come All Ye Faithful'. *Everybody* sang the carols loudly and lustily. The crib in the church was enormous and after mass we could clamber over one another at the altar rail to get the best view. Then there were visits to family and friends before heading home for the dinner.

Weary and full, we would plonk ourselves in front of the fire and read our annuals under the lights of the tree. Another magical Christmas Day almost over. And so to bed, six very happy children.